The Longy Club

BOOKS BY DAVID WHITWELL

Philosophic Foundations of Education
Foundations of Music Education
Music Education of the Future
The Sousa Oral History Project
The Art of Musical Conducting
The Longy Club: 1900–1917

The History and Literature of the Wind Band and Wind Ensemble Series
A Concise History of the Wind Band
Volume 1 The Wind Band and Wind Ensemble Before 1500
Volume 2 The Renaissance Wind Band and Wind Ensemble
Volume 3 The Baroque Wind Band and Wind Ensemble
Volume 4 The Wind Band and Wind Ensemble of the Classic Period (1750–1800)
Volume 5 The Nineteenth-Century Wind Band and Wind Ensemble

For a complete list of the currently available works of David Whitwell visit:
whitwellbooks.com

David Whitwell

The Longy Club
1900–1917

SECOND EDITION

EDITED BY CRAIG DABELSTEIN

WHITWELL BOOKS • AUSTIN, TEXAS, USA

The Longy Club, 1900–1917
Second Edition
David Whitwell
Edited by Craig Dabelstein
www.whitwellbooks.com

Whitwell Books
P.O. Box 342673
Austin, Texas, USA

Copyright © David Whitwell 2011
All rights reserved

All images used in this book are in the public domain except where otherwise noted.

Composed in Bembo Book
Published in the United States of America

The Longy Club (paperback) isbn 978-1-936512-14-0

Contents

Pre-Longy Chamber Winds Societies in Paris   1

Georges Longy, 1868–1930   13

Season One, 1900–1901   21

Season Two, 1901–1902   27

Season Three, 1902–1903   35

Season Four, 1903–1904   41

Season Five, 1904–1905   51

Season Six, 1905–1906   65

Season Seven, 1906–1907   81

Season Eight, 1907–1908   99

Season Nine, 1908–1909   113

Season Ten, 1909–1910   129

Season Eleven, 1910–1911   135

Season Twelve, 1911–1912   145

Season Thirteen, 1912–1913   155

Season Fourteen, 1913–1914   165

Season Fifteen, 1914–1915   179

Season Sixteen, 1915–1916   189

Season Seventeen, 1916–1917   197

The Longy Club Repertoire   209

On the Search for the Longy Club Performance Materials   213

About the Author   227

Acknowledgments

Along with those mentioned in the chapter, 'On the Search for the Longy Club Performance Materials,' the reader is indebted to Mr. Craig Dabelstein, the editor of this book, for the very great number of hours he has spent in creating this new edition. I am not only grateful for his highly professional work but must point out that but for him this book would have never been again available.

David Whitwell
Austin, 2011

Pre-Longy Chamber Winds Societies in Paris

IN BALZAC'S 1838 NOVEL, *Les Employées*, a character named Colleville[1] is walking down the street and, turning to a friend, says,

> You should come to our place to hear a concert next Tuesday. We will play a *quintetto* by Reicha.

[1] Another Balzac novel, *Scenes de la Vie Parisienne*, identifies Colleville as the principal clarinet of the Opera-comique.

Balzac captures here a moment in the first generation of important civic wind chamber music—all prior wind chamber music having been performed by musicians serving aristocrats.

Anton Reicha (1770–1836) was one of the most interesting composers of his period. While a student at the University of Bonn in 1789 he met and became a lifelong friend of Beethoven. After moving to Paris in 1808 he found little appreciation for his compositions,[2] most probably being too austere for the French taste. He became well established as a professor at the Conservatoire and his students included Liszt, Berlioz, Gounod and Franck. In his autobiography, Berlioz speaks highly of Reicha as a teacher and in a eulogy which he published in a Paris newspaper upon Reicha's death:

[2] Including a beautiful Symphony for wind band.

> It is to be noted that, despite the apparent severity of Reicha's precepts, none of the living professors has been more prompt than he to recognize an innovation, even if contrary to all admitted rules, if a happy effect resulted from it, and he saw there the germ of progress. In considering how tight the diapers still are in which they would like, in the schools, to keep musical art, one must confess that this merit reveals, in one so gifted, a great honesty of talent and a reasoning ability of the highest order.[3]

[3] *Journal des Debats*, 3 July 1836.

The year before Berlioz began his studies with Reicha in 1826, an encyclopedia of music by John Sainsbury was published. Here we find a rare contemporary portrait of Reicha.

Reicha is still in the vigor of life, of middle stature, and most urbane manners, his general courtesy greatly endearing him to strangers, to whom he is uniformly obliging. He has often expressed to this writer his wish to write an oratorio for the English in the style of their favorite Handel.

In private life he is cheerful and amiable; his favorite amusement is a game of tric-trac. His rooms are decorated with a profusion of elegant and curious articles, which have been presented to him by numerous individuals in public and private life, as testimonies of friendship and of the respect and admiration due to his genius and perseverance.

Anton Reicha, by Claude-Marie-François Dien, 1815

The wind quintet mentioned in Balzac's novel is one of a number of such works, which are also mentioned with some enthusiasm by John Sainsbury in 1825.

Reicha's skill has been shown in a variety of compositions, but especially in some admirable quintets, composed expressly for the flute, clarinet, cor Anglois [sic], French horn and bassoon; these are performed frequently at *L'Ecole des Fils d'Apollon*, and, indeed, on all occasions when first-rate performers on the appropriate instruments assemble together.

No description, no imagination, can do justice to these compositions. The effect produced by the extraordinary combinations of apparently opposite-toned instruments, added to Reicha's vigorous style of writing and judicious scoring, have rendered these quintets the admiration of the musical world.

Berlioz in his autobiography, even though it was written much later, also recalled that these 'quintets for wind instruments were the fashion for a time in Paris,' although he found them interesting, but rather cold.

Another nineteenth-century composer who wrote of these quintets was Ludwig Spohr.

> Two days ago I heard two more quite new quintets of Reicha, which he wrote for the morning-concerts ... They were played at a rehearsal, which appears to me to have been given solely for the purpose of fishing for more subscribers to the morning-concerts, among the numerous persons who were invited ... It is sad to see what means artists here are obliged to resort to, in order to procure support for their undertakings. While the Parisians press eagerly forward to every sensual enjoyment, they must be almost dragged to intellectual ones ...
>
> I found the composition of these two new quintets, like those I had previously heard at Kreutzer's, rich in interesting sequences of harmony, correct throughout in the management of the voices and full of effect in the use made of the tone and character of the different wind instruments, but on the other hand, frequently defective in the form. Mr. Reicha is not economical enough of his ideas, and at the very commencement of his pieces he frequently gives from four to five themes, each of which concludes in the tonic. Were he less rich, he would be richer. His formal sections also are frequently badly connected and sound as though he had written one yesterday and the other today. Yet the minuets and scherzo, as short pieces, are less open to this objection, and some of them are real masterpieces in form and content. A German soundness of science and capacity are the greatest ornaments of this master.

The reservations of Berlioz and Spohr aside, it seems clear that the popularity of Reicha's quintets served to stimulate wind chamber music during a new era in which performance was oriented toward the public rather than the court. Reicha was the God Father of a French movement in wind chamber music which is still surprisingly strong.

It was only after the final deposition of Napoleon that the great civic music institutions of France began to flourish, including thousands of bands, orchestras and choirs organized under the banner of the Orpheon Society. Among the chamber music societies which were formed in the nineteenth century one of the most important was the formation in 1879, by Paul Taffanel (1844–1908), a distinguished flutist and opera conductor, of the *Société de Musique de Chambre pour Instruments à Vent*.

Paul Taffanel

For the next fourteen years this ensemble gave regular concerts in Paris at the Salle Pleyel, a hall still used for music today, and actively commissioned new works—notably the *Petite Sinfonie* (1885) by Charles Gounod. Other new works for chamber winds created for this ensemble include the Lazzari *Octuor* (1889), the *Octuor* and *Suite Gauloise* by Gouvy, two suites by Dubois, the *Sextuor* by Boisdeffre and works by d'Indy and Pierné. One is surprised to find very few performances of music from the Central European School. Even Reicha, whom the French probably associated with Bonn and Vienna, is missing.

Etching by J. Grigny showing a concert by Camille Saint-Saëns, Pablo de Sarasate and Paul Taffanel on 2 June 1896 at the Salle Pleyel in Paris, on the occasion of the fiftieth anniversary of Camille Saint-Saëns' first concert at the Salle Pleyel in 1846.

The original members included, in addition to the flutist Paul Taffanel, principal flute of the Paris Opera and of the *Société des Concerts du Conservatoire*, and the oboists Gillet and Sautet, the clarinettists Mimart, Grisez and Turban, Garique and Dupont on horn, and the bassoonists Leon Letellier, Espaiquet and François Villaufret.

The initial concert of the *Société de Musique de Chambre pour Instruments à Vent* was performed on 6 February 1879 in the Salle Pleyel and consisted of the following compositions:

Beethoven	Octet op. 103
Bach	Flute Sonata in B minor
Barthe	*Aubade* for wind quintet
Rubinstein	Quintet for piano and winds.

The repertoire of the remaining concerts of the first year was, 20 February 1879:

Mozart	Serenade K. 375
Beethoven	Sonata for horn
Pessard	Prelude for wind quintet
Spohr	Quintet op. 52 for piano and winds
Schumann	*Romances*, op. 94

20 March 1879:

Beethoven	Quintet op. 16 for piano and winds
Beethoven	Trio op. 87
Mozart	Quintet K. 452 for piano and winds
Lassen (arr.)	*Three Pieces* for wind quintet

April 1879:

Beethoven	Sextet op. 71
Weber	Sonata for clarinet
Mendelssohn	*Concertstuck*
Kreutzer	Sextet
Deslandres	Scherzo
Grandval	Suite for winds

6 The Longy Club, 1900–1917

The *Société de Musique de Chambre pour Instruments à Vent* repertoire of the following thirteen years included the same mix of small and larger size wind ensembles and solo wind work. In addition to the repertoire listed above, the following years included,

Alary, G., *Cavatine et Intermezzo*, for flute, oboe, 2 clarinets, horn and bassoon.
Bach, Brandenburg Concerto no. 4 (arranged).
Beriot, C. de, *Sonate*, for flute and piano.
Berlioz, H., *Trio des Ismaelites*.
Bernard, E., *Divertissement*, for 2 flutes, 2 oboes, 2 clarinets, 2 horns and 2 bassoons.
Boisdeffre, R. de, *Septuor* op. 29, for piano, flute, oboe, clarinet, horn, bassoon and contrebasse.
———., *Pieces*, for flute and piano.
Brahms, J., Serenade op. 16, for winds and strings.
———., Horn Trio.
Colomer, B. M., *Nonetto* op. 51, for flute, 2 oboes, 2 clarinets, 2 horns and 2 bassoons.
Diemer, L., Allegro, Andante, Scherzo, Final, for flute, oboe, clarinet, horn and bassoon.
Durand, J., Romance, for flute.
Ehrhart, J., *Valses*, for piano, flute, oboe and clarinet
Godard, B., *3 Pieces*, for flute and piano.
Gounod, Charles, *Petite symphonie*, for flute, 2 oboes, 2 clarinets, 2 horns and 2 bassoons.
Gouvy, *Ottetto* op. 71, for flute, oboe, 2 clarinets, 2 horns and 2 bassoons.
———., *2eme Ottetto*, for flute, oboe, 2 clarinets, 2 horns and 2 bassoons.
———., Serenade, for flute, oboe, clarinet, horn and bassoon.
Grandval, C. de., Suite, for flute and piano.
———., *Valse melancolique* for flute and harp.
———., *Trois Morceaux* for English horn and piano.
Hartmann, E., Serenade op. 43, for flute, oboe, 2 clarinets, 2 horns, 2 bassoons, cello, contrebasse.
Herzogenberg, *Quintette* op. 43, for piano, oboe, 2 clarinet, horn and bassoon.
Hummel, *Septuor* op. 74, for piano, flute, oboe, horn, strings.
O'Kelly, *Menuet de la Reine*, for flute, oboe, clarinet, 2 horns and 2 bassoons.
Lachner, F., *Ottetto* op. 156, for flute, oboe, 2 clarinets, 2 horns and 2 bassoons.
Lalo, E., *Aubade*, for flute, oboe, clarinet, horn, bassoon and strings.
Lazzari, S., *Octuor* op. 20, for flute, oboe, clarinet, English horn, 2 horns and 2 bassoons.
Le Borne, F., *Aquarellen*, op. 20, for winds and strings.
Lefebvre, Ch., *3 Pieces*, for flute, oboe, clarinet, horn and bassoon.

———., *Meditation*, for flute, oboe, 2 clarinets, 2 horns and 2 bassoons.
———., Intermezzo-Scherzando, for flute, oboe, 2 clarinets, horn and bassoon.
Mozart, Serenade K. 384a
———., Adagio for clarinets and basset horn.
Novachek, R., *Sinfonietta*, for flute, oboe, 2 clarinets, 2 horns and 2 bassoons.
Onslow, *Sextuor* op. 30, for piano, flute, clarinet, horn bassoon and contrebasse.
Périlhou, A., *Divertissement*, for winds.
Pfeiffer, *Pastorale*, for flute, oboe, clarinet, horn and bassoon.
———., *Sextour*, for piano, flute, oboe, clarinet, horn and bassoon.
Raff, *Sinfonietta* op. 188, for 2 flutes, 2 oboes, 2 clarinets, 2 horns and 2 bassoons.
Reinecke, C., *Undine*, op. 167, for flute and piano.
———., *Ottetto* op. 216, for flute, oboe, 2 clarinets, 2 horns and 2 bassoons.
Rheinberger, J., *Nonetto* op. 139, for flute, oboe, clarinet, horn, bassoon and strings.
Rietz, J., *Concertstuck* op. 41, for flute, oboe, clarinet, horn, bassoon, and piano.
Röntgen, J., Serenade op. 14, for flute, oboe, clarinet, 2 horns and 2 bassoons.
Rubinstein, A., *Ottetto*, for piano, flute, clarinet, horn and strings.
Saint-Saëns, C., *Tarentelle* op. 6, for flute, clarinet and piano.
———., Romance, for flute and piano.
———., *Caprice sur des Airs Danois et Russes*, for piano, flute, oboe and clarinet.
———., arr. Taffanel, *Feuillet d'Album*, for flute, 2 oboes, 2 clarinets 2 horns and 2 bassoons.
Schubert, Variations for flute and piano.
Schumann, *Fantasiestücke*, op. 73, for clarinet and piano.
Spohr, *Quintetto* op. 52, for piano, flute, clarinet, horn and bassoon.
———., *Nonetto* op. 31, for flute, oboe, clarinet, horn, bassoon and strings.
Strauss, R., Serenade op. 7, for 2 flutes, 2 oboes, 2 clarinets, 4 horns, 2 bassoons and contrebasse.
Taffanel, *Romance et Saltarelle*, for flute oboe, clarinet, horn and bassoon.
Tchaikovsky, *Arioso d'Eugene Oneguine*, for flute and piano.
Thuille, Ludwig, *Sextuor* op. 6, for piano, flute, oboe, clarinet, horn and bassoon.
Widor, Ch. M., Suite, for flute and piano.

Société Moderne pour Instruments à Vent

In 1895 Taffanel was offered an important position conducting opera and he brought his involvement in his famous ensemble to an end. The group was reformed by the oboist Georges Longy and clarinetist Prosper Mimart, professor of clarinet at the conservatoire. This ensemble continued only for a brief time.

At the same time, the flutist, Georges Barrère (1876–1944), created a new ensemble under the name *Société Moderne pour Instruments à Vent*. This group was responsible for commissioning, among other works, the Roussel *Divertissement* op. 6 for piano and winds (1914) and the Schmitt *Lied et Scherzo* op. 54 (1910), for 10 winds. A publication in 1911 made an interesting observation about this ensemble.

Georges Barrère, New York, 1908

[4] *Metronome* (NY), 1911

> This society has proved a stimulus to modern composers, enabling them to realize the expressive qualities, peculiar sonority and special effects resulting from the combination of flute, oboe, clarinet, French horn and bassoon employed in single or double quintette with or without piano. During the sixteen years of its existence this society has produced no less than 100 new compositions by 50 different composers and has been subsidized by the Government in recognition of its service to general musical advancement. Colonne, Massenet, Saint-Saens, Widor, d'Indy and Faure are a few of the many prominent musicians bearing testimony to the unique achievements of this organization.[4]

As this account implies, this ensemble existed until 1911 but its founder, George Barrère, left Paris in 1905 to assume the position of Principal Flute with the New York Symphony. As we know by a published article in 1907,[5] soon after his arrival in New York Barrère had founded a woodwind quintet, the New York Symphony Quintet. The article about this ensemble begins,

[5] *Metronome* (NY) April, 1907, p. 16.

> That musical culture and taste is greatly on the increase and that there is a decided demand for the artistic in musical performances can be demonstrated in no stronger way than by calling attention to and discussing the objects of such an organization as 'The New York Symphony Quintet.'
> What more delightful combination can be imagined than the associating of a Flute, an Oboe, a Clarinet and a Bassoon, strengthened and ennobled by the peculiar tonal qualities of a French Horn?

This article concludes with an interesting letter addressed to Barrère.

> In continuing the work of *Société Moderne pour Instruments à Vent* in New York, which you founded so successfully in Paris, you will contribute to the art in America, by introducing many interesting works too little known there, to the American public.
>
> My best wishes are with you. I have no doubt your enterprise will be crowned with success.
>
> Most devotedly,
>
> Camille Saint-Saëns

In addition to Barrère on flute, the other members of the quintet were the Italian oboist, Cesare Addimando; the French clarinetist Leon Leroy, who had been a soloist with the Garde Republicaine Band in Paris; the Viennese hornist, Hermann Hand, who also was a member of the Metropolitan Opera Orchestra; and the French bassoonist, Auguste Mesnard.

The Barrère Ensemble

By 1911 Barrère decided to enlarge his New York ensemble in order to perform larger works similar to those done in Paris by the *Société de Musique de Chambre pour Instruments à Vent*. The first concert by this ensemble was performed on Monday afternoon, 28 February 1911, at the Stuyvesant Theatre in New York City. The program, assisted by Arthur Whiting on harpsichord, was,

Haydn	Octet in F
Handel	Sonata in B minor for harpsichord and flute
Mozart	Serenade in C minor
Bach	Sonata in E♭ for harpsichord and flute
Beethoven	Octet op. 103

The second concert, on March 7, was much more extended.

Part I: German Composers
Reinecke	Octet op. 216
Thuille	*Sextette* op. 5

Part II: French Composers
Pierné — *Pastorale Variee dans le style ancient*, op. 30
d'Indy — *Chanson et Danses*, op. 50
Hahn — *Cimetiere de Campagne*
Caplet — *Suite Persane*

The members of this ensemble were,
Flutes—Barrère and Rocco Guerriere
Horns—Josef Franzel, H. Heyer
Oboes—Albert de Bussacher and Irving Cohn
Bassoons—Benjamin Kohon and Emile Barbot
Clarinets—Henry Leon Leroy and Harry Christman
Trumpet—Carl Heinrich.

The oboist, Georges Longy, whom as we have seen above, was a co-founder with the renewed *Société de Musique de Chambre pour Instruments à Vent* in Paris in 1895 after Taffanel left to become a full-time opera conductor. The brief life of this reformed ensemble was no doubt due in part to the fact that Longy left for America in 1898 to accept a position in the Boston Symphony Orchestra. He became the Principal Oboe and one of the early French musicians of an orchestra which then rehearsed in German.

It was he who founded the Longy Club wind ensemble in Boston in 1900.

Mr. Longy probably influenced the musical life of Boston more than any other one man.[1]

    Olin Downes, Music Critic, *New York Times*

Georges Longy, 1868–1930

WHEN GEORGES LONGY ARRIVED IN BOSTON in 1898 from Paris to become the Principal Oboe of the Boston Symphony he found an all-German orchestra which rehearsed in German. Through the influence of his musicianship, and the almost immediate hiring of more wind players from Paris, the Boston Symphony soon became a 'French' orchestra, a reputation it enjoyed through most of the twentieth century. Who was this man?

A native of Abbeville, France, by age eighteen Longy had obtained the first prize in oboe at the Paris Conservatory as a student of Georges Gillet, and was a member of the Lamoureux Orchestra. At age twenty he became the Principal Oboe of the Colonne Orchestra and in 1898 was made an *Officer d'Academie* by the French government.

After his arrival in Boston, Longy's influence was soon felt throughout the musical activities of the city. In 1899 he became the conductor of the Boston Orchestral Club, with whom he gave American premieres of major works by Saint-Saëns, Berlioz, Debussy, Enesco and Moussorgsky. He founded the Longy Club (1900), Boston Musical Association (1919), the Longy School of Music (1915), conducted the MacDowell Club Orchestra (1915–1925) and the Cecelia Society (1916). He also founded the New York Chamber Music Association in 1913.

He was a formidable personality, tempered with an old world sense of manners, as is recalled by a guest pianist with the Longy Club, Heinrich Gebhard:

Boston, Massachusetts, 1898

[1] *Boston Transcript*, Nov. 4, 1930.

> After my return from a concert tour, following my studies with Leschetizky, Longy invited me to play with the Longy Club, which he had just founded. Now, as a young concert soloist, I had a natural inclination to play as if I were the whole show, instead of giving the winds of the club a chance. Tactfully and kindly, Longy reminded me several times during the first rehearsal that the winds needed to be heard, as well as the piano. I tried to heed, but I'm sure my idea of holding myself down wasn't quite correct.

At the following rehearsal, Mr. Longy didn't hint any more. He would say, 'Less pedal, please.' Now, Leschetizky taught his pupils to use the pedal for other effects besides mere loudness, so by habit I would still make loudness, by the pedal. Next, Longy was saying, 'That foot, Mr. Gebhard. Please watch that foot.' I was conscience-stricken, but my foot would insist on acting every so often in spite of my good intentions. By the third rehearsal, Mr. Longy was saying, not 'Less pedal,' but 'No pedal.'

I should mention now that these rehearsals in Longy's house in Roxbury were attended by the family pet, a big but peaceful dog. He would simply come into the room, crouch down and remain quiet. When the fourth rehearsal came around, the dog disappeared under the piano as soon as I sat down to it. At this time, some comment was made about the animal's deserting his usual post, but no one thought any further about the matter.

As I played along, I tried faithfully to keep down the volume of the piano part. Then, before I knew it, my foot started for the pedal. But it never arrived. Naturally, I was startled, and the rehearsal broke off for everyone to see what was the matter. The huge paw of the dog was planted in such a position that I couldn't touch the pedal. Longy acted just as innocently surprised as any of the rest of us. But afterward, those who knew Longy better than I did told me they were sure that Longy had spent a week teaching the dog to keep anyone's foot off the pedal.[2]

Another nice anecdote was told by Clement Lenom,[3] who sat, as second oboe, next to Longy for many years.

By degrees Longy acquired the ability to play for a minute and a half on one breath. Every summer he would spend his vacation mostly in farming and fishing. At first he wouldn't touch his oboe at all. Then, about a month before he had to return to the orchestra, he would begin to practice. After he got into the swing he would practice three or four hours a day.

He was a very serious musician, but very good-natured. I remember two funny things he did. Once the Longy Club was going to play a piece which needed some drum-taps. But the club had no drum. 'I'll take care of that,' Longy told us. When the time came for the drum, Longy tapped with his oboe on a silk hat beside him on the floor, where the audience couldn't see it.

And speaking of hats. A good while ago, when jazz was new [Mr. Lenom called it *jhahss*, which sounded very well] Longy and I and some other fellow musicians got into a discussion about it. Longy didn't say much, then he sat down at a table and began scribbling on a paper, then tearing a piece off, writing some more and tearing that off, and so on.

'Mon Dieu, Longy, what is the matter with you?' we asked him.

'You wait,' he said, and kept on writing on scraps of paper. Then he asked for a hat, and threw the papers in and mixed them up.

[2] Laning Humphrey, 'Longy in Oddments,' *Boston Transcript*, Nov. 1, 1930.

[3] Lenom, a popular oboe teacher in Boston, as an older man married a young student. Curiously, then, I actually was able to correspond with Mrs. Lenom and was surprised, until I did the math, that she did not know Longy, nor had ever heard the Longy Club.

'Everybody take one,' he said, holding the hat up high so that nobody could look inside. There was a little music on each paper.

'What's this for?'

'I have written a *jhahss*,' Longy told us. 'You shall see. Now, everybody play.'

Which we did. You should have heard it! It was so good we kept on playing it. Then someone banged on the door of the hotel and someone asked for Mr. Longy.

'Mr. Longy,' he said, 'the manager says the people below you think someone here has gone crazy.'

'Tell the manager it is all right,' Mr. Longy said. 'I have written a *jhahss* and we are playing it now.' [4]

[4] Ibid.

The Longy Club

As a student in Paris Longy was familiar with the famous wind chamber music ensemble, the *Société de Musique de Chambre pour Instruments à Vent*, as his teacher, Georges Gillet, was a member of this ensemble. When this ensemble disbanded in 1895, Longy was one of the persons who attempted to re-establish it. It is no surprise, therefore, that in 1900, soon after his arrival in Boston, Longy founded such an ensemble in Boston under the name The Longy Club. The relationship between the Paris and Boston ensembles was strengthened by the fact that two other members of the Longy Club were children of members of the Paris ensemble, clarinetist Georges Grisez and the oboist Auguste Sautet. Longy announced his intention to form this ensemble of professional wind players as follows:

Georges Gillet, 1900

> I propose to give a series of public concerts in Boston, at which a number of works especially written for wind instruments will be performed. These will consist of solos, duos, trios, quartets, and the like. Many of the selections will also require the additions of piano, strings or voice. The public hitherto has had very little opportunity to hear such works performed; and yet the great masters, Bach, Handel, Haydn, Mozart, Beethoven, Schumann, Brahms and others, wrote highly interesting compositions for these instruments. There is no lack in the number, the variety, or the excellence of the pieces, but the difficulty in organizing a company of artists of homogeneous talent has naturally caused this form of concert to be of infrequent occurrence. At the present time the array of artists composing the Boston Symphony Orchestra makes possible any desired combination of instruments, and the obstacles formerly existing have been obviated.

> The principal instruments which will form the fundamental elements of these concerts will be the Flute, the Oboe, the Clarinet, the Horn and the Bassoon.

The Longy Club began giving concerts in 1900 and continued for seventeen years. The following papers provide the repertoire of those concerts as well as many of the newspaper reviews which are interesting for their documentation of Boston taste at the time.

The Last Days of Longy and the Memorial Concert in Boston

Major Henry Higginson, one of the primary benefactors of the Boston Symphony, took a trip to Paris in 1912 as he was interested in engaging Fernand Gillet, first oboist with the Concerts Lamoureux and the Paris Opera.

> I am worried about M. Longy, the first oboist of the Boston Symphony since 1898 and who plays so beautifully. He is getting so fat that I think he might burst. I would like you to come to Boston and play second oboe so that if he does, you will be there to take over.

Henry Lee Higginson, by John Singer Sargent, 1903

Gillet responded that he only played first oboe, but should an opening arise he would consider Higginson's offer, but not until then. After the retirement of Longy, Gillet did come to Boston.

After this incident, Longy played with the orchestra for another twelve years, through the first season under Koussevitzky. Koussevitzky apparently did not like Longy's French tone and this led to conflicts. This relationship led to Longy's retirement, but we must report that at Longy's final concert Koussevitzky joined in the orchestra's applause and shook his hand. Upon Longy's final concert with the orchestra the leading critic in Boston, Philip Hale, observed,

> Thus he played a leading part in the musical life of Boston for nearly 25 years; often conducting in the face of discouragement, often achieving surprising results with the material at this disposal …
>
> To him there was good music and there was bad music. He did not inquire first of all into the nationality of a composer …
>
> As a master of the oboe his influence was equally beneficent. His phrasing in the Symphony concerts and in the club named after him was a gratuitous lesson to violinists, singers and pianists. For he was much more than a florid rhetorician. No matter how short and comparatively insignificant was the phrase, it was always a thing of beauty.[5]

Upon his retirement from the orchestra, Longy left Boston to return to his farm in France. His small estate there he called 'Le Cornemuse' and he raised poultry, maintained some two hundred cattle but no longer played oboe. This farm had been a gift from a wealthy Boston society leader, Mrs. Elise Hall.

Mrs. Hall had married a prominent surgeon of New York and Santa Barbara and soon after her marriage began suffering a loss of hearing. Her husband told her she should learn to play a wind instrument in order to 'blow out the tubes of her ears.' So, at age forty-seven she began to study saxophone with Longy. Being a Francophile, who had lived briefly in France, she became a strong supporter of Longy, including creation and funding of an orchestra, which he conducted. These performances introduced much French music to Boston, including performances by Mrs. Hall and her saxophone. She commissioned famous composers to write for her, including Debussy.

---

[5] *Boston Herald*, April 26, 1925. In this article Hale includes some curious and now forgotten musical associations with hanging, 'Mr. Longy was not deterred from choosing the oboe for his instrument by the old French slang: 'to play the oboe,' i.e., to be hanged. 'Justice plays the oboe for she rigs the gallows for the mournful dance.' The French delighted in jests connected with executions. The hanged not only played the oboe, he 'danced the branle of the bishops,' for he gave by his feet a benediction to those standing near. The cord that knotted his neck was called the E string of the hangman.'

Even after Longy had departed from Boston to France, Mrs. Hall followed him there, taking a chalet in Piccardy next to his where Longy continued to give her a lesson every day.

We have a first-hand account of Longy in retirement on his farm in France from none other than Arthur Fiedler, later the famed conductor of the Boston Pops but then a young man living in Europe.

> On a rainy day, one summer, Arthur Fiedler dropped in on Longy from Paris. You couldn't call him up—he had no telephone, nor, for that matter, were there any in the village …
>
> Longy, pipe in hand, clattered up in wooden shoes to give a joyful reception. Afterall, solitude is not good without a break. Off Longy rushed Fiedler to play billiards with him in the village saloon. The population of the village numbered only about 30 or 40—with men to the number of 6. Yes, the old man wielded an able cue, according to Fiedler.[6]

[6] Told by Louis Speyer, English hornist in the Boston Symphony Orchestra from 1918 until 1965.

After five years of retirement, Longy died in France in 1930. Six months after his death, on 3 November 1930, an extraordinary Memorial Concert was given in Boston by the orchestra with Walter Piston conducting (Koussevitzky was present in the audience). The repertoire of the concert consisted primarily of composers whom Longy had introduced to Boston and the soloists included Carlos Salzedo.

But it is the names of the honorary committee of this concert, those who gave their names to honor Georges Longy, who document the influence of his life. Among the names one finds on the honorary committee were:

Ignace Paderewski
Maurice Ravel
Ottorino Respighi
Fritz Kreisler
Pierre Monteux
Vincent d'Indy
Alfredo Casella
Alfred Cortot
Walter Damrosch
Georges Enesco
Eugene Goossens

'A goodly company,' observed the *Boston Herald* for 4 November 1930.

Season One, 1900–1901

The First Concert

THE VERY FIRST CONCERT given by this distinguished wind ensemble occurred on the evening of 18 December 1899, in Association Hall, Boston. In the program the members of the Longy Club were listed as Longy, oboe; André Maquarre, flute; Alexandre Selmer, clarinet; Albert Hackebarth, horn; Hugo Litke, bassoon and Heinrich Gebbard, piano with Arthur Brooke, flute; Auguste Sautet, oboe; Peter Metzger, clarinet; Paul Litke, bassoon and Franz Hain, horn, listed as 'assisting players.'

For this inaugural concert Longy selected the Quintet op. 16, for piano and winds by Beethoven, the B Minor *Sonate* for flute by Bach and the *Divertissement* op. 36, by Emile Bernard (1843–1902) for 10 winds. The *Boston Herald* was enthusiastic.

> The pleasing anticipations to which the announcement of the formation of this club and its object gave rise were fully realized last evening, which were received with enthusiastic favor by the critical audience in attendance. The program was well balanced and of discreet length, and the performances were of the highest order of merit. With the exception of the pianist, the club consists of prominent leading members of the Boston Symphony Orchestra, which is in itself ample endorsement of their high artistic worth. For the performance in regard to both interpretation and playing, there is nothing but the heartiest praise. The occasion was delightfully interesting and the club is to be congratulated on the complete success that attended its opening effort and thanked cordially for the large share of refined pleasure it afforded.[1]

Philip Hale (1854–1934), the influential critic of the *Journal*, was also pleased by this first concert and added an interesting note regarding a brief earlier series of wind chamber concerts in Boston.

> In 1891 and 1892 Mr. Charles Mole, who was then first flute of the Symphony Orchestra, with some of his colleagues gave concerts for the purpose of introducing works written for wind instruments, and at one of these concerts and in Association Hall, Messrs. Mole and Nikisch played the sonata by Bach that was on the program last night.

[1] 'The Longy Concert,' *Boston Herald*, Dec. 19, 1900.

> It is a good thing that Mr. Longy has the courage to make a similar experiment. He himself is an artist of rare talent and he has shown in this city his marked ability as a conductor. His skill in the latter direction was proved last night by the excellence of the ensemble in phrasing, in attack, and in all the details that characterize fine ensemble playing.[2]

Aside from the Bach, Hale was not so enthusiastic for the literature selected for this concert. Of the Beethoven he writes,

> Let us hope that in the future Mr. Longy will give the most of his attention to the moderns. We could well have been spared the quintet by Beethoven, which is familiar, and is one of the youthful works of the composer. It was first played … when the Emperor Francis and his court were in the audience. The work, therefore, has a certain historical evidence, but why should it be played in 1900, when there are modern pieces that are unknown to the public?

He also found no pleasure in the Bernard, which, in 1900, might have been considered 'modern.'

> Emile Bernard was born at Marseilles in 1845. He studied at the Paris Conservatory and he is organist at Notre Dame des Champs, Paris … Bernard is not of the extreme modern French school, and he is inclined to be dry and academic as in this Divertissement, which is well written, with knowledge of the capabilities of the instruments, and with a sense of color. The work, however, is rather deficient in spontaneous melody, and the vivacity is not crisp and sparkling.

The Second Concert

The second concert of the first season was given on 9 January 1901. The *Herald* did not review this concert, but in the *Journal* one can read of the sense of importance these concerts were beginning to establish for themselves.

> It is to be hoped that Mr. Longy will feel sufficiently encouraged with the musical success of his undertaking to warrant the giving of another series of these most excellent concerts. Musical Boston is not so musical after all, for how much do we really hear and become thoroughly acquainted with, outside of the Symphony Orchestra music, a few soloists and a smattering of opera once a year? There was a good sized and applausive audience.[3]

[2] Philip Hale, 'Mr. Longy's Club,' *Boston Journal*, Dec. 19, 1900. It is interesting that the Bach sonata which Mr. Hale points out began the concerts by the Mole and Longy ensembles also appeared on the first concert of Taffanel's famous wind ensemble in Paris in 1879.

[3] 'Second Concert of the New Society of Wind-Instrument Players,' *Boston Morning Journal*, Jan. 10, 1901.

The repertoire of this concert included the Quintet op. 55, for piano and winds by Anton Rubinstein (1829–1894); the *Three Romances*, op. 94, for oboe and piano by Schumann and the Vincent d'Indy (1851–1931) *Chanson et Danses*. This last work in particular, one of the real masterpieces of the chamber wind repertoire, was clearly appreciated by the critic of the *Journal*.

Anton Rubinstein, by Ilya Yefimovich Repin, 1887

> D'Indy's 'Chanson et Danses' was first performed at a concert of the Society of Chamber Music for Wind Instruments in Paris, March 7, 1899. It was heard for the first time in Boston last evening. As might be suspected it is ultra-modern in melodic and harmonic structure, nor is the composer afraid of writing a full fledged tune that is sufficient in its strength to make its way through a labyrinth of harmonic ornamentation, for the these of the first dance fascinates one on its repetition, and haunts the memory. This characteristic melody is greatly enhanced by a most unique accompaniment in the bassoons, but after all it is the melody that remains with one. The chanson is not so clearly defined, but contains all the modern inventions of abrupt modulation, an almost endless variety of tone color, and shows the master hand of one whose natural voice is the orchestra.

The Third Concert

The third and final concert of the first season was given on 13 March 1901, in Chickering Hall, Boston. The program began with an Octet by Louis Théodore Gouvy (1819–1898), a composer for whom the critic, Philip Hale, had little respect. Indeed, he began his review of this concert with a quotation from Tchaikovsky's diary of a tour in 1888, during which the composer mentions meeting Gouvy at the home of Carl Reinecke in Leipzig.

Chickering Hall, Boston, originally published in E. M. Bacon, *Boston: A Guide Book*, 1903.

> M. Gouvy was completely Teutonized, spoke German perfectly, was rather hostile toward his own country (that is, as regards music), and on the whole gave me the unpleasant impression of a man who thinks himself disillusioned and injured, and, not being appreciated by his own countrymen, is consequently disposed to exaggerate the virtues and value of foreigners. It is quite probable that M. Gouvy had some good cause for railing against musical France; but it was painful to me to hear him extol everything German at the expense of France. I had never met such a type of Frenchman before.[4]

Regarding this Octet in particular, Hale found it

> well made for the most part, but here and there are instances of the amateur workmanship which creeps into Gouvy's strongest works, for Gouvy abandoned the law for music, and in his youth he had no solid musical foundation. There are two movements of genuine interest: the 'Swedish Dance' and the rondo finale. They are piquant and characteristic. The Introduction says little, and the Romance is labored.

Neither was Hale enthusiastic for the second work on the program, the Brahms Sonata in F, for clarinet and piano. After mentioning that the composition was first heard in Boston in 1895, Hale wrote,

> It seemed to me then a dull piece and the performance of last night did not change the opinion. The second and third movements are more tolerable than the others.

We suppose that the critic, Hale, just had a bad day before coming to the concert, for he was also unimpressed by the remaining composition on this concert, one of the greatest masterpieces by Mozart, the C Minor Partita for winds.

> Mozart's twelfth serenade is one of the many pieces made to order by the 'glorious boy.' It is crowded with Mozartian formulas, most of them in this instance superficially pretty and meaningless. The Menuet in canon is [little?] more than a clever contrapuntal trick; there is no trace of effort and the music flows naturally in the arbitrary channels.

While the reviewer had little enthusiasm for the actual music, he nevertheless found the level of performance by the ensemble impressive, although hinting that this ensemble was not yet widely known.

[4] Quoted in Philip Hale, 'Chamber Concerts,' *Boston Journal*, March 14, 1901.

Louis Théodore Gouvy

The performance throughout was of a high order of excellence and the audience was appreciative. Mr. Longy prepared carefully these concerts, and it is to be hoped that the artistic results thereby achieved will arouse wider interest in this club another season. There are no such players of wind instruments in any other American city, or for that matter in Germany, and their abilities should be recognized in Boston, their adopted town.

The *Herald* did not review this concert as its critic attended a combined concert of the Harvard and Yale Glee Clubs. Also space in the paper was limited on this date due to the coverage of the death of former President Harrison.

Season Two, 1901–1902

The First Concert

THE FIRST CONCERT OF THE SECOND SEASON was given on the evening of 16 December 1901, in Chickering Hall. Several new players appeared with the ensemble in this season, including Clement Lenom in his first appearance as second oboe, Victor Lebailly as first clarinet and Albert Debuchy and John Helleberg, bassoons.

The repertoire for this concert included the Mozart Quintet for piano and winds; the *Two Rhapsodies* for oboe, viola and piano by Charles Loeffler (1861–1935); and the Octet by Sylvio Lazzari (1857–1944) for flute, oboe, clarinet, English horn, with pairs of horns and bassoons. Of these compositions the *Journal* critic, Philip Hale, was particularly interested in the unusual work by Loeffler.

Charles Martin Loeffler, by John Singer Sargent, 1917

> Maurice Rollinet is a French poet, whose purpose, like that of the Fat Boy in 'Pickwick Papers,' is to make your flesh creep … Rollinet is happiest when he sits in a dank churchyard, happier even than when he sings of the end of absinthe-drinkers, paretic and crapulous old men, and peculiarly atrocious and ingenious murderers … But in the midnight graveyard he is really at home and comfortable. With Job, he makes his bed in darkness: 'I have said to corruption, Thou are my father, to the worm, thou art my mother and my sister.' Health is to him abnormal. The skirts of his Muse smell of the gutter.
>
> Mr. Loeffler chose 'La Cornemeuse' and 'L'Etang' for musical inspiration. There never was such weeping as the voice of the bagpipe player. Now he is dead, but, says the poet, under cold skies, as soon as night weaves his black stuff, at the bottom of my soul, there in the corner of old terrors, I hear his bagpipe groaning as of yore. 'L'Etang' pleased Leon Pourtau, that poet of the clarinet, whose cruel death we are still mourning and Mr. Loeffler's Rhapsodie is dedicated to his memory. The secretive pond with its consumptive frogs and old blind fish is visited by the fantastic moon, which with its flat nose and strange toothlessness is like unto a death's head lighted within, and it peers at itself as in a dark glass.
>
> This admirable and highly imaginative composer, who has just excited wonder even among the Philistines of Berlin, is too true an artist to attempt purely imitative music. Neither with a viola, an oboe and a piano, nor with a full orchestra would he attempt to portray a

pond, fish, frogs or a moon. It is the mood, the spirit of the poem that seizes him and incites him to reproduction. Although this music is not panoramic, it depends for full appreciation on acquaintance with the poetry, and it was, therefore, a pity that no English paraphrase was printed on the program. Yet no sensitive hearer could have failed to recognize the presence of something rare and wildly beautiful

    The performance was of a very high order of excellence. Mr. Loeffler as a viola player needs no praise at this late date ... Mr. Longy as leader proved himself to be a dangerous rival to Mr. Longy, oboist.[1]

[1] Philip Hale, 'Longy Club,' *Boston Journal*, Dec. 17, 1901.

The critic of the *Herald* also wished for the printing of the poetry as necessary for the audience.

As the poems themselves were not printed, it was not easy to deduce haw afar after them the music was ... one could hardly hope to guess in what exact directions Mr. Loeffler's fancies had coursed for their own thoughts and figures. This was a pity; for Mr. Loeffler always has something to say, and, although his meaning may sometimes be occult and far to seek, it is worth pursuing for the poetry and originality which is sure to be in it.[2]

[2] 'The Longy Club,' *Boston Herald*, Dec. 17, 1901.

The Mozart Quintet attracted little comment in the press. Hale only noted that it 'was suavely melodious and inimitably constructed,' and the *Herald* critic praised the pianist, Mr. Gebhard, for 'apportioning the volume of his share discreetly.'

    The Octet by Lazzari did not excite the interest of either critic.

Lazzari ... does not possess great interest beyond that of a novelty and of the unusual tonal effect produced by such a combination of instruments ... The adagio was tedious. [*Herald*]

Sylvio Lazzari was born in Bozen in 1858 ... His octet was written in 1888 and it was first played at Paris March 18, 1899. It is in certain respects an ingenious work, but it is by no means a masterpiece. Here is found a constant desire to shun the commonplace, but the monotony of such avoidance is as boresome as obsequious respect for the platitudinous. The first movement is Weberish, the second pays imitative tribute to Wagner, and the third does not show any marked individuality. Furthermore, there was more than one page where the composer was distinctly groping, and groping painfully. [*Journal*]

Sylvio Lazzari

Hale closed his review by observing,

> There was a small but appreciative audience. It seems strange that when two new works were produced by such accomplished musicians the hall was not crowded. I hope Mr. Longy will not be discouraged … nowhere in this country at least can new compositions be heard in such perfection of performance as now in Boston.

The Second Concert

The second concert of the Longy Club of this season was given on 3 February 1902, and presented the Beethoven Octet; the Charles-Marie Widor (1844–1937) Suite for flute and piano and the André Caplet (1878–1925) Quintet for flute, oboe, clarinet, bassoon and piano.

Philip Hale began his review by again commenting on the disappointing size of the audience.

> Mr. Longy, not a whit discouraged by comparatively small audiences, continues to give concerts in which new works are introduced and admirably played. Here is a true artist, a great artist, master of technic, taste, who sings on his oboe with a purity and beauty of phrasing that any soprano of the very first rank might envy: an oboist of international reputation, who surrounds himself with worthy colleagues.[3]

3 Philip Hale, 'Longy Club,' *Boston Journal*, Feb. 4, 1902.

The Beethoven Octet, a long and difficult work, did not excite the press. The *Herald* hints that the performance may not have been up to this ensemble's usual standard.

> The Beethoven octet is probably as well know to such an audience as these players have, as any work of the wooden wind class, and we only remark upon the generally fair rendering given it … There were portions in which the reading was rough and uneasy, as if some of the players did not altogether appreciate the value of Beethoven's figures, and so forced them as to make them obtrusive and harsh.[4]

4 'Second Longy Concert,' *Boston Herald*, Feb. 4, 1902.

Hale, as before, questioned whether Beethoven was of interest to the modern audience.

> Beethoven's Octet was probably played as a guarantee of good faith for the benefit of those who are inclined to shy at the mere mention of an unfamiliar name. 'Caplet? Who, pray, is he? What business has he to write music? But Beethoven—ah, Beethoven! Anything by him must be good.'

The Octet is one of his youthful works. It suffered transformations and appeared in other forms, and is it in these days worth doing or hearing? Merely as a reminder of how wind instruments were treated in chamber music of that period. There is historical interest—if you wish; but Beethoven is known in the work only in his name.

In contrast both critics enjoyed the minor Widor work.

The Widor was very agreeable … It was not deep, although by no means superficial or commonplace. [*Herald*]

The Suite is well made throughout. How far it is removed from the tootie-tootle of so many 'standard works for the flute' that in miscellaneous concerts almost brought blasphemy to the lips of ordinarily pious hearers and affixed the term: 'water-logged' to the instrument itself! Meaningless bravura passages that alternated with smugly sentimental tunes and thunder or meaningless interludes to rest the flutist—no, Widor departed widely from the time-honored scheme … Mr. Gebhard occasionally forgot due proportion and drowned the flute in the lower register. [*Journal*]

Charles-Marie Widor

Both critics heard the final work, the Caplet Quintet, as being musically uninteresting.

The last had hardly interest enough to repay the trouble it must have cost in preparation and the time required for hearing it. It was serious almost to somberness and occasionally almost to dullness and might rightly be called 'work' as the composer had evidently elaborated it with long drawn conscientiousness.

The scherzo had a nervous oddity in its notions and manners, and the finale might have stirred if it had been played as indicated—allegro con pioco—whereas, the rendering was rather with a smolder than a blaze … It would have been better to represent it by a sample or two than to give the whole. [*Herald*]

André Caplet, by Paul Méjat, 1920

[Caplet's] Quintet is an unequal work. The first movement is clear and firmly knit together. The themes are not of great distinction—indeed one of the themes recalls, or rather hints at the most familiar theme in the first movement of Schumann's piano quintet … The Adagio is somber, dolorous, impressive. It is moody, some might say sullen … Here the composer seems deliberately to forget the limitations of the wind instruments; he attempts to swell them into orchestral force and fury. In the desire to be intense, he forgets the size of the frame, and the result is not satisfactory, at least after one hearing. [*Journal*]

The Third Concert

The final concert of the Second Season was given on 31 March 1902, in the Chickering Hall, Boston. The Herald mentioned that the bassoonist Albert Debuchy was ill and was replaced by Frederick Guenzel.[5]

[5] 'The Longy Club,' *Boston Herald*, April 1, 1902.

This concert began with a performance of the Camille Saint-Saëns (1835–1921) *Caprice sur des airs Danois*, op. 79, for flute, oboe, clarinet and piano. The critic, Philip Hale, found pleasure in the performance, although he could not understand Saint-Saëns' choice of these particular fork songs.

> The airs themselves are not especially characteristic; they are neither wild or piquant; they are, in fact, eminently respectable, as though they were sung by persons with money in the bank.[6]

[6] *Boston Journal*, April 1, 1902.

The *Herald* added,

> The Saint-Saëns Caprice, after its meaningless, commonplace and slapdash introduction is passed, is a pleasant, well ordered arrangement of simple, agreeable airs, full of cleverness in construction and affording opportunity for some virtuosity in performance.

The second work on the program, the d'Indy Trio op. 29, for clarinet, cello and piano was clearly the musical highpoint for Mr. Hale.

> This Trio is in four movements. The first an Overture is in the composer's most austere vein. It is not music for an entertainment or a parlor. It is introspective; it is without sensuous charm; the themes are not at once alluring, and the development is almost wholly intellectual. It no doubt would repay careful study. It seemed last night prolix. The second movement, a Divertisement, is thoroughly delightful, in animation, rhythm, melody that suggests folk-song and dance; nor is admirable contrast lacking. Furthermore, the movement is admirably constructed, and the dash and swing of the chief section are irresistible. The third movement, a 'Chant Elegiaque,' is nobly somber and impressive ... The Finale, an Allegro energico, is less interesting in the character of the material, but it abounds in passages of strength and beauty. The more of d'Indy's music we hear, the more we honor him for his technical equipment, his high thoughts and pure aims, his disdain of the commonplace, his shrinking from the easy success with which so many composers are contented. It is impossible to think of d'Indy writing music that is cheaply agreeable, tunefully ignoble. He has his own style,

and he has fashioned it with infinite pains, until it seems to be the only possible expression of his dignified and rich thoughts. The Trio, on the whole, was played effectively, at times with uncommon brilliance … Mr. Lebailly was fluent and intelligent; Mr. Gebhard played with spirit, but occasionally with an enthusiasm that works injury to his colleagues, especially Mr. Schroeder, when the cello part was in the depths of his instrument.

For the *Herald*, this work had

diversity, interest, sentiment and value. The elegiac slow movement is deeply tender. Mr. Gebhard, who was at the piano, appeared to be in a somewhat nervous mood.

The final composition on this concert was a premiere performance of the Arthur Bird (1856–1923) Serenade op. 40 (1898), which had won the Paderewski Prize of 1901 as the finest chamber work by an American composer. This honor made the critic Philip Hale more suspicious than curious to hear this performance by the Longy Club.

The fact that it is a prize piece would naturally awaken suspicion if not prejudice against it, for experienced composers who fully expect to win a prize refrain as a rule from marked originality, and walk calmly in well-trodden paths. They refrain studiously from the exotic, from that which might startle, perplex, annoy. There was a time when Mr. Bird by orchestral pieces gave much promise, for he displayed melodic charm, and warm and varied harmonic and orchestral color. His ways for some time have been ways of pleasantness and ease, and he writes more and more conventionally. Surely he had no idea that this piece would ever be played by such admirable artists as those who did everything last evening to put his work in a favorable light. He might have written it for the ordinary wind instruments of a small German town. The music is smooth and respectable. The Adagio owed its charm chiefly to the fine playing of Mr. Lenom. The Scherzo is of an operetta character and the Finale includes a common ditty and a sufficient amount of commonplace counterpoint. The character of the judges in his competition is such that we are left to wonder concerning the character of the other chamber music entered for the prize. What must these other pieces be!

The critic of the *Herald* was no less interested to hear this work, due to its publicity.

> Considerable curiosity attached to the production of the last number, because it has recently been named as the first selection for the Paderewski prize for a chamber music composition, which has been long held in abeyance, but which was awarded by a ready and complete agreement of the judges. It falls into the large category of works which for one or another reason is not easy to take in or to pass upon at a first hearing, even though the originality, merit and good workmanship may be at once apparent. It is bright, enlivening, full of activity and bustle, having also its graver moments, but the degree of approval to be accorded it cannot be decided at once … The unusual combinations of so many wind voices, with no strings to bind their tones together, and no piano to increase definiteness by the emphasis of its percussion, made the inner texture of the composition hard to trace, and many may have found it inclined toward thickness or monotony in spite of the author's variety of hymn, his fertility of figuration and his frequent uplifting of his themes to the freshest flute and most piquant oboe registers. The music held attention well, and was evidently liked and approved, even by those who were in doubt just how to make up their minds about it. It is unquestionably skilful, ingenious, thoughtful, well founded and well evolved music and a credit to American composition.

Philip Hale closed his review with praise for this second season and again hints that Boston had yet to fully appreciate the art of this ensemble.

> Thus ended a series of concerts conspicuous for interest and display of artistry. The subscribers already owe much to Mr. Longy for his catholicity and taste in selection, his skill as the oboist and the leader of the club, his enthusiasm and courage. It would seem that in a city where so many talk passionately about their enjoyment of music, concerts of such an unusually high character would be more liberally encouraged. Let us hope that Mr. Longy will not lose heart.

Season Three, 1902–1903

AN ARTICLE IN THE *BOSTON JOURNAL* announces the beginning of the third season listing the regular members of the Club being the same as the previous year, with the exception of a new second clarinetist, Augusto Vannini. The newspaper mentions that subscription sales for these concerts begin the following day and recommends them to the readers.

> There is no need at this late day of dilating upon the unique features and high artistic excellence of these concerts, which would be impossible in any other city except Paris or Brussels. The programs this season are of unusual interest.[1]

[1] This item, cut from the newspaper, carries no date but is found in a scrapbook of reviews of the Longy Club kept by Georges Longy which is now in the Boston Public Library.

The First Concert

The first concert of the third season was given on the evening of 24 November 1902. This concert presented the Quintet op. 43, for oboe, clarinet, horn, bassoon and piano by Heinrich von Herzogenberg (1848–1900), a product of the Vienna Conservatory and a teacher at the Hochschule in Berlin; the Sextet for flute, oboe, English horn, clarinet, horn and bassoon by Edmond Malherbe (1870–1963);[2] and the Octet for flute, oboe, two clarinets, trumpet, horn and two bassoons by Paul de Wailly (1854–1933), a work dedicated to Longy.[3]

Philip Hale heard the Herzogenberg work as undistinguished.

Heinrich von Herzogenberg, ca. 1900

> The work of a solid musician, who is now in another world, where he is no doubt absorbed in higher contrapuntal problems. He was an industrious and fecund musician who knew thoroughly his trade. Unfortunately his ideas are generally as commonplace as his workmanship is smooth … Music lexicons will speak respectfully of his labors; they well acquaint posterity with his industry; and the works themselves will surely go into the great bin of oblivion, which, according to Sir Thomas Browne, is not to be hired; but the bin is there, capacious, and with mouth open for well-made symphonies, anxiously written operas, and all manner of chamber-music that was heard once and possibly praised on the night of the performance by friends and pupils.[4]

[2] Malherbe studied at the Paris Conservatoire and obtained numerous prizes there, including the Prix de Rome.

[3] De Wailly was a student of Franck.

[4] Philip Hale, 'Longy Club,' *Boston Journal*, Nov. 25, 1902.

On the other hand, Hale found the Malherbe Sextet to be quite an interesting composition.

> It contains ideas which are well expressed; there is a sense of tonal color, especially in the Andante and Presto; there is melody and there is grace. There is true poetic feeling in the Andantino, and the colors are finely blended. The Finale is a fluent movement that demands abandon as well as accuracy and general technical skill.

Hale's comments on the final work suggest that he was generally suspicious of the composer, de Wailly.

> De Wailly's octet is a disappointment. The composer is rich, a club man, a society swell, who takes himself seriously and is taken seriously, it seems, by some of the Parisian critics. Surely, this work does not do him justice, for it often seems the crude effort of an amateur.

The critic of the *Herald* did not discuss the individual compositions of this concert, writing 'It is impossible to swell now upon the performance at such length as would be pleasant.'[5] He did provide an interesting observation that suggests one or more members of the ensemble may have been privately complaining over the financial arrangements for these concerts.

[5] 'The Longy Concert,' *Boston Herald*, Nov. 25, 1902.

> That honorable and unique group of players, the Longy Club, is heartily welcomed back to the platform, where it is to be hoped they will meet this season a larger and richer remuneration than was accorded last year. Honors are good to get, but such musicians ought to have also a generous material recompense for what is done so well as their work is. Mr. Longy seems to have a special talent for finding interesting and edifying music of which the public knows practically nothing, so that his programmes provide instruction as well as pleasure.

The Second Concert

The second concert of this season was given in Chickering Hall on the evening of 5 January 1903. The *Herald* found this entire concert praiseworthy.

> It is sometimes said in Paris that it is useless to train up there a fine wooden-wind player, because as soon as he has made himself of some consequence he is engaged for Boston and taken away thither ... With the performances of the club, there is seldom a word of fault possible

to be found; the men know their music and how to deal with it. The programmes, extended and catholic as are Mr. Longy's knowledge and taste, are less uniform in merit and interest, because sometimes novelty has to do duty for stronger recommendations. But last evening's selections were all good in themselves and well arranged, so that matter and manner were both to be approved.[6]

[6] 'The Longy Concert,' *Boston Herald*, Jan. 6, 1903.

This concert began with the Serenade by Julius Röntgen (1855–1932) for flute, oboe, clarinet and pairs of horns and bassoons. The *Herald* only cites the composer as being a native of Leipzig, but previously an influential musician and professor in Amsterdam. Philip Hale, of the *Journal*, mentions the composer's background as well, but goes on to doubt the final worth of this composition.

Julius Röntgen, ca. 1932

> The first two movements of the Rontgen serenade were conventional and dull, and no rays of the other Rontgen could find originality or true beauty in them. They were the work of an honest Leipziger—of Dutch descent. It is true—but a Leipziger born and bred and the music had the familiar smell of Richter, Hautmann and other worthies. Where such movements are on a program, there should be a footnote: 'Conversation is allowed during the allegro and scherzo.'[7]

[7] Philip Hale, 'Longy, Oboist, Leader, First Performances,' *Boston Journal*, Jan. 6, 1903.

The second work on this program was the d'Indy *Fantasy on popular songs*, for oboe and piano, which the *Herald* called 'brilliant.' Hale noted, 'the performance gave Mr. Longy a great opportunity for the display of his unapproachable tone and exquisite artistry. Such a musician honors the town which he chooses for his abiding-place.'

Both critics found the final composition, André Caplet's *Suite Persane*, for double wind quintet, to be most unusual and interesting (which it certainly is!).

> And finally the quaint, ingenious and delightful 'Persian' suite of A. Caplet was played ... There were a strange sensuous charm and a wild, remote excitement in the different sections of this, and it brought a delightful evening to a romantic conclusion. [*Herald*]

> Caplet's Suite Persane ... is an illustration of three fantastic Persian poems, and the composer has used Persian melodies, as Saint-Saens and Claudius Blanc did in groups of songs. The first poem, 'Scharki,' is an erotic nocturne. The second 'Nihawend,' is as follows in paraphrase: 'As in a misty distance, dancing shades approach and take on human form to laugh in the sweet joys of love. They bloom in postures of grace and

pleasure. Becoming human, they seem to diffuse the odors of flowers and sunbeams.' The third poem, 'Iskia Samaise,' describes the dancing fakirs, who fall in weariness, ecstasize and then leap all the more furiously. The three pieces are of more than exotic interest; but the one that seems to a Western hearer the most expressive of the poetic mood is the second, which is beautiful in many ways, such music as caused the lovers in 'The Arabian Nights' to swoon with rapture and desire. The opening of the first is effective, and the constant return of the theme, 'the sob of love,' is skillfully managed. The third disappoints from lack of the frenzy that is rightly anticipated by the poet's description, and there is little suggestion of the madness of the scene. Caplet has succeeded in coloring the passages vividly, even when he does not take refuge in sheer exoticism. The Suite is well worth hearing and it was played with marked effect. [*Journal*]

The Third Concert

The final concert of the third season was given on the evening of 5 March 1903. Both extant reviews mention the small audience which appeared for this concert. The *Herald* attributed this on poor weather,[8] but Hale, in the *Journal*, gave blame to the dictates of 'society.' [9]

[8] 'Yesterday's Chamber Music,' *Boston Herald*, March 6, 1903.

[9] Philip Hale, 'Longy Third Concert of Wind Instruments,' *Boston Journal*, March 6, 1903.

> And there were so few to hear it. Such performances are rare, even in Paris, or Brussels, the homes of wind-instrument players. These members of our orchestra excite the admiration of musicians in the cities they visit. Are we too much accustomed to them that we miss the opportunity of hearing them? It does not seem to make any difference whether Mr. Longy and his associates produce new works or give the best of the classic repertory. The result is the same, the 'patrons and patronesses' of music have not decreed that these concerts should be fashionable. Mediocre singers or pianists, either local or visitors, are approved, and the word is passed that they should and must be heard. But these artists—and I use the word discreetly—are passed by. Mr. Longy has made a brave endeavor. I should not blame him if with dignity he withdrew from the field. The abandonment of his concerts on account of non-support would be a reproach to themusic-lovers of Boston and a blow to the prestige of the boastful city.

This concert began with the Sextet op. 6, for flute, oboe, clarinet, horn, bassoon and piano by Ludwig Thuille (1861–1907). The *Herald* thought this an excellent work to open a concert and Hale mentioned that the work had been first performed in Boston by the New England Conservatory Chamber Music Club earlier the same year, adding,

Thuille was a fellow-student of Richard Strauss in Munich, when they both walked meekly in the conventional paths of respectability. The sextet is a thoroughly amiable work, well made, pleasant to hear, without evidence of striking originality, and with some pages of true beauty … All in all a work well worth doing.

Next came a Sonata for two oboes and bassoon by Handel, which the *Herald* found the most 'alive' of the three compositions on the program. This performance made Hale wish that audiences could come to know more of the instrumental music of this master.

Ludwig Thuille, George Grantham Bain Collection, Library of Congress

Handel, as is known to Macaulay's schoolboy, was addicted to the oboe. He wrote trios for oboes and bassoon when he was a youngster, all through his tumultuous life he was faithful to his early love … It is a pity that we hear so little of the instrumental music of the grand master who is now considered by many as a mere oratorio-monger. Think of the wealth of melody in his operas which is given to few of the untuneful declaimers and strivers after 'diction' to sing Handel's music.

The major composition on this program was the *Sinfonietta* op. 188, by Joachim Raff (1822–1882), for pairs of flutes, oboes, clarinets, horns and bassoons. On this occasion both critics found merit in this composition.

The Raff was entertaining and laudable, its being sumptuous yet not cloying and without his not unusual affectation, pomposity or ad captandum display. Its use of the wooden wind quartet, intensified and enriched by the horns, showed fancy, feeling for color and musicianly skill. [*Herald*]

Joachim Raff, by August Weger

The feature of the concert was the superb performance of Raff's Sinfonietta. The work was written at Wiesbaden … and the composer arranged it for four hands. Raff is undeservedly neglected in these days, as he was during his pathetic life—pathetic because full of ideas, eager to strike out on new paths, nobly ambitious, he was obliged to write pot-boilers that he might live out his meager life. Mr. Longy is to be thanked heartily for reminding us of the great talent of this composer. The skill developed with extraordinary richness of resources, ever tuneful, ever euphonious, beautifully and now gorgeously colored. For Raff heard his music as he wrote it, not when it was performed. The man's color-sense was most acute; his blending of tonal colors was confident and unerring. Even passages of routine are here kaleidoscopic. It is impossible to speak too highly of the performance, which must be justly counted as a memorable one, a glory of a season. [*Journal*]

Season Four, 1903–1904

During the fourth season the Longy Club ventured for the first time away from Boston to give a concert in New York City. This season also marked the point at which the printed programs began to list all ten winds as 'Members of the Club,' rather than listing some as members and some as 'assisting artists.' For the season the artists were André Maquarre and Arthur Brooke, flute; Longy and Clement Lenom, oboe; Peter Metzger and Augusto Vannini, clarinet; Albert Debuchy and John Helleberg, bassoons; Albert Hackebarth and Frank Hein, horn and Heinrich Gebhard, piano.

Beginning with the first concert the ensemble was now heard in the Potter Hall, 177 Huntington Avenue, and the programs list a new Manager, J. Sauerquell. Subscription tickets for the three concerts sold for four dollars.

The First Concert

The first concert of the fourth season, given on the evening of 30 November 1903, began with the Suite op. 4, for flute, oboe, clarinet, horn, bassoon and piano by Charles Quef (1873–1931).[1] This was followed by a performance of the Carl Reinecke (1824–1910) *Undine* flute Sonata, performed by Mr. Maquarre. The final composition was the Mozart E♭ Partita, K. 375. On the occasion of this concert one finds a review by a new critic, one much in love with his own voice and nearly always finding some relationship between music and food, as on this occasion.

[1] Charles Paul Florimond Quef was born in Lille, France. As a student at the Paris Conservatoire he took first prize in organ performance.

> In the midst of the richer and graver things of a full musical season the passionless intellectuality of an occasional program of wind instrument music comes almost as refreshingly as the glass of sorbet in the course of a long, highly savored repast. The range of possibility in tonal effects and even in mere extent of scale is small, to be sure, and there usually is a certain naiveté and simplicity that relieve tension and give new, even though but slight, sensations.[2]

[2] 'Longy Club Opens its Music Season,' *Boston Journal*, Dec. 1, 1903.

This same critic called the first composition on this concert, the Quef Suite, 'quaintly conceived.' The *Herald* considered the composer,

Potter Hall, New Century Building, Boston, ca. 1910

while not rigidly academic in his views concerning composition, by no means a wild-eyed revolutionary. The suite is interesting and would stand more than one hearing.³

3 'Longy Club's First Concert,' *Boston Herald*, Dec. 1, 1903.

Each reviewer considered the Mozart Partita to be the most outstanding work heard on this concert.

The last number was the strongest and made the most impression … The minuet left the hearers quite astir. [*Journal*]

Mozart wrote this serenade at Vienna in October, 1781, for the sister of a Mrs. Von Hickl. If he wrote it for a woman, there was more than a compliment in his intent, for, as he wrote his father, he wished von Strack, a daily visitor, to hear some of his music, so he composed it with extra care. Jahn, the faithful admirer, saw all sorts of wonderful things in this music: he ascribed a chivalric character to the first movement; he wondered at the lamenting second theme of the same movement; he found in the adagio a dialogue of lovers, and in the finale the echoes of a simple mirthful folk. The oboes were added by Mozart later. Some

---

Fourth Season, 1903-04

Chamber Music for Wind Instruments

by

The Longy Club

FIRST CONCERT

Monday Evening, November 30, at 8 o'clock

in

POTTER HALL,   177 Huntington Ave.

New Century B'ld'g

SUBSCRIPTION TICKETS, with Reserved Seats for the Series, FOUR DOLLARS, on sale at Box Office, Symphony Hall, Massachusetts and Huntington Avenues, MONDAY, Nov. 23, at 8.30 a.m.
J. SAUERQUELL, *Manager*.

PROGRAMME.

C. QUEF.   SUITE, op. 4, for Flute, Oboe, Clarinet, Horn, Bassoon and Piano.
 I. Entrée (Allegro.)
 II. Andantino.
 III. Rondo. Finale.
Messrs. A. Maquarre, G. Longy, P. Metzger, A. Hackebarth, A. Debuchy and H. Gebhard.

REINECKE.   SONATE, "Undine," for Flute and Piano.
 I. Allegro.
 II. Intermezzo.
 III. Andante tranquillo.
 IV. Allegro molto agitato.
Messrs. A. Maquarre and H. Gebhard.

MOZART.   SERENADE in E flat major, No. 11, op. 375, for two Oboes, two Clarinets, two Horns and two Bassoons.
 I. Allegro maestoso.
 II. Adagio.
 III. Menuetto.
 IV. Allegro.
Messrs. G. Longy, C. Lenom, P. Metzger, A. Vannini, A. Hackebarth, F. Hein, A. Debuchy and J. Helleberg.

Mason and Hamlin Pianoforte.

SUBSCRIPTION TICKETS, with Reserved Seats for the Series, FOUR DOLLARS, on sale at Box Office, Symphony Hall, Massachusetts and Huntington Avenues, MONDAY, Nov. 23, at 8.30 a.m.
J. SAUERQUELL, *Manager*.

one has even added two English horns, and Pleyel turned the piece into a string quintet. If the average hearer is a bit less discerning, or less imaginative, than the enthusiastic Jahn, nevertheless the work holds plenty of matter to interest and even move him. [*Herald*]

Finally, the *Herald* mentioned that this concert had a large audience and the *Journal* promised that in the next concert the public would hear a new work by Loeffler which would include a part for the 'saxaphone.'

The Second Concert

Beginning with this concert one finds a new format which appears regularly during the following years: presenting guest soloists in the intervals between the major works of the wind ensemble. This idea, no doubt one intended to broaden the audience, finds expression on this occasion in the appearance of Mr. and Mrs. Gilibert, who sang duets from Offenbach, Weckerlin and Messager, with additional arias by Matini, Weber and Massenet, rendered by Mr. Gilibert.

This concert also marks the first appearance with the wind ensemble of Mrs. Elise Hall, a lady whose contributions to the musical life of Boston is quite amazing. She only began the study of the saxophone at age forty-seven, and then for purposes of health and at the recommendation of her husband, Dr. Richard J. Hall, a prominent Boston surgeon. She studied with Longy and in a short time was performing in public. In addition, she commissioned many works for saxophone, including works by master composers such as d'Indy, Schmitt and Debussy! She was very highly regarded in Boston, as can be seen in the following rather typical press notice.

Elise Hall

4 'Boston Orchestral Club,' *Boston Globe*, Dec. 30, 1906.

> Mrs. Hall has played in Boston enough times to make plain to the initiated the high grade of her artistry. Every year she plays abroad with orchestras of international reputation and often compositions written and dedicated to her by some of the best modern composers, her personal friends.
>
> Despite the proportions of her present-day attainments, she is an earnest and continuous student, and with the humility of true greatness affirms that she knows 'very little.'[4]

This article reminds the reader that in 1899 Mrs. Hall had founded an earlier musical organization, called 'The Amateurs,' in Santa Barbara, California, and then founded the Boston Orchestra Club.

> The early and continued success of the club was due to Mrs. Hall's appreciation and respect for art, while in several instances scores calling for rare instruments not to be procured in this country necessitated her ordering them made abroad, as she would consider no substitute …
>
> For the instruction of less experienced players and that the orchestra should have all necessary parts, professional musicians, mostly from the Symphony, have been paid members of the club.
>
> The dollars necessary for each year's expenses have reached well into the thousands, and for the greater part of the club's lifetime these expenses have been met by Mrs. Hall unaided.
>
> Up to the advent of the Orchestral Club, modern French music—which at the present time is so distinctly a school by itself—was practically unknown to America.

Among the new works introduced to Boston by the Orchestral Club, on 5 January 1903, was the premiere of a composition by Longy himself. This was his *Impression*, composed for Mrs. Hall, for saxophone, three horns, harp, strings and antique cymbals. Upon hearing this work the *Journal* noted, 'It is a pleasure to learn that Debussy and d'Indy are now at work on pieces for this somber, melancholy, mysterious instrument.'[5]

On the second Longy Club concert of this season Mrs. Hall was the soloist in the Loeffler, *Ballade Carnavalesque*, for saxophone, flute, oboe, bassoon and piano, a work dedicated to her.

The wind ensemble itself performed two major works, an Octet by Haydn and the Gouvy *Petite Suite Gauloise*, op. 90, for flute and octet.

[5] 'News Notes on Music,' *Boston Journal*, Jan. 6, 1903.

An Extra Concert in New York City

On 8 March 1904, the Longy Club gave its first concert in New York City, in the Mendelssohn Hall. An unnamed critic reflects a rather cold atmosphere for wind ensemble music in New York.

There are in Paris, London and Berlin excellent ensemble organizations of wind instruments, but that branch of the musical industry has never flourished conspicuously in America.⁶ The lack of tonal variety and color in a composition written exclusively for wind instruments militates successfully against its wide popularity. Even the help of a piano does not improve the monotony of color. Indeed there are some finely attuned musical ears which refuse to hear the slightest real tonal unity between the piano and a wind instrument of any description whatsoever. Composers of former days wrote rather frequently for combinations of woodwind, or brass, or both; but it must be remembered that those were the experimental days in music. With the exception of Brahms, none of the later composers showed a marked preference for exploiting wind instruments outside of the orchestra. There are many musical persons, too, who agree with the old German joke, that there is only one thing worse than a flute concerto, and that is—two flute concertos!⁷

⁶ Curiously ignoring Sousa who was at his heights in popularity.

7 'Longy Club Concert,' *Musical Courier* (New York), March 16, 1904.

Apart from their performance of the Mozart Quintet for piano and winds, the program the Longy Club presented New Yorkers was certainly not one to turn this attitude into one of enthusiasm. The concert began with the Mozart, followed by the Reinecke *Undine* flute Sonata, a Trio by Handel for two oboes and bassoon, and the Caplet *Suite Persane* for ten winds. The reviewer was not moved by the choice of literature and reserved his only real praise for the piano.

The most difficult problem was that of intonation, and it was solved with care and with success on the whole. The technic of all the players, individually and in ensemble, left nothing to be desired. The Mozart number of them all ranked highest in musical value, and the Caplet suite ranked lowest. It is pretty, but nothing more. Reinecke has written many notes in his flute sonata, but not one striking musical or harmonic idea. There is no reason apparent why the work should be named 'Undine.' The Handel trio is by Handel.

An unalloyed musical joy was the dignified and luminous pianism of Heinrich Gebhard. As an ensemble pianist it would be difficult to name his superior. He is an analyst who pays full tribute to the letter of his score, without, however, passing by its lyrical and imaginative ingredients. He adapted himself with remarkable facility to the tonal and dynamic exigencies of the wind instruments, and that is an achievement deserving of no unstinted praise. Mr. Gebhard added materially last week to his large clientele of admirers in New York.

Carl Reinecke, by Alfred Naumann, 1893

The Third Concert

Returning to Boston for the final concert of the fourth season, on 28 March, the ensemble encountered a level of enthusiasm from public and press it had never before enjoyed. One wonders if the tour to New York contributed in some degree to this change in local attitude. Certainly the larger audience must be credited largely to the guest artist, Armand Forest, the Concertmaster of the Opera Comique Orchestra in Paris. Philip Hale wrote after this concert,

> It is pleasant to see, at this ending of the fourth season of Mr. Longy's concerts, that the music-lovers of the town have at last found what their founder has been doing for art, and have decided to support him in his work. A year or two ago, these men were rewarded by rows of empty seats and the future of their undertaking looked dark. Henceforth success seems assured.[8]

[8] Philip Hale, *Boston Journal*, March 29, 1904.

PROGRAMME.

V. D'INDY,   CHANSON ET DANSES, op. 50, Divertissement for Flute, Oboe, two Clarinets, Horn and two Bassoons.
    I. Chanson.
    II Danses.

BACH,   SONATA in B minor, for Violin and Piano.
    Andante.
    Allegro.
    Andante.
    Allegro.

WAGNER,   PRELUDE to the third act, "Tristan und Isolde," for English Horn Solo and Small Orchestra.
    ENGLISH HORN SOLO: Mr. Longy.

A. CAPLET,   SUITE PERSANE for two Flutes, two Oboes, two Clarinets, two Horns and two Bassoons.
    Scharki (Allegretto quasi Andante.)
    Nihawend (Andantino.)
    Iaka Samaise (Vivo.)

The Pianoforte is a Mason and Hamlin.

A second reviewer also notes this change in the fortunes of the ensemble.

> The Boston audience is sometimes accused of being cold, but this charge cannot be laid against the large and enthusiastic audience which greeted the Longy Club last night. The programme selected was of unusual merit and the people were quick to show their appreciation of it …
>
> It my now be said that the Longy Club is thoroughly established as one of the important factors in the musical life of this city. It is no longer an experiment and the liberal patronage and appreciation given the club during the year show that there is a demand for just such an organization. Much credit is due Mr. Longy and his colleagues for the good start made. The further influence and benefit to be derived from their efforts will no doubt continue to grow from year to year.[9]

[9] 'The Longy Club,' *Boston Advertiser*, March 29, 1904.

The concert began with a real masterpiece for wind ensemble, exactly the kind of work which should have been played in New York, the d'Indy *Chanson et Danses*, for flute, oboe, two clarinets, horn and two bassoons. The *Advertizer* thought this work, 'rich in tone color and contained some beautiful melodies. It was finely given by the club and was well received.' Hale, on the other hand, was still deaf to the medium itself.

> It is undoubtedly difficult to find music for wood wind that is so skillfully written as to make an entirely pleasant impression upon its hearers and d'Indy, able master of orchestration though he was, was not able to avoid the almost inevitable in his song and dances with which Mr. Longy and his men began their concert. The song, a rather somber little affair, had no very definite message, while the dances of the oriental type rather than French cannot be called especially beautiful. It goes without saying that both movements were played with all the finish and technical beauty possible, but even those qualities hardly vitalized the work.[10]

[10] Hale, *Boston Journal*, March 29, 1904.

Next Mr. Forest appeared. The surviving program lists only the B minor violin Sonata by Bach (which the nearly always unhappy Mr. Hale labels 'a drearily, monotonous collection of finger exercises'), although the reviews reveal the presence of a small orchestra, consisting of members of the Boston Symphony Orchestra, conducted by Wilhelm Gericke (1845–1925), who participated in the encore, Saint-Saën's *Rondo Capriccioso*. Here one wonders if the reviewers were at the same concert. Hale found, 'the orchestra rather at a disadvantage in its little stage-enclosure, and the music came out lacking in clearness,' whereas the *Advertizer* maintained, 'we must call attention to the beautiful effect of hearing an orchestra in a small hall. Every bit of shading, every instrumental tone-color is perfectly preserved, and effects are obtained which are infinitely superior to those given by any orchestra in a large hall.'

Wilhelm Gericke, originally published in *The History of American Music*, by Louis Charles Elson (New York: Macmillan Co., 1904).

Taking advantage of the strings present, Longy next appeared as an English horn soloist in his own arrangement of the Prelude to Act Three of Wagner's *Tristan*. Both reviewers paid tribute to Longy, the *Advertizer* calling him the 'King of the oboe and English horn' and the *Journal* mentioning his 'exquisite art' and promising the work, 'has never been heard with such absolute beauty in this city before.'

After all of this, the audience seems to have been unmoved by a repetition of the Caplet *Suite Persane* played in New York, even though it is an outstanding composition. Hale did not even discuss this work and the *Advertizer* suggested, 'Perhaps if it had been played earlier in the evening it might have fared better.'

Season Five, 1904–1905

DURING THIS SEASON THE LONGY CLUB had several new members: Daniel Maquarre appears, beside his brother, as second flute; Georges Grisez, a new member of the Boston Symphony Orchestra also appears as first clarinet in this ensemble, and a new pianist's name appears, Alfred de Voto. The first program listed Albert Hackebarth as first horn, but the reviews record he was 'not present on account of indisposition' and that he was replaced by Frank Hain, who usually played second horn. That seems to have been the end of Mr. Hackebarth, for beginning with the second program, Mr. Hain is listed as first horn and a new member, Heinrich Lorbeer, joins as second horn.

The First Concert

The first concert of the fifth season was given on 17 November 1904, in the Potter Hall. From several press accounts one gains the impression that by this date the Longy Club had clearly gained an enthusiastic following in Boston.

> The now famous Longy Club inaugurated its fifth season with a program that was simply delightful and left nothing to be desired, unless indeed it be the perfectly natural desire for more; one hour of such a treat seems too short … The enthusiastic recall of the artists at its close tells better than words the pleasure it afforded.[1]

> This fine organization, whose like does not, and probably could not exist anywhere else in America, is at last coming into its own. For two years, at least, Mr. Longy, its founder, struggled against coldness and neglect on the part of those who might have been expected to support his venture. He kept on his way bravely and hopefully and now the future of his labor seems secure. The audience last night was larger than any the club has yet drawn, and the attendance will doubtless grow in a healthy way.

> The concert was thoroughly enjoyable, which cannot always be said of this special form of music. Often wood-wind, even re-enforced by horns, grows monotonous and cloying. But the program was so admirably made last night that nothing of that feeling was possible.[2]

[1] *Boston Traveler*, quoted in the Longy brochure printed in 1906.

[2] 'The Longy Concert,' *Boston Journal*, Nov. 18, 1904.

Seldom has the Longy Club given a more attractive concert than that of yesterday evening. From the organization we have learned to expect perfection of performance and catholic taste in the making of programmes, but it has not always been easy to find works for wind instruments alone that are agreeable to listen to.[3]

Even the hard to please critic, Philip Hale, who in this year moved to the *Boston Herald*, had to admit, 'the concert gave much pleasure,' and commented twice on the appreciative audience.[4]

The program began with the *Concertstuck* ('Idyllische Scene'), op. 41, by Julius Rietz (1812–1877) for wind quintet and piano. The program described this as a premiere performance, which no doubt refers to the composer's transcription (from orchestra) for wind ensemble and piano. The critics enjoyed this work for its pleasant character, but none of them took it as a serious composition. The *Journal* called it

[3] R. R. G., 'Potter Hall: Longy Club Concert,' *Boston Transcript*, Nov. 18, 1904.

[4] Philip Hale, 'Longy Concert,' *Boston Herald*, Nov. 18, 1904.

> amiable music, if not of any great distinction. The Andante, with its horn phrases overlaid with flute lace work as its most salient characteristic, pleased in a modest way, and the rustic wedding sort of flavor that marked the final movement was gay and unaffected.

The *Transcript* heard it as not just rustic, but indeed only suited as garden music.

> To begin the concert there was a composition by Julius Rietz, a most respectable composer of Dresden, who knew how to write gracefully and prettily, even if he had not much to say. His concert piece is much after the order of a serenade; were the players stationed in the arbor of an old garden, to play for guests after supper, the music could not fail to have pleasure.

Philip Hale, in the *Herald*, had a similar reaction, but for him it recalled a specific memory:

> Its performance brought up pleasant memories of afternoons spent in an open-air restaurant on the bank of the Elbe.
> There was a sheet iron scenery representing an Alpine glacier, and real water trickling in the foreground vied with the foaming beer in the endeavor to persuade the guests that it was cool. Women gossiped over their knitting and commented on the unmistakable fondness of betrothed couples drinking blissfully out of one glass; men struggled heroically with sausages and two cent cigars.

```
            Fifth Season 1904-05                                    PROGRAMME

        Chamber Music for Wind Instruments        J. RIETZ,      Concertstück (Idillische Scene) for Flute, Oboe, Clarinet,
                                                                 Horn and Bassoon with Piano accompaniment, op. 41.
                        by                              I. Moderato assai. Allegro con fuoco.
                                                            II. Andante sostenuto.
                                                                III. Molto Allegro
                                                                 (First time.)

                The Longy Club                    G. PIERNÉ,     Pastoral variée (in the ancient style) for Flute, Oboe,
                                                                 Clarinet, Trumpet, Horn and two Bassoons, op. 30.
                                                            Andantino. (Introduction.)
                                                            Tema in Canone.
                                                              1st Double.  Scherzosamente.
                                                              2d Double.   Tourbillon.
                                                              3d Double.   Tempo di menuetto.
                                                              4th Double.  Alla siciliana.
                                                              5th Double.  Final.
                                                                 (First time.)

                    FIRST CONCERT                 N. W. GADE,    a) Ballade.
                                                  CH. M. WIDOR,  b) Introduction and Rondo for Clarinet and Piano,
                                                                 op. 72.
                                                                 G. GRISEZ and A. de VOTO.
          Thursday Evening, November 17, at 8 oclock             (First time.)

                          in                      E. BERNARD,    Divertissement op. 36, for two Flutes, two Oboes, two
                                                                 Clarinets, two Horns, and two Bassoons.
         POTTER HALL,         177 Huntington Ave.        I. Andante sostenuto. Allegro molto moderato.
                                                            II. Allegro vivace.
                    New Century B'ld'g                          III. Andante. Allegro non troppo.
```

The band played on, and it played music that sounded like Rietz's Concertstuck—this same Idyllic Scene. Possibly the music was by Mueller or by Lange, but we are inclined to think it was by Rietz. It did not irritate, it did not excite, it did not divert from gossip or from eating and drinking. No one kept count of the number of movements. The music went with the scenery and the guests, but it was not nearly as well played as it was last night.

The program lists the second composition as a premiere performance as well, the Gabriel Pierné, *Pastoral variee*, 'in the Ancient Style,' op. 30, for flute, oboe, clarinet, trumpet, horn and two bassoons. The trumpeter, Louis Kloepfel, joined the Longy Club for this performance, which three of the critics thought to be the musical highlight of the entire concert.

The gem of the evening was the Pierne pastoral piece, in which a near old-fashioned theme was given a set of little variations highly amusing as well as exceedingly clever. The use of the bassoon was skilful, and the total effect of the short composition was most happy. It was played in masterly fashion, as, indeed, was everything. [*Journal*]

Gabriel Pierné, by Franz Benque, 1898

After a few bars of introduction, which carried the imagination irresistibly to the mountains d'Indy sang of in his symphony for orchestra and pianoforte, came the theme, a delightful theme, given out by the oboe and repeated in canon by the clarinet. And then there were variations—only five, and all short; a scherzo in miniature; a brilliant bit called 'Tourbillon,' verily, a tiny hurricane; a charming minuet, with brilliant work for the trumpet; a sicilenne, and then the finale. Probably the whole performance lasted no more than five minutes, but everybody in the hall was delighted with the grace and melodic charm of the little work. It certainly must be repeated some day. [*Transcript*]

Pierne's pastoral, performed there for the first time, is delightfully piquant. The theme, announced in canon form, is varied ingeniously. The variations are short, and there is just enough of them. They are of quaint beauty and the indisputable technical skill of the composer is supplemented by fine taste and imagination. The performance was of the highest order, both technically and aesthetically. [*Herald*]

At this point the stage was given over to two of the new members of the club, Georges Grisez and Alfred de Voto, who performed the Widor *Introduction and Rondo*, op. 71, for clarinet and piano and a *Ballade* by Niels Gade (1817–1890). As Grisez was also a new member of the Boston Symphony Orchestra, there must have been considerable curiosity to hear him in a solo performance. The only reservations of the critics were with regard to his tone.

The first Longy Club concert was also made interesting by the appearance of Mr. Georges Grisez, the new clarinet player of the orchestra. Mr. Grisez comes of a musical family, his father, Leon Grisez, being a distinguished player of the clarinet in Paris, where he has been soloist of the Pas de Loup and Conservatoire concerts, while his grandfather was an admirable bassoon player. Mr. Grisez, a very young artist, has a fluent technique with much brilliancy of execution and a musical way of phrasing. While his tone is sweet and clear, as yet it is not large, and at times it seems lacking in richness. With time, however, it will probably increase. [*Transcript*]

Mr. Grisez, the new clarinet of the Symphony orchestra, exhibited tone and sustained song in the ballade, and his virtuoso qualities in Widor's piece. His tone is pure and pleasing, without, however, the melancholy richness that is characteristic of the lower tones of the instrument; in fact his tone is not warmly emotional. On the other hand, his technique is fluent and brilliant and he phrases with understanding. He is a young player, and he will no doubt develop. He may yet gain in elasticity and in variety of tonal emotion. [*Herald*]

Mr. Grisez, in his clarinet solos, showed much beauty of phrasing and high virtuosity, although at times the mellowness of his tone was not fully sustained. Mr. De Voto, at the pianoforte, acquitted himself with perfect taste and a clear knowledge of what ensemble playing should be. [*Journal*]

The final work on this first concert was the Bernard *Divertissement* op. 36, for ten winds. Although this work is still performed throughout the world today, the critics of 1904 paid little attention to it; only the *Transcript* mentioned that it is 'so well written that the lack of strings does not make itself so clearly felt as usual.'

The Second Concert

The second concert of the fifth season was given on the evening of 19 January 1905 and featured, for the second year in a row, Mrs. Hall and her saxophone.

The concert began with a work the critics found quite weak, the Lacroix, *Sextuor* for wind quintet and piano. Judging by Hale's review, this composer's name was not one well-known in Boston.

> Lacroix is no doubt an organist. When a young composer leaves the Paris Conservatory he either plays a church organ or sets music to some ingeniously improper operetta; sometimes he does both with marked success. If Lacroix studied at the conservatory, he was not an honor man, but this should not prejudice one against him. The fate of the prix de Rome and that of the college valedictorian is often sadly the same. Lacroix's sextet shows that he has studied, for his technic is fluent; indeed, the music shows more technic than inspiration. The composer's melodic vein is not rich. Only in the second movement is there a truly spontaneous theme of old-fashioned French character, clear, well defined and with a grace that is rather elegance, and this theme is dangerously near the conventional salon romance of the years just before Gounod began to write songs. The third movement, a fugue, is deftly made and is not too long.[5]

5 Philip Hale, 'Longy Club's Second Concert,' *Boston Herald*, Jan. 20, 1905.

The *Transcript* thought even less of this composer.

> The first movement of the composition is exceedingly uninteresting, although well-made, and the slow movement, while really charming, is distinctly commonplace; the melody sounds like that of a French Sir Arthur Sullivan. The fugue, too, is trivial, the most agreeable of the parts being the finale, a lively, vivacious bit of music pleasant to hear.[6]

It was, needless to say, Mrs. Hall, her saxophone, and two new compositions commissioned by her, which most attracted the attention of the press. The new works were a *Legende* by Caplet, for saxophone, oboe, clarinet, bassoon, two violins, viola, cello and string bass, and a Lento in C♯ Minor, for solo saxophone, two clarinets, bassoon, string bass, harp, and three timpani by none other than Longy himself.

The *Transcript*, after a very polite rejection of the music, commented on the performance of Mrs. Hall and the progress she had made as a player during the previous year, but also gave some rare and valuable hints of how the saxophone was heard in the years before jazz clarinets in America were responsible, or so some suggest, for redesigning the mouthpiece to produce the far more brilliant sound usually heard today.

> The interest of the occasion was mostly aroused by the two pieces for saxophone, both of which were written to be performed by Mrs. Hall. Heretofore there has been little literature for the saxophone, and it is the art of Mrs. Hall that has inspired such composers as Caplet, Mr. Longy and Mr. Loeffler to make experiments for the instrument, to see what may be done with it in the way of chamber music. Mr. Longy's piece is peculiar in that it requires greater bravura in saxophone playing than we have been accustomed to hear. The music is practically a saxophone solo, the other instruments being used chiefly for color or dramatic effect. The composition proves conclusively the work of the saxophone for establishing a certain somber, tragic mood. This is also true of the Caplet Legend. The music is indeed romantic and distinguished by beautiful melody, but the course of the melody seems unnecessarily involved. In hearing it, one longs for greater simplicity. However, although it may be doubted if either Mr. Longy's or Caplet's piece will ever gain a place in the repertory of chamber music, there is no question that both composers have done useful service in proving to the world the value of the saxophone in chamber music. Mrs. Hall, who has gained appreciably in her art since she last appeared in public, played admirably indeed, with very beautiful tone, with frequent exquisite phrasing, and often with extreme brilliancy of execution. If the saxophone ever gains recognition as an instrument for chamber concerts, it will be largely due to Mrs. Hall.[7]

[6] R. R. G. 'Potter Hall: Longy Club,' *Boston Transcript*, Jan. 20, 1905.

[7] R. R. G. 'Potter Hall: Longy Club,' *Boston Transcript*, Jan. 20, 1905.

> **Fifth Season 1904-05**
>
> Chamber Music for Wind Instruments
>
> by
>
> **The Longy Club**
>
> SECOND CONCERT
>
> Thursday Evening, January 19, at 8 o'clock
>
> in
>
> POTTER HALL,   177 Huntington Ave.
>
> New Century B'ld'g
>
> **PROGRAMME.**
>
> E. LACROIX,   Sextuor for Flute, Oboe, Clarinet, Horn, Bassoon and Piano.
>   I. Assez vite.
>   II. Calme.
>   III. Fugue.
>   IV. Vif.
>
> G. LONGY,   a) Lento in C sharp minor, for Saxophone Solo, Two Clarinets, Bassoon, Double-bass, Three Kettledrums, and Harp.
>
> A. CAPLET,   b) Legende for Oboe, Clarinet, Saxophone, Bassoon, Two Violins, Viola, 'Cello, and Double-bass. *
>
> MOZART,   Serenade No. 12, in C minor, for Two Oboes, Two Clarinets, Two Horns, and Two Bassoons.
>   I. Allegro.
>   II. Andante.
>   III. Menuet in Canone.
>   IV. Allegro.
>
> *Mrs. R. J. Hall will play the Saxophone in these two selections, which have been specially composed for her.
>
> The Piano is a Mason and Hamlin.
>
> Third Concert Thursday Evening, March 2, at eight.

Philip Hale gives an almost identical description of his impression on the nature of the instrument as he knew it.

> The pieces by Longy and Caplet were composed especially for Mrs. Hall and for the display of the saxophone and the performer. We believe that Mr. Longy wrote the saxophone part as a sort of etude for his pupil, and that the instrumentation was supplied by Caplet, who is interested in the instrument, for which few have written intelligently; for they have cared chiefly for its bravura possibilities and have treated it as they would treat a clarinet. But such composers as d'Indy, Debussy and Caplet recognize the value of its mysterious and peculiarly mournful tones and these experimenters with timbres see a future for the saxophone in chamber music. Mr. Longy's Lento is frankly a show piece of a better kind. It makes demands on the sustained song and the facility of the player, and thus it is effective.
>
> Pieces by Caplet have been played at the concerts of this club. The Legende was written for an occasion, and it is more or less experimental music. The opening is charming; a legendary mood is suggested and then the mood is quickly dispelled. The musical thought seems needlessly and ineffectively tortured. There is seldom any true continuity of line or mood. When there is beauty, it is generally beauty of color without reference to enrichment of a line or the accentuation of an emotion. There are interesting harmonic progressions, but in a work of this kind one has a right to expect either beauty of thought or some sustained and persuasive emotion; Caplet's music is not clear in thought, and the

emotion is so vapid, so restless, that instead of leaving a definite impression it irritates. By beauty of thought we do not mean smug euphony; there are blasted heaths, desolate sand dunes, grim rocks, blighted and spectral trees, both in music and in nature, and supreme beauty today contains the element of fantastic or wild irregularity, as centuries ago Plotinus found the surest form in flickering or leaping or ever-changing fire. In this irregularity there must be some definite purpose, though the mood be as a summer haze or as those nightmare mountains, the Diablerets. Caplet's music lacks the essential purpose.

The two pieces served Mrs. Hall admirably. There are some who dislike the saxophone and to some the instrument is an acquired taste, as caviar, olives or the prose of Mr. Meredith; yet the saxophone has sonorously noble qualities, and after Caplet and the others are through with their experiments, they may succeed in varying chamber music and yet keeping it in its proper place without the pretension of rivaling an orchestra. Mrs. Hall has gained greatly in technical proficiency, in quiet mastery of tone, in authority of song and bravura, in continuity of rhythm. Her performance last night was engrossing; it was much more to the hearer than the satisfaction of his curiosity. Mrs. Hall in a word played with the enthusiasm of a devoted amateur and the proficiency of the accustomed professional. She was heartily applauded, as were her colleagues throughout the concert.[8]

[8] *Herald*, Jan. 20, 1905. Another interesting early description of the saxophone tone is found in a discussion of Mrs. Hall in the *Boston Globe* for Dec. 30, 1906, where a critic wrote, 'it resembles the combination of clarinet, English horn and cello, but has an utterance of more resounding depth than either of the above.'

The final work on this concert was one of the most important and beautiful wind ensemble works ever written, the great C Minor Partita, K. 384a, by Mozart. Curiously, these early Boston critics never seem to fully grasp the importance of this work. Hale was not even sure if he had heard it before at these concerts [he had], 'these serenades of Mozart and of his period sound much alike.'[9] The *Transcript* critic, at least, recognized that it was the best music on the program.

[9] *Herald*, Jan. 20, 1905.

The number that called forth the most enthusiasm was the Mozart Serenade, which, after the rest, seemed remarkably simple, straightforward and fresh. The closing allegro in particular was thoroughly delightful.

An Extra Concert

On 12 February 1905, the Longy Club appeared on a series of concerts in Chickering Hall organized by a H. G. Tucker as a benefit for the Perkins Institute for the blind. *The Boston Journal* reported 'the audience was large and enthusiastic and the program was worthy of their enthusiasm. It was a revelation of the possibilities of wind instruments for chamber concerts.'[10]

The ensemble performed the Bernard *Divertissement*, which they had played on their January concert as well as the Gouvy *Suite Gauloise*, the Thuille *Sextette* for piano and winds and a Trio by Handel which appears frequently on their programs. This Trio, which earlier critics scarcely bothered to mention, was considered by Louis Elson of the *Advertizer* to surpass the famous Beethoven Trio—an opinion surely no one alive today would share!

[10] 'With the Longy Club at Chickering Hall,' Feb. 13, 1905.

> The Handel was quaint and interesting and was charmingly played. It is shorter and much more attractive than Beethoven's trio for 2 oboes and English horn, which we hope that the Longy Club will not resurrect. This Trio was full of very ingenious counterpoint. The players were twice recalled.[11]

[11] Louis C. Elson, 'The Longy Club Concert,' *Boston Advertizer*, Feb. 13, 1905.

Alternating with these compositions were some solo performances by members of the wind ensemble. Elson thought this an excellent way to avoid the 'monotony which might have resulted from a succession of concerted pieces for wood-wind,' and, while it made the program a bit long, 'gave an excellent opportunity for the laity to study some of the instruments, with which they were but slightly acquainted, more minutely.'

Aside from his views on the literature, this same critic found nothing but praise for the members of the ensemble themselves.

> The Longy Club plays more equally this season than ever before. The artists are almost perfectly balanced. M. Longy is the prince of oboists, M. Lenom is exquisite on the English horn as well. M. Maquarre's flute playing is as good as any we have in this country, and MM. Debucky and Grisez are thorough on bassoon and clarinette respectively. The horns are also well played.

A Newark, New Jersey, Concert

The 1906 Longy Club brochure quotes a review (without date) from the *Newark Evening News* which suggests the ensemble may have made another tour this season to the New York City area. The repertoire mentioned in this review includes the Beethoven Quintet for piano and winds, as well as several solo and duets by members of the Club. This review is interesting to read for in it we can easily sense the enthusiasm of the review, and his town, in hearing a serious wind ensemble for the first time.

> Among the musical organizations in this country, the Longy Club, wood-wind choir devoted to the interpretation of chamber music … is unique. In all the art centres of Europe and in many of the smaller cities of the Continent such bands are not uncommon and in their special field are important factors in promoting the enjoyment and happiness of those who are interested in aesthetic pursuits and in the manifestation of fine art in any form. It was not until 1899, when Georges Longy, the French oboe player, who had been brought to this country by the management of the Boston Symphony Orchestra, associated himself with several other virtuosi in that superb band and founded the Longy Club, that American could boast such an organization and inquisitive music-lovers could hear performances of compositions that previously had been as a sealed book to them. When it is understood that many of the great composers have written music in solo or concerted form for the different instruments in this combination, and that the literature from which selections can be made for concert purposes is so varied and rich that very interesting programs can be arranged, the value of such a club to the musical public as a means of enlarging its knowledge of comparatively unknown works cannot be over-estimated or prized too highly.
>
> Until last season the Longy Club had confined its labors to Boston and other New England cities. Last year it sought recognition in New York, and met with such a cordial reception on its debut that it was encouraged to reappear there this year.
>
> Composed as it is of members of the Boston Symphony, its virtuosity in ensemble playing ranks it with the famous Kneisel [string] Quartet, also an outgrowth of Mr. Higginson's symphonic band.[12] As an agent capable of providing new sensations for music-lovers satiated by hearing much of the best music in well-known forms, or for others curious about novel compositions by creative genius, it is more interesting than any of the many fine chamber music organizations now assisting in spreading the gospel of art and melody throughout the country.

[12] 'Mr. Higginson's symphonic band' is a reference to the Boston Symphony Orchestra.

The Third Concert

The third and final concert of the season was given on 2 March 1905. The program began with a *Pastorale* by Jean Huré (1877–1930) for three flutes, oboe, English horn, two clarinets, horn and two bassoons. The reviewer of the *Journal* found this work, 'heavy and without any clear or definite message,' but then he was rather cool toward the entire program.[13] On the other hand, two newspapers were rather pleased with this new work. It was, said the *Herald*,

> a work of unusual charm and distinction. The harmonic expression is ultra-modern, but there is no too anxious search after originality, and there are no passages that seem deliberately bizarre. The chief theme is frankly melodic and it is developed with no little skill. The color effects are always interesting and often beautiful, and the finale is as engrossing as it is unexpected.[14]

The *Transcript* was even more enthusiastic.

> The most attractive number of this programme was the Pastorale by Jean Hure, a young French composer quite unknown in this country. The man must possess and instinctive feeling for orchestral color, since he has succeeded, far beyond some of his betters, in writing a composition for wind instruments alone that has as much body and depth of sound as though there were a solid background of stringed instruments. The piece sounds always delightful to the ear, with an ever-varying play of tonal color, and it is also pleasantly melodious, the melody being of a character that charms and at the same time establishes a definite and delicately felt mood. Harmonically the music seems spontaneous, despite its audacities. This Pastorale is tender and subdued, like a poetically conceived painting of summer twilight—till close to the end, when everybody is surprised by a sudden outburst of lively gayety. This is a bit of music that will bear repetition, for the pleasure aroused by its beauty of sound, its charming melody and its imaginativeness is far from slight.[15]

The next work on this concert was the *Fairy Tales*, for clarinet, viola and piano by Robert Schumann. This work seemed to please none of the critics. The *Transcript* suggested that it would never be performed if it were not for Schumann's name, while the *Journal* called it, 'scarcely worth while.' The *Herald*, going further, hints that Schumann was no longer quite sane when he composed this work.

[13] 'Last Concert of Longy Club for this Season,' *Boston Journal*, March 3, 1905.

[14] 'Longy Club's Last Concert,' *Boston Herald*, March 3, 1905.

[15] R. R. G., 'Potter Hall: Longy Club,' *Boston Transcript*, March 3, 1905.

Schumann's 'Fairy Tales' were written only a year or two before his brain was clouded. The third movement is charged with the exquisite melancholy peculiar to Schumann, and, admirably played, it made one forget the dryness of the other movements, which are, indeed, barren of ideas, nor does the occasional torture of rhythm bring any lively interest.

The Mozart Concerto for flute and harp, performed on this occasion by André Maquarre, Heinrich Schuecker, and with piano accompaniment, received only slightly more enthusiasm from the critics. The *Herald* reminds the readers that, 'if ever there were two instruments that Mozart disliked, they were the flute and harp,' but has to admit the concerto is 'mild and agreeable music.' The *Transcript* voiced nearly the same ideas, asking, 'who else would have been able to write a concerto for two such unlikely instruments as the flute and harp together?' 'Mozart wrote music,' continued the *Transcript*, 'that even today can be listened to with pleasure.' The *Journal*, which devoted only a sentence to each composition, declared the Mozart, 'pleasing by reason of its dainty beauty.'

Having shown so little enthusiasm for Schumann and Mozart, how would the critics hear the Gouvy Octet, which brought this concert to a close? 'Limped,' said the *Journal*. 'Raw ... not of striking interest,' said the *Transcript*. 'Dry and conventional,' said the *Herald*, which added some background:

> Gouvy's Octet was written in 1879 and first played the next year in Dresden. Taffanel and his colleagues brought it out in Paris in 1881, and it soon made its way throughout Europe; but the literature for wind instruments in ensemble was not then so rich as it is today. Gouvy was a painstaking musician, whose works at their best are second-rate German rather than French.

As this was the final concert of the season, two of the newspapers gave a brief retrospective of the season.

> It is not necessary to speak of the artistic qualities of the performance throughout the evening. It was of the high standard that characterizes the concerts of this club, which are among the choicest features of our local musical life. The concerts this season have been varied and of unusual interest. That they have not drawn crowded houses is a serious reflection on the musical taste and enthusiasm of the city. [*Herald*]

The season just ending has proved, on the whole, more interesting than have those of past years. Mr. Longy has been successful in finding more agreeable music to play, and, of course, the club now having been in existence five years, it is possible to repeat the compositions that have been most favorably received. Although there has been no audience this winter so large as that which rushed to hear Mr. and Mrs. Gilibert last year, it would seem on the whole, as though the average audience this season has been larger than heretofore. If so, it is to the credit, if somewhat belated, of Boston, for such playing as that of the Longy Club is seldom heard in any city of the world. [*Transcript*]

Season Six, 1905–1906

THE PROFICIENCY OF THE LONGY CLUB may be assumed from the fact that its members were all members of the Boston Symphony Orchestra, but any lingering doubt of their proficiency is certainly put to rest by the fact that they began their sixth season by performing three different programs in a single week's time!

The Club had now reached a level of confidence and self-awareness as can be seen in the printing of an impressive brochure which gave the history and goals for the ensemble, reviews and brief histories of the various wind instruments. The brochure also included pictures and biographical notes on the members of this season's ensemble. These brief entries contain much interesting information.

André Maquarre (flute) was born in Brussels in 1875, won first prize in flute at the Paris Conservatoire and also studied composition with Massenet. He joined the Boston Symphony Orchestra in 1898.

Daniel Maquarre (flute) was born in Brussels in 1881 and by age 15 had, like his brother, won first prize in flute, under Taffanel, at the Paris Conservatoire (there were two more brothers, trombonists, in this family who won first prizes at the Conservatoire!). He joined the Boston Symphony Orchestra in 1902 and also taught at the New England Conservatory of Music.

Clement Lenom (oboe) was born in Belgium in 1865 and took first prize in oboe at the Brussels Conservatoire. After studying with Gillet in Paris he performed with numerous orchestras before joining the Boston Symphony Orchestra in 1901. He also studied with Massenet and composed a number of ballets. The French government awarded him an 'Officier "Academie" in 1897.'

Charles Grisez (clarinet) was born to a family of musicians (his father Leon was a famous clarinetist; his grandfather, Espaignet, a famous bassoonist), began study at age 9 and by age 18 he won first prize in flute at the Paris Conservatoire. He joined the Boston Symphony Orchestra as Principal Clarinet in 1904.

Paul Mimart (oboe) was born in Vincennes, France, in 1876. He studied with his father, Chief Musician at the Artillery School of Vincennes, and his brother, clarinet professor at the Paris Conservatoire, as well as studying composition with Franck. Paul Mimart taught at the Scola Cantorum, where d'Indy was Director, and was a member of the Opera Comique Orchestra before coming to the Boston Symphony Orchestra in 1905.

Franz Hain (horn) was born in Terplitz, Bohemia, and graduated from the Prague Conservatory at age 19. He held positions in Hamburg and Carlsbad before being brought to Boston by Artur Nikisch.

Heinrich Lorbeer (horn) was born in Weida, Germany, in 1865 and studied at the Leipzig Conservatory under Gumpert. He held positions in St. Petersburg and Leipzig (the Gewandhaus, under Reinecke and in the Opera under Mahler and Nikisch) before coming to Boston.

Peter Sadony (bassoon) was born in Wiesbaden, Germany, in 1867 and studied in Berlin. He held positions in Regensberg, Berlin, Rega and Flamberg (under Mahler). He joined the Boston Symphony Orchestra in 1905.

John Helleberg (bassoon) was born in Aalborg, Denmak, in 1858, but received his education in Norway. Before joining the Boston Symphony Orchestra in 1901, he was a member of the Theodore Thomas Orchestra, the Philadelphia Symphony, Metropolitan Orchestra and the New York Orchestra under Damrosch.

A Special Concert with Vincent d'Indy

On 11 December 1905, the Longy Club had the opportunity to appear in public under the baton of Vincent d'Indy in a concert of his music. The composer was in America to lecture at Harvard on, 'Cesar Franck, Man, the Artist, and his Influence on Modern French Composers.' According to an account in *The Boston Globe*, 12 December 1905, d'Indy noted that 'Franck's influence on modern French composers was greater than had been generally recognized, and that his pupils had started a new regime in musical circles in France, having drawn away from the influences of the theatre to compose symphonies and quartets of great merit.' D'Indy left immediately after the Longy Club concert for Paris, due to the illness of his wife.

Vincent d'Indy, ca. 1900

> POTTER HALL 1905
> MONDAY AFTERNOON, DECEMBER 11, at THREE O'CLOCK
>
> SPECIAL CONCERT
> BY
> The LONGY CLUB
> AND
> Mr. VINCENT D'INDY
>
> ASSISTING ARTIST
> Mr. JOSEF KELLER, Violoncello
>
> ARTISTS
>
> | | |
> |---|---|
> | Mr. VINCENT D'INDY | Piano |
> | Mr. JOSEF KELLER | Violoncello |
> | Mr. G. LONGY | Oboe |
> | Mr. A. MAQUARRE | Flute |
> | Messrs. G. GRISEZ and P. MIMART | Clarinets |
> | Mr. F. HAIN | Horn |
> | Messrs. P. SADONY and J. HELLEBERG | Bassoons |
>
> Programme
>
> 1. V. D'INDY . Chanson et Danses, Op. 50, for Flute, Oboe, two Clarinets, Horn, and two Bassoons
>   I. Chanson
>   II. Danses
>
>   The Longy Club
>   Mr. Vincent d'Indy, Conductor
>
> 2. V. D'INDY . Fantaisie for Oboe on Popular French Themes, Op. 31
>
>   Messrs. Vincent d'Indy and Georges Longy
>
> 3. V. D'INDY . . Trio, Op. 29, for Piano, Clarinet, and 'Cello
>   I. Ouverture (Modéré)
>   II. Divertissement (Vif et animé)
>   III. Chant élégiaque (Lent)
>   IV. Finale (Animé)
>
>   Messrs. Vincent d'Indy, G. Grisez, and J. Keller
>
> THE PIANOFORTE IS A MASON & HAMLIN

This was a very special event and the excitement of both performers and public was clearly reflected in the beginning lines of the *Journal's* review.

> A large and very distinctively musical audience was present at Potter Hall yesterday afternoon when the Longy Club gave a special concert with the assistance of Vincent D'Indy. The occasion was extraordinary. Here was the finest company of wood-wind players on this continent, if not in the world, conducted by the greatest composer of chamber music now living, and playing his very works for the entire program.

> Nothing quite like it has ever been experienced in Boston before, and it cannot but be remembered long by those who were 'there to see,' even though they need not all have been worshipers of the D'Indy cult.[1]

The *Globe* also noted the importance of the occasion, but also commented on the heightened sense of musicality contributed by the composer's participation.

> The distinguished French composer, Vincent D'Indy, appeared before a critical and very friendly audience pretty well filling Potter Hall yesterday afternoon. It was a signal honor to one of Boston's musical organizations, and the auditors were in a mood to appreciate keenly the somewhat unusual situation. It is no disparagement to the club to say that the same compositions (all D'Indy's and all heard for the second time at the Longy Club's hands) gained new charms under the gifted Frenchman's direction. For, whether as conductor or pianist, his influence was pronounced throughout the concert. His method in either capacity is placid but extremely forceful; and the subtle charm of this 'composer's own' hearing is wellnigh impossible to put into words.[2]

The first work on this concert was d'Indy's *Chanson et Danses*. Although the Boston critics had never been especially enthusiastic about this work, which nearly everyone today considers a masterpiece, this performance seemed to earn more respect, especially because of the influence of the composer's conducting.

> The 'Chanson and Danses,' played at the beginning by flute, oboe, two clarinets, horn and two bassoons, are pretty clear sailing and full of exquisite melody; that haunting air that comes back after the dance and breathes a final peace on the scene is one of D'Indy's masterpieces. The playing here was delightful, doubtless made more perfect by the composer's conducting. [*Journal*]

> The 'Chanson et Danses' called for the whole strength of the club, the special part borne by Mr. F. Hain, horn and Mr. Maquarre, flutist, being worthy of particular mention. Mr. D'Indy conducted with much evidence of musicianly ability, bringing to the fore the wonderfully poetic trend of the wild and haunting melodies of the second paragraph. [*Globe*]

[1] 'D'Indy Leads in his Own Works,' *Boston Journal*, Dec. 12, 1905.

[2] 'M. Vincent D'Indy,' *Boston Globe*, Dec. 12, 1905.

A solo work for the composer and Mr. Longy, the *Fantaisie on Popular French Themes*, op. 31, followed. While the *Globe* found this composition to be, 'verile and intensely modern, the exquisite modulations leading from one theme to another being as enjoyable as the rollicking airs themselves,' the *Journal* found little of genuine musical interest.

> Spite of the beautiful way in which Mr. Longy interpreted the music, it seemed scarcely worth while. It was dull, and it suggested the thought that if the sorrowful tunes used as themes were popular in France, the Gauls must be a much more serious people than we have taken them to be.

All the newspaper critics agreed that the musical highlight was the final work, the Trio op. 29, for clarinet, cello and piano.

> But it was in the trio ... that the greatest delight was experienced. The overture began with a semi-Caledonian fashion of theme, a sort of 'skirling' introduction, followed by a succession of rich unison passages. In the second movement the lively air for clarinet, leading to a sedate passage for cello, was one of the gems of the concert. Beautiful as was the finale, 'Anime,' the 'Chant Elegiaque' proved its full equal in interest. A lovely clarinet 'miserere' them with a singular chiming prelude, was succeeded by a unison passage supported by sweeping piano chords, suggesting music suitable for a dim and vast cathedral interior. [*Globe*]

> The trio ... came last, an appropriate sort of 'magnum opus.' It is truly a colossal work, full of intense ernestness, a deal of fascination, and a musicianship that almost appeals by its cleverness. The 'divertissement' movement especially is a marvel of difficulties, and Mr. Grisez, the clarinetist, covered himself with glory for his extraordinary performance of it. [*Journal*]

The critic of the *Transcript*, who had heretofore worked up little enthusiasm for this 'little concert,' suddenly was taken by this composition.

> Then for ending came the trio ... Rich and fertile were the melodies of it. Rich and warm was the development. Feeling played through the music, now delicate, now deep, now light and gay—tempered feeling always, but feeling that was singularly pure. Design and delineation,

imagination and execution were nearly perfectly fused. It was more human music than any of d'Indy's that we have heard in the last fortnight. For once we that listened forgot the mind that we have honored for the man that was like ourselves. There was sheer zest of life in him and in his music after all.[3]

3 H. T. P., 'Potter Hall: D'Indy and the Longy Club,' *Boston Transcript*, Dec. 12, 1905.

An Extra Concert in Chickering Hall

Six days after the d'Indy concert, the Longy Club wind ensemble performed a completely different concert as part of a series in Chickering Hall, Boston, sponsored by H. G. Tucker. This concert consisted of the Beethoven Quintet op. 16, for winds and piano; the Charles Gounod (1818–1893) *Petite Sinfonie*, a Haydn Octet, in addition to solo works, the Franz Doppler (1821–1883) *Hungarian Fantasie* for flute and a Duet for oboe and piano by Georges Guilhaud.

The surviving review says the Doppler made Mr. Maquarre 'the hero of the day, being recalled again and again.' The Beethoven went well, but, the critic notes, the pianist, Mr. de Voto, 'seemed a triffle vague at first.' In comparison to the 'modern' music one often heard in these concerts, the newspaper reflects that the Beethoven Quintet, 'is a work which one does not have to be a music student to enjoy, and of which the public never tires.'[4]

Charles Gounod, 1863

4 'Longy Club Concert,' *Boston Advertiser*, Dec. 18, 1905.

The First Concert

The following day the Longy Club gave their official 'first concert' of the sixth season, the third completely different program in one week!

This concert, according to the *Advertiser*, enjoyed a 'good-sized audience, but it is a pity that the hall was not crowded, for the Longy club is the … best organization of its kind in this country.'[5]

The *Journal*, in reference to a work by Fauré, complained that the Longy Club 'is still enthusiastic over the modern French school of music.'[6] Elson, of the *Advertiser*, also mentions this leaning toward French culture (the critics seem to have forgotten that the players were mostly French-speaking!), although his comments seem to contain a bit of prejudice towards the wind ensemble and like most prejudice its basis lies in ignorance.

Franz Doppler, by Ágost Elek Canzi, 1853

5 Louis C. Elson, 'The Longy Club Concert,' *Boston Advertiser*, Dec. 19, 1905.

6 'Sixth Season of Longy Club,' *Boston Journal*, Dec. 19, 1905.

The programmes of the Longy club of woodwind instruments are always quite out of the ordinary run of concert repertoires. That given last night, in Potter Hall, was no exception to this rule. Of course, the French school was preponderant, for France is the home of the wood-wind, and its musicians have written more compositions for this combination than all the composers of all other nations combined.

What one would give to see his face if he were told that the amount of this kind of wind ensemble music produced in France was in fact only small and insignificant compared to the vast repertoire of the German-speaking countries!

POTTER HALL   177 Huntington Avenue

SIXTH SEASON, 1905-1906

Chamber Music for Wind Instruments

By

The LONGY CLUB

MEMBERS of THE CLUB

FLUTES: Messrs. A. Maquarre and D. Maquarre   HORNS: Messrs. F. Hain and H. Lorbeer
OBOES: Messrs. G. Longy and C. Lenom   BASSOONS: Messrs. P. Sadony and J. Mollenberg
CLARINETS: Messrs. G. Grisez and P. Mimart   PIANO: Mr. A. de Voto

FIRST CONCERT

Monday Evening, December 18 : At eight o'clock

ASSISTING ARTISTS

F. MÜLLER, Oboe   O. FRITZSCHE, Bass Clarinet
M. HESS and C. SCHUMANN, Horns

Programme

1. ANDRÉ CAPLET   Quintette for Flute, Oboe, Clarinet, Bassoon, and Piano.
       I. Allegro (Brillamente).
       II. Adagio.
       III. Scherzo.
       IV. Finale (Allegro con fuoco).

2. (a) GABRIEL FAURÉ   Nocturne in E-flat minor, Op. 33, for Flute, two Oboes, two Clarinets, two Horns, and two Bassoons.
       Transcription by GABRIEL GROVLEZ.

   (b) CH. LEFÈBVRE   Intermezzo scherzando, for Flute, Oboe, two Clarinets, Horn, and Bassoon.

3. MOZART   From the Concerto in E-flat major, for Oboe and Piano.
       (a) Romanza.
       (b) Rondo.

4. WALTHER LAMPE   Serenade, Op. 7, for two Flutes, two Oboes, two Clarinets, Bass Clarinet, four Horns, two Bassoons, and Contra-bassoon.
       I. Allegro con grazia.
       II. Allegro scherzando.
       III. Adagio.
       IV. Molto vivace.

MASON & HAMLIN PIANOFORTE

The Second Concert of the Series will take place Monday Evening, January 22.

The first work on this program was the Quintet by Caplet for flute, oboe, clarinet, bassoon and piano. This composer seems never to have interested the Boston critics; in this case two did not even mention this work at all and the *Advertiser* passed the work by with the observation that it was 'on the whole, more remarkable for length than for depth.' Only the critic of the *Herald* gave space to this work, but his comments may not have been pleasing to the composer.

> As a whole, it is an agreeable rather than a strongly individual composition. The melodic thought is flowing, if at times thin. In the opening allegro there is a curious suggestion of an inversion of the familiar theme of the first movement of Schumann's piano quintet. The scherzo, which, by the way, was not played with the steady precision characteristic of this club, is more striking than the adagio, which is forgotten as soon as it is heard.[7]

7 'Hear Longy Club in Potter Hall,' *Boston Herald*, Dec. 19, 1905.

The next two works on the program seem to have been presented as new works from France, the Fauré *Nocturne* op. 33, transcribed by Gabriel Groviez for flute and pairs of oboes, clarinets, horns and bassoons and the Charles Lefebvre (1843–1917) *Intermezzo scherzando* for flute, oboe, two clarinets, horn and bassoon. Again the critics could not reflect much excitement for these latest works from Paris. The *Journal* merely wrote that the 'Fauré is interesting in a mild sort of way, and the LeFebvre is rather pleasing.' In a similar fashion, the *Herald* observes, 'The transcription of Fauré's nocturne seemed muddy in spots, and it has little musical interest, but the Intermezzo [Lefebvre] sparkles and it was played brilliantly.' The *Globe* used the same word, 'muddy' for the harmony of the Fauré and an even more strange picture of the Lefebvre.

> [It was] not particularly stirring to the emotions, it faded through modulation after modulation, always with oboe repeating the final phrase, and always with a muddy harmony below. It was, however superbly played, and was balanced by an 'intermezzo scherzando' … a syncopated, humorous, laughing, quaint thing—almost like the musical joke of a hunchback.

Following the tradition which had been observed for some time of featuring solo works for variety, Longy himself now performed two movements from the E♭ Concerto of Mozart.

Three newspapers failed to even mention this performance and in the fourth, the *Advertiser*, the critic, Elson, presented a strange discussion indeed.

> In listening to this number one could not but remember that Schumann did not understand this instrument as well as the older master. The oboe is an 'exigent' in holding back the breath, as other wind instruments are in calling it forth, and the composer must bear in mind that the oboist, more than other wind-instrument players, demands periods of rest, to restore his lungs to their normal condition.
>
> Mozart fully comprehended this, and his concerto is very practical for the chief instrument. In the deeper passages M. Longy even attained the fullness and nobility of the English horn, while in the lighter phrases all the naiveté and delicacy of the oboe was revealed. The rondo of this work was, however, in that old vein, established by Ph. Em. Bach, in which a chief theme is repeated until it is bored into the memory, which is a defect. The moderns are not as fond of repetitions as their fore-fathers were.

The final work on this concert, the Walther Lampe (1872–1964) Serenade op. 7, for two flutes, two oboes, two clarinets, bass clarinet, four horns, two bassoons and contrabassoon required the assistance of four additional players: Max Hess and C. Schuman on horn, Florian Müller on oboe[8] and Otto Fritzsche on bass clarinet. The critics were more interested in the larger instrumentation than in the music itself.

[8] Florian Müller later became Principal Oboe in the Chicago Symphony and later still professor of oboe at the University of Michigan.

> The combination of instruments allows massive effects, and there is continual ensemble rather than a free use of solo passages. Lampe is modern both in harmonic treatment and in tonal colors. He evidently knows and admires Richard Strauss, but his music is not bizarre purely for the purpose of exciting the musically orthodox hearer. [*Herald*]

> [The Lampe] was rather heavy for a chamber concert. It has beauty and a limited quantity of melody, but its great merit is that it calls out every quality of the wood and wind instruments whose possibilities in the past have been considered rather limited. [*Journal*]

> This score was large enough to place the orchestra upon a symphonic footing. But the work itself was not of the epic character of a symphony, nor even of the sinfonietta type.

> The old serenade was a lighter style of Suite or Partita, and this less ambitious vein was properly adopted by the composer. If the work was not especially thrilling from any ideas expressed, it was at least a very interesting study of a particular kind of orchestra, and it held the attention throughout. [*Advertiser*]

> This evening concluded with a most satisfying number scored for instruments rarely seen even today ... It is a serenade, by Walther Lampe, in four beautiful movements, every one of which is full of unusual feeling. As for its tone color, the thing is positively bewildering. [*Globe*]

One review of this concert has not yet been mentioned. This reviewer of the *Transcript* abandoned the usual composition by composition impressions and instead was moved to write a little essay on the appropriateness of using the wind choir to express the 'comic' in music. The present writer regards this not so much an expression of this particular concert, as a reflection of a generation or more of French and English (and American!) wind band and wind ensemble music. One simply cannot study the German, Italian or Czech wind literature of the second half of the nineteenth century (which was largely unknown to the Boston audience) and arrive at conclusions such as these. From first word to last, it is all utter nonsense.

> Composers, even the composers of earlier centuries, seem always to have written for combinations of wind instruments in the comic vein, or at most in the spirit of light, bright fancies. When orchestras were smaller than they are now, the wind voices were more assertive. The elder composers, when they were writing for orchestra, sought full loud colors, and not half tints and faint suggestions from the acid oboe, the mournful flute and the hoarse bassoon. They were the composer's staple reds and blues, where now they are only odd and especial tints that he seeks for odd and particular effects. Yet even in these days, as soon as composers gathered wind instruments by themselves, they began to use them lightly. The oboe, the clarinet, the bassoon they set to dancing, and the traits of the instruments themselves were bound to turn the frolic into dancing. It was making a minuet for Pierrot and Columbine. Or if even they were made to sing grief—these whimsical voices—that was because it must be the aching grief, like a child's, of Pierrot or Columbine when they add for an instant a pitiful little glimpse of sorrow. Composers of our day usually select these odd stops from their fuller orchestral organ for the same old-time uses. Or at most they employ them to represent to the listening mind those plentiful moods of our

own time that no other instruments seem to characterize half so well—the moods that make us hunt out the quiet moonlit like, that its stillness may lull the restlessness of the day and its work.

Faure's Nocturne was such music, while Lefebvre's Intermezzo perfectly embodied the other, the comic function, of a wind choir. Andre Caplet had thought too seriously with his pianoforte and quartet of woodwinds. He was making Pierrot read Hamlet. Nevertheless, Mr. Longy and his associates played it, as they played all, with a grace that was in itself as interesting as the music which it clothed. With the Faure to show the path, they led us to the still lake. With Lefebvre they led their tonal sport. With Mozart they took down a lot of old humor and old fancy from its shelf in a museum and made it live its tranquil life again. To do that was cleverest of all.[9]

9 'Two Chamber Concerts,' *Boston Transcript*, Dec. 19, 1905.

The Second Concert

The second regular concert of the sixth season was given on 22 January 1906, and due to the return appearance of the popular vocalists, Mr. and Mrs. Gilibert, a very large audience attended. But it was also a varied program of unfamiliar works, which moved one critic [10] to cry, 'Here was a programme modern enough to gladden the heart of the iconoclast,' and another to offer the following colorful summary:

10 'Second Concert by Longy Club,' *Boston Herald*, Jan. 22, 1906.

> Mulled wind and caviar, that is a concert of wind instruments. The taste for it must be acquired and comes slowly. But when it is there, the true musical gourmet is made. He sits down to his ortolans, then, and his terrapin and truffles, knowing at last what it is to live and wring out of his senses their last refinement of pleasure. The faithful audiences that are regularly attracted to the Longy Club concerts treat themselves to the same sort of sublimated enjoyment. Almonds and spiced liqueurs for them, and Mr. Longy and his company of wind instruments to provide them.[11]

11 'Potter Hall: The Longy Club,' *Boston Transcript*, Jan. 23, 1906.

The concert began with the *Sinfonietta* op. 48, by Rudolf Novacek (1860–1929), for flute, oboe and pairs of clarinets, horns and bassoons. This composer, observed the *Transcript*,

> had perfect feeling for the character of the band for which he was writing, and yet while writing for them was writing for himself. Brave little themes to start off with, and little tunes in the adagio, and a lively finish—these he gave his pipes and horns in just the fashion in which they could deliver them best. The club played this with perfect finish. Indeed the whole concert was an example of finish, delicacy and spice.

Next came the vocal numbers, works by Hüe, Gounod and Grétry and they returned later with works by Chausard, Debussy and Vidal.

The Saint-Saëns, *Caprice sur des Airs Danois et Russes*, op. 79, for flute, oboe, clarinet and piano, received little notice by the critics; the *Journal* found these *Airs*, 'intensely fascinating by their highly developed technical skill',[12] but the *Herald* heard them as lacking, 'the charm of other of Saint-Saëns' works and gives a curious effect of thinness.'

The final wind ensemble composition on this concert was the *Divertissement* by Albert Périlhou (1846–1936), an organist in Paris, for pairs of flutes, oboes, clarinets, bassoon and four horns. This work was 'almost too novel' for the *Transcript*, but made 'a profound impression' on the *Journal*. The *Herald* provides an outline of this composition, which it said served,

[12] 'Second Concert of the Longy Club Last Night,' *Boston Journal*, Jan. 23, 1906.

> rather to exploit the virtuosity of the members of the club than of the club as a whole, for only in the last movement, a bouree, were all the instruments used in ensemble. The first movement is an andantino for flutes and clarinets; the second, an allegro for the oboes and bassoons; the third, an allegro for four horns. The several movements of the work were played admirably and each group of players was obliged to acknowledge the applause.

The Third Concert

The Longy Club Wind Ensemble's final concert of the sixth season was given on the evening of 26 February 1906, before a large and enthusiastic audience. By this time the ensemble seems to have developed a regular audience for itself, indeed the *Journal* observed, 'There were many who loudly expressed regret that the club is content with three concerts a season when other organizations feel justified in giving half a dozen.'[13]

The reader will recall the review of the previous concert by the critic of the *Transcript*, who was moved to metaphors of food. This madman must have received encouragement from some quarters for in describing this concert he returns to food and then, somehow, expands those metaphors to literature!

[13] 'Longy Club Gives Closing Concert,' *Boston Journal*, Feb. 27, 1906.

There may be many whose feet Mr. Longy has not yet lured to his concert hall and whose fancy he has not yet caught with the rich condiments of his unusual collection of instruments and the unusual music that they play. Mr. Longy sets forth a banquet of spices, of rare and delicate and even daring dishes; and the generality cleave to their beef and potato and will not be won. But the true musical gourmet who has found Mr. Longy out, or your inveterate concert-goer—for the moment wearied, if that may be, with the safe and tried diet of violin and piano—who grows adventurous and hankers for the spice of Mr. Longy's band, these probably know a keenness of pleasure beyond any telling to the crass taste that will not be wheedled from its humdrum preference for orchestra or fiddle. The faithful who sit with Mr. Longy bravely put the ordinary and the expected behind them. They have deliberately placed their imaginations under experiment. Along with the accustomed sounds of the piano, the voice, the violin, go their accustomed moods into limbo. Flute and oboe, clarinet and bassoon, instead become their guides and lead them out of the common world into the haunts of fays and gnomes. Go to a Longy concert and you shut your Carlyle to open your Andersen or Grimm. Close your eyes and these instruments will conjure up dragons that puff awful (and harmlessly fanciful) fire. Princesses will be rescued from thorn-covered castles of brass. Choruses of outlandish birds will sing to you from forest that might have been grown by Aubrey Beardsley. You will mingle with fantastic people who do impossible feats in a fantastic world. Your fancy has been bidden to leave logic and consistency behind and to romp at will, freed of their numbing tyranny.[14]

What inspired such prose? The first composition on this concert was a woodwind quintet by Fritz Kauffmann (1855–1934). The critics barely mention it, the *Advertiser* calling it 'ingenious rather than inspired'[15] and for the *Journal* it was merely, 'interesting.'

The second work was a Trio op. 28, 'Schilflieder' (after the poems of Lenau) for oboe, viola, and piano by August Klughardt (1847–1902). Two reviewers did not mention this composition, but two found this the most interesting work on the concert, Elson, in the *Advertiser*, judging, 'the first, third and fourth … the best movements of this beautiful suite.' The gourmet-bibliophile critic of the *Transcript* continues in his madness.

Klughardt's five fantasies for piano, oboe and viola belonged to another world entirely. While they were heard Andersen was shut and we turned to Byron. These fantasies were in no frolic humor to consort with fays and fight with dragons. Lenau aside, they walked with Manfred along his crags, and pictured forth his too too solid flesh, and

[14] B. K. 'Two Chamber Concerts,' *Boston Transcript*, Feb. 27, 1906.

[15] Louis C. Elson, 'The Longy Club Concert,' *Boston Advertiser*, Feb. 27, 1906.

August Klughardt, 1902

sang his very real discontent with this very real and disordered world. Klughardt has not made earth-splitting music, it is true; but he had furnished the solidest thing of the evening.

Most of the critical attention was given over to the Raff *Sinfonietta* op. 188, for ten winds, which was a regular part of the Longy Club repertoire. The *Journal* found this work 'full of strength and beauty,' while the *Globe* heard it more as we do today, 'It shows the composer's remarkable fluency, his great technical skill, his sense of color, and, alas, at times, his intrinsically commonplace thought.'[16] This last observation was one with which Louis Elson, in the *Advertiser*, both joined and elaborated on.

[16] 'Longy Club,' *Boston Globe*, Feb. 27, 1906.

> Raff had a fatal facility. He could toss off a composition in any form without disturbing his emotional nature a particle. It was said of him that if he desired to write a string quartette he would compose half-a-dozen as experiments and then dash off his composition. No man was a greater master of routine than he.
> We find something of this deceptive ease in the sinfonietta which ended this programme. It was suave, flowing, and utterly without effort: but utterly without passion or great emotion as well. It is a dangerous thing to be the Chesterfield of Music. Yet the perfect leading of the voices, the sweet fluency of each movement, had its peculiar charm. Raff had a full comprehension of the tone-colors with which he was dealing, and won the effects that he aimed at.

The *Globe* closed its review with a perspective of the season just concluded.

> Appearances are often deceitful in a concert hall, for musicians, like the hare in the fable, have many friends; but it is fair to infer that the audiences this season were larger than in preceding seasons. The club deserves the hearty support of all those that are interested in concerts of the highest grade. Such players of wind instruments are not found except in a few of the largest European cities, and it is doubtful whether any one of the foreign clubs surpasses the Longy in ensemble and in virtuosity.

Season Seven, 1906–1907

An Extra Concert in Newport

THE LONGY CLUB WIND ENSEMBLE began the 1907 season with a concert in nearby Newport, Rhode Island. This was one of several extra concerts during this season, which was perhaps possible because for the first time the personnel of the club remained the same as in the previous season.

The Newport concert was sponsored by the Newport Philharmonic Society and held in the Masonic Hall on the evening of 1 November 1906. Two extant reviews suggest by their careful discussion, even to the point of describing the various wind instruments, that any kind of serious wind ensemble performance was something extremely rare in Newport. The *Herald* even seemed obligated to devote some lines to defining the concept of chamber music itself.

> A large and appreciative audience gathered last night in Masonic Hall to listen to the playing of the Longy Club. Those who were absent missed a rare opportunity of hearing music of a high order, rendered by artists of great skill and taste; with a volume of power, conspicuous harmony, and a true interpretative feeling, worthy of sincere and grateful praise. Chamber music, with wind instruments, of which the talented members of the Longy Club are excellent exponents, is perhaps the finest form of chaste, classic music. Speaking in a wide and general sense, chamber music is any music not specially designed for church or theatre. The term was originally derived from the fact that kings, patrons of music, had the concerts given before them, in their audience chamber, the musicians being frequently attached to the royal household.
>
> Chamber music is thus taken to represent in outward musical expression all that is highest and purest in human thought. The softness, sweetness and harmonious blending of the various instruments was very marked last night, and demonstrated unusual capacity on the part of the individual players. They proved themselves musicians of superior talent and principle—of principle, because they were all evidently deeply penetrated by the spirit and action of the text.[1]

[1] 'Longy Club Concert,' *Newport Herald*, Nov. 2, 1906.

The concert began with the Novacek *Sinfonietta* op. 48, for eight winds. The *Herald* heard this work as 'powerfully rendered, and was the keynote to the whole program,' while the

Daily News described it as 'piquent, so characteristic of the Slavish spirit,' and especially liked its 'extremely beautiful adagio.'[2]

[2] 'An Unusual Concert,' *Newport Daily News*, Nov. 1, 1906.

Newport Philharmonic Society

MASONIC HALL

Thursday Evening, November 1, 1906, at 8:15 o'clock

Chamber Music for Wind Instruments

By

The LONGY CLUB

FLUTES: Messrs. D. Maquarre and A. Brooke
OBOES: Messrs. G. Longy and C. Lenom
CLARINETS: Messrs. G. Grisez and P. Mimart
HORNS: Messrs. F. Hain and H. Lorbeer
BASSOONS: Messrs. P. Sadony and J. Helleberg

Program.

NOVÀČEK	. .	Sinfonietta, op. 48, for Flute, Oboe, two Clarinets, two Horns and two Bassoons.

    I. Allegro molto.
    II. Presto.
    III. Adagio.
    IV. Allegro molto vivace.

BEETHOVEN	. .	Quintet, op. 16, for Piano, Oboe, Clarinet, Horn and Bassoon.

    I. Grave—Allegro, ma non troppo.
    II. Andante cantabile.
    III. Rondo (Allegro ma non troppo.)

a, PERILHOU	. .	Tale, for two Flutes and two Clarinets.
b, GRIEG	. .	Four small pieces, for Flute, Oboe, two Clarinets and two Bassoons.

    1. In my Native land. 2. Birdling. 3. Solitary Wanderer. 4. Dance of the Elves.

c, MENDELSSOHN	. .	Scherzo, op. 16, for two Flutes, two Oboes, two Clarinets, Horn and two Bassoons.
HAENDEL	. .	Trio No. 2 in D minor, for two Oboes and Bassoon.

    I. Adagio.
    II. Allegro.
    III. Affettuoso.
    IV. Allegro.

WEBER	. .	Grand Duet, op. 47, for Clarinet and Piano.

    I. Allegro con fuoco.
    II. Andante con moto.
    III. Rondo (Allegro.)
    MESSRS. G. GRISEZ AND A. G. LANGLEY.

RAFF	. .	Sinfonietta, op. 188, for two Flutes, two Oboes, two Clarinets, two Horns and two Bassoons.

    I. Allegro.
    II. Allegro molto.
    III. Larghetto.
    IV. Vivace.

ASSISTING ARTIST:

MR ALFRED G. LANGLEY

The Steinway Grand Piano is kindly furnished by J. H. Barney, Jr. & Co.
154 Thames Street

THE LONGY CLUB
7th Season, 1906-1907

PHILHARMONIC SOCIETY
11th Season. 9th Concert of the Society

WARD, THE PRINTER, CLARKE ST., NEWPORT

As might be expected, the critics gave most notice to the second work, the Beethoven Quintet op. 16, for piano and winds. The *Herald* called the performance lofty and beautiful, while the *Daily News* was drawn to elaborate on Beethoven's sense of wind characterization.

> The wood-wind instruments are capable of wonderful effects, when in the hands of artists like the members of the Longy Club. The clarinet is no longer a simple pipe—it has a soul; the oboe no longer speaks shrilly—it also breathes and lives; it is positive, it is melancholy, it is tender and it soothest; the notes of the bassoon are rich and mellow, and the horn gives body.
>
> Beethoven was the first to give character to the different instruments, a matter in which he showed rare instinct and imagination; and his famous quintet … was the tour de force of the program. The opening movement is in one of the master's gayest moods, its ending simply delicious. The smoothly flowing andante, and the brilliant finale all received just interpretation.

The following compositions, most for smaller ensembles, were not discussed by the newspapers: the Périlhou, *Tale*, for pairs of flutes and clarinets; arrangements of four short works by Grieg, for six winds; the Mendelssohn Scherzo op. 16, arranged for nine winds; the Handel Trio in D Minor, for two oboes and bassoon, and the Weber, *Grand Duo*, op. 47, for clarinet and piano.

The final work on this concert was the Raff *Sinfonietta*. While the Boston critics had not been enthusiastic over this piece, the *Newport Daily News* found it, 'rich in coloring,' and the *Herald*, 'thrilling and magnificent.'

Both papers praised the level of performance repeatedly and the *Herald*, which devoted few words to any of the actual compositions, explained in summary,

> To attempt a detailed critical analysis of each number would be wearisome and futile, even if one had the special capacity necessary thereto; because the grand spirit of unity and artistic touch—of time, tone, temper, musical beauty and soulfulness, was the distinct characteristic of their playing.

The First Concert

The first regular concert of the seventh season was given on the evening of 14 November 1906. The *Journal* suggests the audiences were continuing to grow in size.

> … an audience whose size showed that the fine work of the unique organization of artists is growing in popular favor of the sort that means a happier box-office. Mr. Longy's struggle to make a place for his company of players seem to be nearly over, and all lovers of rare and good music should rejoice. A little more of public support and the victory will be completely won.[3]

3 'Longy Club Opens 7th Season in Triumph,' *Boston Journal*, Nov. 15, 1906.

In spite of such evidence of a growing public, not to mention the club's considerable record of achievement by this date, the reviews of the critics after this concert are unenthusiastic in tone. It would appear that the unusually large proportion of transcriptions contributed to the cool response to this program. The *Journal*, with all due tact, noted, 'Last night's concert was by no means an epochal one, nor so interesting as some that have gone before,' while Philip Hale in the *Herald* spared no words, 'The transcriptions were not so effective. Handel's air and variations seemed stupid.'[4] For the *Globe* the question of the legitimacy of the medium itself seemed to come up all over again.

4 Philip Hale, 'First Concert by Longy Club,' *Boston Herald*, Nov. 15, 1906.

> Of course this class of compositions appeals only to a limited circle; but those students and enthusiasts who are fond of unusual combinations of instruments and novelty in musical works find the artistic interpretations by Mr. Longy and his associates a source of great delight.[5]

5 'Longy Club Concert,' *Boston Globe*, Nov. 15, 1906.

The concert began with a new woodwind Quintet in E Major ('on French popular themes') by Henry Woollett (1864–1936), which, as a brand new composition, seemed to interest the critics the most. The critic of the *Transcript* began by trying to put this work in some sort of aesthetic perspective.

> A few French composers still write chamber music for wind instruments, and so uphold an honorable convention of French music and cultivate a field where their lightness and neatness of touch, their grace of bizarre or poetic fancy, their delicacy of taste and polished elegance

of expression find agreeable conditions. Unlike most other composers of our time, they write it not as a trifling pastime or as an amiable tour of force, but from innate aptitude and sincere inclination.

They believe that such music may still have vitality, and that there is no need to crib it in old forms or to clothe it with archaic utterance. It may be quite as interesting, they say, and much more alive when it is written in the newest and freest of ultra-modern fashions. In this way, Mr. Woollett wrote the quintet that the Longy Club played for the first time here. His form is free and individual, even to a finale which is no rippling allegro and whirling presto, but a simple, deeply felt and earnestly modulated song. His harmonies are as individual and imaginative. Fancy shapes them and feeling for the delicate differences of his instrumental voices colors them … It is only in the slow movements that his imagination warms him and his hand goes free. Yet even there is this ultra-modern speech quite the natural voice of wind instruments?[6]

[6] H. T. P., 'New and Old Music by the Longy Club,' *Boston Transcript*, Nov. 15, 1906.

The other newspapers had views of considerable variety.

A pretty, fluttering thing of no great depth or cohesion, and occasional platitudes, but generally pleasing by reason of its grace and melodious simplicity. [*Journal*]

The quintet by Woollet is modern, but not especially ultra-modern in form or harmonic thought. The opening movement is logically developed, but it interests by its poetic episodes rather than by the treatment of the chief theme. The second movement, an andante, is a fine example of romantic melancholy and it has genuine lightness, and the contrasting section has more musical worth. The finale, moderato, is an agreeable relief from the conventional ending of suites for wind instruments, in which fuss and fury generally predominate. [*Herald*]

The scherzo of the Woollett quintet displayed the beautiful tonal qualities of the five instruments, the movement being played with a daintiness and grace needed no string accompaniment. [*Globe*]

After offering the audience this new composition, the club now presented transcriptions of a number of familiar works. For a sextet of flute, oboe, with pairs of clarinets and bassoons, one heard the 'Air Varie,' from Suite V of Handel, a Weber Minuetto, and four short works by Grieg, 'In my countryland,' 'Young bird,' Lonely Traveller,' and 'Elf's dance.'[7] This was followed by three works for solo oboe and piano.[8]

[7] A recording of members of the Longy Club playing the 'Elf's Dance' exists.

[8] The 'Allegro' from Sonate Nr. 2, in E♭, by Bach; Romance by Schumann and the 'Highlander's March' from *Scotch Scenes* by Godard.

The concert closed with the Beethoven Octet op. 103, a composition of which the critic, Philip Hale, seemed to have an unusual knowledge. He mentions the relationship with the string Quintet op. 4, and interestingly adds that the Octet was, 'entitled originally a Partita and written in his early years at Bonn, was not published until after his death.' The only other newspaper to discuss this work was the *Transcript*, which saw it as the masterpiece that it is.

> Listen especially to the slow movement and to the minuet. There is suave and tender song in the one, gracious and wooing in melody, warm in spontaneous expression, and so rich and varied in its coloring that the listener forgets for the moment that here are only oboes, clarinets, horns and bassoons, and in another instant realizes that only these could give such felicitous tints. In the scherzo, similarly, there is apt instrumental humor. The different voices speak a little tonal comedy that is all brightness and gayety. The blending in both matter, manner and speech is nearly perfect.

An Extra Concert in Providence, Rhode Island.

On 16 November 1906, the Longy Club gave a concert in Memorial Hall, Providence, sponsored by the Providence Musical Association. The program included all the transcriptions and solo oboe works which had been given in Boston two days earlier, but in a characteristic symbol of this wind ensemble's ability the two major works were replaced by two different ones, the Raff *Sinfonietta* and the Beethoven Quintet op. 16. The only extant review is a brief one, observing in part:

> The combination is a somewhat unusual one and the concerts given by the organization are unique and interesting. The club has long enjoyed much popularity in Boston and vicinity, but has never before appeared in this city.
>
> The programme of chamber music which they offered was a choice one, and it was interpreted with the skill which might be expected from such experienced players.[9]

9 'Chamber Music Concert,' *Providence Journal*, Nov. 17, 1906.

An Extra Concert in Chickering Hall

On 6 January 1907, the Longy Club gave an extra concert in Boston as part of a series of concerts organized by H. G. Tucker in Chickering Hall. The club shared this concert with a young singer, Miss Mary Desmond, who received due praise from the critics.

The wind ensemble began the concert with the Franz Lachner (1803–1890) Octet op. 156, for flute, oboe, and pairs of clarinets, horns and bassoons, a work for which one finds little enthusiasm in either of the two extant reviews of this concert. While the *Herald* passed this work off merely as, 'often dull,'[10] the *Globe* offered more detail.

[10] 'Longy Club and Miss Desmond,' *Boston Herald*, Jan. 7, 1907.

> The afternoon began with the opus 156 of the voluminous Herr Lachner ... The work lacks somewhat in ideas, but its four movements have each its own well-marked characteristics. Of course there is not possible to the wind choir the variations and shading of tone that the strings can produce, and the consequence is a monotony of color which almost forbids a concert entirely of this kind of music.

Franz Lachner, by Fritz Luckhardt

Program

Octet. In B flat major. Op. 156. For Flute, Oboe, two Clarinets, two Horns and two Bassoons. . . . . *Lachner*
    Allegro
    Adagio
    Scherzo
    Finale
    (*First time*)

Songs. Gens duce splendida. Alto aria from "Hora Novissima." . . . *H. Parker*

Quartet. Adagio. }
    Allegro Scherzando. } . . *Wouters*
    For two Flutes, Oboe, and English Horn.
    (*First time*)

Songs. Beloved it is morn. . . *F. Alyward*
    Summer Noon. . . *Margaret Ruthven Lang*
    Berceuse. . . . . *Godard*
    Love the Pedlar. . . . *German*

Trio. In A minor. Op. 188. For Oboe, Horn, and Pianoforte. . . . . *Reinecke*
    Allegro moderato
    Scherzo (molto vivace)
    Adagio
    Finale (allegro ma non troppo)
    (*First time*)

MASON & HAMLIN PIANOFORTE

> The opening allegro of the octet is simple, almost rudimentary, in its construction; its three themes run sweetly their courses—and then repeat. The adagio which follows is a clever piece of scoring, the eight instruments being handled in antiphonal quartets of shifting makeup. The scherzo helped along by comical little agilities of the fat old bassoons, and by the device of giving one of them a tender little phrase to sing half a tone flat in its ending.
>
> A brilliant finale flashes more dramatic feeling forth than any of the earlier stanzas.[11]

[11] 'Three New Works,' *Boston Globe*, Jan.. 7, 1907.

Following some songs by Miss Desmond, the club presented a Quartet by François Wouters (1849–1924) for two flutes, oboe and English horn. Both critics thought this a better composition than the Lachner, although the *Globe* found the lack of a bass instrument very limiting.

The final wind ensemble work on this program was the A Minor Trio, op. 188, for oboe, horn and piano by Reinecke. The *Herald* made no comment of this work which the *Globe* called, 'a thoroughly stupid composition, whose very arrangement forbids the pianist to be heard distinctly under pain of "blanketing" his colleagues.'

The Second Concert

The second regular concert in Boston by the Longy Club was given on the evening of 16 January 1907. Perhaps Longy was stung by the cool reception which the critics gave the first formal concert, with its numerous short, popular transcriptions, for now one finds him organizing a concert of major original wind ensemble works new to Boston. The result was not only very extensive, but very receptive press coverage. The *Advertiser* ciritc, Louis Elson, reflects this in his overview of the concert and adds some interesting information.

> Mr. Longy is known for his tact and taste in programme-making and the list of the concert of last night, in Potter Hall, was a striking example of this good quality. Every number on the programme had its points of interest. The scores were larger than usual, the three last numbers were new to Boston, and to the full forces of the Longy Club there were added Mr. Tritsche, bass clarinette, Mr. Kloepfel, trumpet, Mr. Ludwig, cymbals, Mr. Rettberg, kettledrums and Mr. H. Schuecker, harp ... Altogether this was one of the best concerts that the Longy Club have ever given and we freely forgive its starting nearly 20 minutes behind the time.[12]

[12] Louis C. Elson, 'The Longy Club Concert,' *Boston Advertiser*, Jan. 17, 1907.

> POTTER HALL 1907
>
> Wednesday Evening, January 16, at eight o'clock
>
> SECOND CONCERT
>
> OF
>
> ## Chamber Music for Wind Instruments
>
> BY
>
> # The Longy Club
>
> ### MEMBERS
>
> Flutes: Messrs. D. MAQUARRE and A. BROOKE
> Oboes: Messrs. G. LONGY and C. LENOM
> Clarinets: Messrs. G. GRISEZ and P. MIMART
> Horns: Messrs. F. HAIN and H. LORBEER
> Bassoons: Messrs. P. SADONY and J. HELLEBERG
> Piano: Mr. A. de VOTO
>
> ### ASSISTING ARTISTS
>
> Messrs. O. FRITZSCHE, Bass Clarinet; L. KLOEPFEL, Trumpet; C. F. LUDWIG, Cymbals;
> A. RETTBERG, Tympani; SCHUECKER, Harp.
>
> ### Programme
>
> 1. S. LAZZARI . Octuor (Op. 20) for Flute, Oboe, English Horn, Clarinet,
>   Two Horns, and Two Bassoons
>   I. Introduction (Poco lento). Allegro con fuoco
>   II. Adagio
>   III. Finale: Allegro scherzando
>
> 2. MOUQUET . . . . . Pan (Sonate for Flute and Piano)
>   I. Pan et les Bergers
>   II. Pan et les Oiseaux
>   III. Pan et les Nymphes
>   Messrs. D. MAQUARRE and A. DE VOTO
>   (FIRST PERFORMANCE)
>
> 3. LACROIX . Variations Symphoniques for Flute, Oboe, English Horn,
>   Clarinet, Bass Clarinet, Two Horns, and Bassoon
>   (FIRST PERFORMANCE)
>
> 4. REYNALDO HAHN
>   Le Bal de Béatrice d'Este Suite, for Two Flutes, One
>   Oboe, Two Clarinets, Two Horns, Two Bassoons,
>   Trumpet, Tympani, Cymbals, Harp, and Piano
>   I. Entrée de Ludovic le More
>   II. Lesquercade
>   III. Romanesque
>   IV. Ibérienne
>   V. Léda et l'Oiseau
>   VI. Courante et Salut final au Duc de Milan
>   (FIRST PERFORMANCE)
>
> The third and last concert of the series will take place on Wednesday evening,
> February 6, 1907
>
> MASON & HAMLIN PIANO USED

This concert began with an *Octuor* op. 20, by Sylvio Lazzari, for flute, oboe, English horn, clarinet, two horns and two bassoons. While Elson found this composition 'skillfully made, but it scarcely seemed to have a raison d'etre,' the *Transcript* thought it, 'gives pleasure by the richness of its harmonies and its warm blending of the peculiar voices of the several instruments.'[13] The famous Boston critic, Philip Hale, also seemed pleased with this work.

[13] H. T. P. 'Reynaldo Hahn and Beatrice d'Este,' *Boston Transcript*, Jan. 17, 1907.

> Lazzari's octet ... has been heard here but it gained by repetition. The first movement is melodically charming, the thematic treatment is masterly, and the effects gained by contrasting and blending timbres

are often delightful. The second movement gives much promise in the opening, but the interest is not maintained till the end. The finale is agreeable.[14]

[14] Philip Hale, 'Longy Club Gives Second Concert,' *Boston Herald*, Jan. 17, 1907.

The composition which followed, a sonata for flute and piano called simply *Pan*, by Jules Mouquet (1867–1946), created unusual enthusiasm among all the critics who heard this performance, beginning with Hale:

> Mouquet's Pan … is a truly poetic work, one of the most noteworthy, if not the most noteworthy contributions for many years to the repertory of the flute. The three movements portray Pan with the shepherds, the birds and the nymphs. These movements are characterized by exquisite fancy and uncommon finish in workmanship. The musical thought is refined and original, and the variety of expression in both cantabile and bravura passages is surprising. [*Herald*]

> The most beautiful and inspired music of the evening was Mouquet's 'Pan,' a sonata in rather free form for flute and piano. This breathed of the woods, caught the scent of the forest dells, and spoke of the wild creatures of Greek mythology. [*Journal*[15]]

[15] 'Longy Club Gives Many Novelties,' *Boston Journal*, Jan. 17, 1907.

> Mouquet's sonata … was notable in its kind. It used the flute in its full and undulating tones and not in the shrill and skipping bravura of many a tawdry show-piece. It gave them the voice of song and it colored them with quick and warm imagination. [*Transcript*]

> The 'Pan' is a great addition to the concert repertoire of the flute. The chief difficulty in writing a sonata or concerto for this instrument is that it lacks the varied tone-colors of the stringed instruments, or of the clarinette. It is brilliant in the upper register and sentimental in the lower, and cannot get very far from either of these two qualities. Wherefore the Germans have reviled it and have made the conundrum—'What sounds worse than a flute?' Whereunto the answer is appended, 'Two flutes!'
>
>   But the French deal more tenderly and wisely with the fine instrument and manage to bring forth beautiful effects from the romantic tube.
>
>   Moquet has written three movements of well-contrasted character. The first jovial, the second ruminative, the finale brilliant. The style of each may be gathered from the mottos added to the movements. They are taken from the Greek and run as follows:
>
>   1. (Allegro Giocoso) Pan and the Shepherds. 'Oh Pan! Who dwellest in the mountains, sing to us from your sweet lips a song. Sing to us and play upon your pastoral pipe.'

2. (Adagio) Pan and the birds. 'Seated in the shade of the solitary wood, Oh, Pan, why dost thou draw from thy flute such delicious sounds.'

3. (Allegro) Pan and the nymphs. 'Silence, in the shade of the oak trees. Silence, fountains splashing upon the rocks. Silence, sheep which bleat beside your young. Pan himself sings with his harmonious pipes. Around him with lightest steps dance the nymphs of the waters and of the woods.'

The sonata was free in form. The second movement had a meditative quality, such as Debussy's faun had one afternoon. [*Advertiser*]

The next work on the concert was the *Variations Symphoniques*, for flute, oboe, English horn, clarinet, bass clarinet, two horns and bassoon by Lacroix. This work seemed to the critics to fail to meet the musical level of the rest of the program.

The piece belongs, on the whole, to the class of compositions that are characterized as 'well made.' They remind one of the unfortunate women who are lumped together as 'estimable persons.' The first variations are ingenious, and they also have musical value, but the weariness of labor becomes apparent, and the final pages are as the working out of problems which interest chiefly the worker. [*Herald*]

Lacroix's 'Variations Symphoniques' ... is an ambitious affair, well and clearly written, sincerely musical and generally highly dignified in style. But after the first few variations the theme palled somewhat and its interest waned. All that a highly artistic performance could do for it was done. [*Journal*]

Lacroix's symphonic variations ... was less fertile in melodic invention and harmonic detail, and less wooing in its fused or contrasted tonal colors—an ingenious exercise in music for wind choir and little more. [*Transcript*]

The final work on this concert was the lengthy and impressive *Le Bal de Beatrice d'Este*, by Reynaldo Hahn (1874–1947), for oboe, pairs of flutes, clarinets, horns, bassoons with trumpet, timpani, piano, harp and percussion. The level of interest in this work was so high that one newspaper, the *Transcript*, printed a lengthy article about it before the concert—something quite rare for the Longy Club. This article quotes a correspondent, probably from Paris, a Mr. K. B. Hill, who writes of Hahn's place in the Parisian musical scene.

> The French composers of the younger generation are not all adherents of d'Indy, Debussy, or even Faure. There are even those who follow the standard of Massenet with his constant exploitation of sentimental emotion. Chief among these is Hahn, who is known widely for his pleasing songs dealing chiefly with one or another phase of the tender emotion, and for his personal gallantry toward the fair sex ...
>
> Orchestrally, he is said to have absorbed from his teacher, Massenet, the art of delicate and appropriate instrumental coloring, a pure melodic style, and clarity of outline.[16]

After the concert this same newspaper published a fairly extensive biography of this famous lady, Beatrice d'Este. The writer saw the entire Italian court scene vividly presented in Hahn's music.

> There is the sweep of harps, the ordered beat of drums, the acclaim of trumpets; the measured progress of the cortege. The impression is of stately and graceful formality. Then the dances—perhaps the dances of the peasant maidens from every corner of Italy ... The suite is artificial music, deliberately archaic, polished often to the last touch of elegance or piquancy, subdued as often to courtly form, sharpened now and then with fantastic contrast and superficial always. Yet with a little sympathetic imagination of the breath of a Renaissance pageant and the faint, far fragrance of Beatrice herself blow lightly through it.[17]

From the review in the *Advertiser* one learns that Longy conducted his ensemble for the first time, rather than appearing as principal oboe.

> The most important score of the concert was Hahn's Suite, which was fully orchestral, save for the absence of the strings ... Hahn, the young Venezuelan is not a seeker after mysteries or tonal ugliness; he is a melodic and even a sentimental composer, and this Suite has a directness of tune in its short movements that ought to float it to popularity.
>
> It is a free Suite, giving an occasional dance movement of the old type, but also several freer romantic touches ... Mr. Longy directed the little orchestra and read the work finely, giving the pomp and circumstance of the more bombastic movements with appropriate power, yet portraying the quaint old style of the Romanesca equally well.

Only the *Herald* seemed to withhold genuine enthusiasm for this composition.

Reynaldo Hahn, by Gaspard-Félix Tournachon (Nadar)

[16] 'Reynaldo Hahn, a New Suite and the Longy Club,' *Boston Transcript*, Jan. 14, 1907.

[17] H. T. P., 'Reynaldo Hahn and Beatrice d'Este,' *Boston Transcript*, Jan. 17, 1907. Hahn's score contains no fixed program.

> Mr. Hahn, who of late has been as much interested in Mozart as he formerly was in Massenet—and imitation though in a diluted form is unmistakable admiration—is said to be a pet of all the ladies, in which respect he resembles Hildebrand Montrose. This charge may come from less successful composers in Paris, and as he purposes to visit the United States this season, let us give him the benefit of the doubt.
>
> The suite played last night contains pretty as well as quaint pages … Hahn makes a brave attempt to be pleasantly archaic in this suite by the use of old modes, and he is at times fairly successful, though he falls far below Delibes, whose music to 'Le Roi s'Amuse' is a masterpiece in its suggestion of the formal grace and elegance of bygone years.[18]

[18] The mention of Mozart refers to Hahn having conducted a concert in Salzburg on the 150th anniversary of Mozart's birth.

The Third Concert

The final regular concert of the Longy Club's seventh season was given on the evening of 6 February 1907. Although the program consisted of three very solid musical works, the Beethoven Trio op. 11, for clarinet cello and piano, the Strauss Concerto op. 11, for horn and the Arthur Bird Serenade, the critics still complain that the musical public of Boston still had not come to fully appreciate this ensemble and its music.

> An audience somewhat larger than usual was in attendance. As yet, however, these remarkably interesting events, made brilliant by what is perhaps the finest body of woodwind players in the world, are not assayed at their true value by musical Boston. Next year there ought to be a general awakening to the wonderful charm of the concerts and the genius of Mr. Longy, their founder, and all of his men.[19]

[19] 'Longy Club's Season at an End,' *Boston Journal*, Feb. 7, 1907.

The Beethoven Trio seemed to have been a composition well known to the critics, especially in its version for violin. On this occasion they reminded the readers that this was an early work, Louis Elson of the *Advertiser* adding 'Beethoven was as yet only a somewhat sturdier Haydn'[20] and that there was nothing yet unique in the writing for clarinet. Elson, again, discussed this point at some length:

[20] Louis Elson, 'The Longy Club Concert,' *Boston Advertiser*, Feb. 7, 1907.

> Beethoven's trio is interesting rather from its infrequent performance than from any special skill of clarinette treatment … It was composed in 1798, before Beethoven was 30. But even in his later years, in his Pastoral Symphony, for example, Beethoven did not fully understand the effects of this comparatively new instrument. It had been introduced into the symphonic orchestra ten years before this trio by Mozart, but

it was not until Weber composed 'Der Freischutz' and Mendelssohn his 'Scotch Symphony' that the full tone-color of the king of the wood-wind was understood.

Philip Hale, of the *Herald*, adds some interesting anecdotes about this composition.

> The theme of the variations was taken from an opera by Weigl, 'The Corsair,' which was produced the year before.
>
> There is a story that a famous Viennese publisher showed the theme to Beethoven and asked him to vary it; that he composer did not know the author of the tune until he had completed his work, and then he was exceeding wroth …
>
> However this may be, the music is delightfully, not stupidly, old-fashioned. In the adagio and in some of the variations there are suggestions of the later Beethoven, so that the hearer today can the more readily understand a remark made by a German music journal, when the trio first appeared, viz: 'With his uncommon knowledge of harmony and his serious taste Beethoven could do good things if he were willing to write in a more natural manner.'[21]

[21] Philip Hale, 'Longy Club Gives its Last Concert,' *Boston Herald*, Feb. 7, 1907.

Richard Strauss was at this time, of course, a very much talked about composer and, indeed, the *Transcript* attributed the large audience at this concert to the mere appearance of his name on the program.[22] Philip Hale, in discussing this performance, seems to express a general dislike for concerti and also adds a remark in defense of this then young and controversial composer.

[22] 'Two Chamber Concerts,' *Boston Transcript*, Feb. 7, 1907. This critic also points out that middle-aged persons then living in Munich could still remember Strauss's father 'pottering about the opera house and concert rooms there.'

> There was a time when flute, oboe, clarinet, and horn concertos were heard in symphony orchestra concerts, and even bassoon and the trombone were not slighted as solo instruments in orchestral concerts of the first rank. One by one they have dropped out, and it is only a question of time when the cello will join them. May the day soon come! …
>
> It may not be amiss to add, in view of the absurd pother about 'Salome,' raised especially by otherwise estimable persons who have not read Wild's tragedy or seen the opera, that this concerto is a moral work.

All the critics agreed that the soloist on this occasion, Mr. Hain, was brilliant. The *Transcript* noting, 'Such purity of tone, such surety in blowing and embouchure, such perfect shading have not been heard upon this instrument since the great Xaver Reiter left this city.'

The final composition on this program was the Bird Serenade for ten winds. Only the *Journal* found this work weak, 'It is a pleasant and rather fanciful work, but not of any great eloquence or persuasive beauty.' The other critics liked the work; the discussion by Elson, of the *Advertiser*, is worthy of including here for its interesting detail.

> The Serenade by Arthur Bird was doubly welcome. It was good music and by a native composer, for Bird was born in Cambridge in 1856. He has lived so long abroad (he resides in Berlin we believe) that he is better known in Germany than in America, and his compositions are respected abroad. Yet this Serenade was brought forth under American influence, for it was composed in competition for the Paderewski prize (for the encouragement of American composers) in 1901. It won the prize.
>
> It is written for a double quartette of regular wood-wind instruments plus two horns. It must be borne in mind that the serenade (in its orchestral and chamber music sense) was a species of Suite, somewhat shorter and less ambitious than the regular suite, as the orchestral suite is less developed than the symphony. But this Serenade was more ambitious than many works of its school.
>
> Mr. Bird's composition is in clear form. No part of this concert indulged in any radical vagaries, but every number held to the established laws of musical architecture. There was nothing very impassioned in the Serenade, and a 'hot bird' was no more in evidence than its usual concomitant, but there was geniality, and charm, and fine musicianship everywhere in it. The Adagio seemed to be the gem of the work; it had a pensive melancholy, and the oboe was played here with all the breadth and nobility of an English horn.
>
> Generally one gets a drone bass (a 'Musette') in the Trio of the Scherzo, but in this the effect was given in the Scherzo itself. There was some splendid bassoon work in the finale, and the attractive and masterly counterpoint here was emphasized by the incisive three-note figure with which it began. Altogether this Serenade is one of the best recent American compositions and will bear frequent repetition.

Philip Hale adds an intriguing comment.

> It is a pity that Mr. Bird has taken life so easily of late years. He was a composer of true promise, and his critical articles published in sundry musical periodicals show him to be a man of much acumen and fastidious taste.

An Extra Concert in Hotel Somerset

The final concert by the Longy Club wind ensemble during this season was one of a series of chamber music concerts organized by a Miss Terry in the Hotel Somerset given on 11 February 1907. The wind ensemble performed the Novacek *Sinfonietta* op. 48, the *Fantaise-Caprice* for clarinet and piano, and some brief single movements: the *Air Varie* by Handel, an *Andante* by Wouters and a *Scherzo* by Mendelssohn. These were separated by various arias sung by a young contralto, Miss Lilla Ormond.

The only review the following day remarked, as one so often reads, on the unique nature of the Longy Club.

> It is late in the day to praise the virtuosity of the ten players of the club or to try to persuade words to impart the exotic fascination of much of the music that they play. They waited patiently for our public to learn both, and discover the pleasure of them. They have their reward now and deservedly, and yesterday afternoon it came in part from a public to whom the charm seemed new.

Season Eight, 1907–1908

The First Concert

THE EIGHTH SEASON OF THE LONGY CLUB again saw the continuation of the same personnel. The first concert, given on the evening of 18 November 1987, consisted entirely of compositions being heard for the first time in Boston. In general, however, these compositions failed to gain the enthusiasm of the critics. Philip Hale, in the *Herald*, for example, wrote,

> The performance of the wind players was excellent, both in ensemble and in solo. It is a pity that there is not more music of distinction written for such admirable artists. Yet it is a pleasure to hear them, even in forced or commonplace work.[1]

[1] Philip Hale, 'Longy Club Gives its First Concert,' *Boston Herald*, Nov. 19, 1907.

The critic of the *Transcript* wrote in a similar vein.

> It only remains to add that the standard of ensemble performance as regards finish, precision and spirited interpretations were on the high level which invariably characterizes these artists. That Mr. Longy and his associates could not raise these works to true distinction can not in any way be laid at their collective door.[2]

[2] E. B. H. 'Potter Hall: The Longy Club,' *Boston Transcript*, Nov. 19, 1907.

An important new critic appears for the first time at these concerts, the now well-known Olin Downes (1886–1955), writing for the *Boston Post*. He joined in the condemnation of the literature.

> The choice of numbers performed was an unfortunate one, which resulted in a very dull concert … It is a matter of regret that the abilities of such a superb band of virtuosi should have been wasted on such poor stuff.[3]

[3] Olin Downes, 'Longy Club Concert,' *Boston Post*, Nov. 19, 1907.

The *Advertiser*, on the other hand, took a more understanding view of the repertoire.

> We have often alluded to the difficulty of obtaining an interesting repertoire for concerts of this description, but this difficulty seems to be entirely overcome by the tact and knowledge of M. Longy, who man-

ages to give programmes which are constantly full of interest and do not deteriorate in the lest from season to season. Every concert has the charm of novelty and repetitions are very few.[4]

All the papers mention, in any case, that the audience (critics excepted) was enthusiastic. The *Journal* mentioned 'one of the most attentive and most enthusiastic in applauding was the conductor of the Boston Symphony, Dr. Karl Muck.'[5] The *Advertiser* reminded the readers how unique this ensemble was, noting that, 'It is a branch of chamber music that has many devotees in France, but Germany, England and America are comparatively barren in this field of music.'

[4] 'The Longy Concert,' *Boston Advertiser*, Nov. 19, 1907.

[5] 'Longy Club Opens its 1907–1908 Season,' *Boston Journal*, Nov. 19, 1907.

.. POTTER HALL ..

EIGHTH SEASON, 1907-1908

Monday, November 18, at 8 o'clock

Chamber Music for Wind Instruments

... BY ...

The Longy Club

Members

Flutes: Messrs. D. MAQUARRE and A. BROOKE
Oboes: Messrs. G. LONGY and C. LENOM
Clarinets: Messrs. G. GRISEZ and P. MIMART
Horns: Messrs. F. HAIN and H. LORBEER
Bassoons: Messrs. P. SADONY and J. HELLEBERG
Piano: Mr. A. DE VOTO

Programme

No. 1. GUSTAV SCHRECK, Nonetto (Op. 40) for two Flutes, Oboe, two Clarinets, two Horns, two Bassoons

  I. Largo (Sostenuto): Allegro ma non troppo.
  II. Adagio di molto.
  III. Scherzo (Vivace).
  (FIRST TIME)

No. 2. ALBÉRIC MAGNARD, Quintet (Op. 8) for Flute, Oboe, Clarinet, Bassoon, and Piano

  I. Sombre (Dull).
  II. Tendre (Loving).
  III. Léger (Light).
  IV. Joyeux (Merry).
  (FIRST TIME)

No. 3. JULES MOUQUET, Suite for Flute, Oboe, two Clarinets, Horn, two Bassoons

  I. Adagio.
  II. Aubade.
  III. Scherzo.
  (FIRST TIME)

MASON & HAMLIN PIANOFORTE

The first work on this concert was the Nonetto op. 40, by Gustav Schreck (1849–1918) for oboe and pairs of flutes, clarinets, horns and bassoons. Philip Hale, who enjoyed this composition, mentioned that the composer taught at the Leipzig Conservatory and became the music director at St. Thomas Church, Bach's old position, and had the previous January had a Divertimento for winds performed by winds of the famous Gewandhaus Orchestra. Hale found the work, 'respectable in workmanship,' and added (as a compliment that it was not 'ultra-modern'), 'it contains nothing imaginative or fantastical.'

The *Transcript* also mentions Schreck's teaching institution, but refers to it as the 'staid' Leipzig Conservatory. This critic was even more restrained, writing, following a listing of the larger forms Schreck had composed in,

> From the foregoing list it was doubtless in the nature of a relaxation to have composed this piece for wind instruments, but the task of the listener is not so easy. For the nonett is written on strictly orthodox lines, it is thoroughly academic in style and sentiment. On the whole conspicuously deficient in originality and inspiration, the adagio rises to some intensity of music expression, and the scherzo possesses in a measure, brightness and animation.

The *Journal* described the work with the single word, 'finished,' while the *Advertiser* failed to mention it at all. The one critic who was completely negative toward the Schreck was Olin Downes.

> Schreck's nonett is music of the most tedious and respectable kind. There is a slow introduction and a succeeding allegro in 'sonata form.' A mellifluous andante follows, an andante warranted to produce dense torpor. There is also a scherzo, which, by an effort of the imagination, might be called, 'jolly.' For some unknown reason that we are thankful for, the composer did not see fit to add a rondo finale. In this he showed more wisdom than his successor on the programme.

The 'successor' referred to was Alberic Magnard (1865–1914), whose Quintet op. 8, for piano, flute, oboe, clarinet, and bassoon was the second composition on this program. Although the *Journal* critic found this work 'especially pleasing,' his colleagues were quite disappointed, with two of them quite critical of the Longy Club's pianist.

Unfortunately it was not possible to get a wholly fair idea of the its merits, for the work calls for a far more sensitive and emotional pianist than Mr. de Voto proved himself to be last evening … The quintet played last night is in four movements. As it was heard, it seemed on the whole labored rather than inspired. The melodic thought is thin, and it does not flow spontaneously. The movements are diffuse, and there seems to be no central idea in any one of them. On the other hand, there are instances of effective writing, as in the fugued section in the first movement, and there are pages of striking tonal combinations, unusual effects, impressive at the time and haunting afterward. The work, however, seems largely experimental, and the composer has no firm grip, no decided impression on his own impressionism. [*Herald*]

As a whole this quintet leaves an impression of disappointment. Its themes are not unpromising, there is a definite opportunity for capable development of them. Instead one is chiefly impressed throughout by the struggle between conventional treatment as regards form, and a distinct impulse towards modernity of invention. As an early work, it is possible that the composer was hesitatingly feeling his way towards modernity of invention. As an early work, it is possible that the composer was hesitatingly feeling his way towards individuality of utterance. At any rate, a palpable unevenness was manifested throughout as if inspiration were seeking to imply the moral restraint of technical training … It ought to be owned, however, in justice to Mr. Magnard, that Mr. de Voto was not always happy in his treatment of the piano part. There was a too frequent absence of sonority in tonal effect; his accents were lifeless at times and he did not succeed in infusing vitality into his interpretation. [*Transcript*]

Mr. De Voto is one of the best of chamber musicians, a fact which he proved in the Magnard Quintette, wherein the ensemble was well kept in spite of enormous difficulties. But we could not enjoy the ugly composition. Magnard delights in hideous progressions and in very sudden endings. The first movement of the work was marked (by an odd mistranslation) on the programme as 'Dull!' But the whole work might well be thus marked. [*Advertiser*]

Allberic Magnard got tired of 'Allegro,' 'Antante,' and 'Scherzo,' and 'Finale,' so he wrote 'Sombre,' 'Tender,' 'Light,' and 'Merry.' He should have stopped short at the first title, a most appropriate one for the whole composition. There is, indeed, a kind of purgatory atmosphere throughout. The work from beginning to end is irritatingly forced and artificial in character. This quintet has the opus number 8. It, therefore, must have come after two symphonies, an opera and some smaller works. But there is neither facility nor technical skill in the handling of material, and little of that acute feeling for tone color and the peculiar qualities of each instrument, which is so often a marked characteristic of the French composer. With Berlioz one cries '20 francs, 40 francs' (whatever the sum was) 'for an idea!' [*Post*]

The final composition on the first concert of this season was a Suite for flute, oboe, two clarinets, horn and two bassoons, by Jules Mouquet, a graduate of the Paris Conservatoire and a winner of the *Prix de Rome*. He was the composer of a work for flute called *Pan* which all the critics liked the previous season. This Suite did not live up to the anticipation caused by the memory of that earlier work. Philip Hale, of the *Herald*, for example, wrote, 'The suite performed last night falls far below *Pan* in structure and fancy. There is melody enough, but it is of a cheap and conventional order, and the workmanship is of the factory rather than of the study.' The *Transcript* agreed, 'It must be confessed that the suite played last night accorded with the usual style of winners of the Prix de Rome. For the most part, it was music of a perfunctory order, and lacking in pronounced individuality.'

On the other hand, two critics had praise for this composition. The *Advertiser* called it, 'much the best work of the evening' and the *Post*, after again pointing out that it did not match the interest of the flute sonata, admitted, 'It is, nevertheless, pleasant music, cleverly scored, and at any rate a welcome relief after what had gone before.'

The Second Concert

The second concert of the eighth season was given on the evening of 30 December 1907, and featured as guest artists the Theodorowicz Quartet.

The concert began with a new work by Gustav Bumcke (1876–1963), a Symphonic Poem, *Der Spaziergang*, op. 22, for flute, oboe, English horn, two clarinets, horn, two bassoons and harp. While two newspapers complained that they could not find this composer's name in their biographical dictionaries, Philip Hale, of the *Herald*, seemed much more familiar, which is not to say pleased, with this composer.

> Bumcke lives in Berlin. He is interested in wind instruments, which is commendable; he organizes concerts of wind instruments, which is praise-worthy; not contented with this, he writes music for these

concerts, a questionable procedure. Not long ago a sonata by him for clarinet and piano was published, and some of his countrymen wished that he would be satisfied with admiring wind instruments and organizing concerts of them …

His symphonic poem is interesting chiefly by reason of combination of timbres. Many of these combinations are ingenious and some are new and striking. The purely musical contents of the movements do not seem to be of much worth. The melodic thought is for the most part labored and of very short breath. There is little sustained sentiment. The music is constantly broken rhythmically for the sake of effect, and as a result it is scrappy. The composer has a sense of color, and his decoration is now and then beautiful, but even in this he is apparently an experimenter.[6]

[6] Philip Hale, 'The Longy Club's Second Concert,' *Boston Herald*, Dec. 31, 1907.

POTTER HALL   177 HUNTINGTON AVENUE

The Longy Club

CHAMBER MUSIC FOR WIND INSTRUMENTS
1907 — EIGHTH SEASON — 1908

SECOND CONCERT

Monday Evening, December 30, at 8.15 o'clock

Members

Flutes	Messrs. D. MAQUARRE and A. BROOKE
Oboes	Messrs. G. LONGY and C. LENOM
Clarinets	Messrs. G. GRISEZ and P. MIMART
Horns	Messrs. F. HAIN and H. LORBEER
Bassoons	Messrs. P. SADONY and J. HELLEBERG
Piano	Mr. A. DE VOTO

Programme

GUSTAV BUMCKE . "Der Spaziergang" (Symphonic Poem), Op. 22
For Flute, Oboe, English Horn, Two Clarinets, Horn, Two Bassoons, and Harp
  I. Morgenwanderung
  II. Rast
  III. Träumen im Walde
  IV. Kleines Intermezzo
  V. Abend

HECTOR BERLIOZ . . . . Trio des Ismaëlites (from "L'Enfance du Christ")
For Two Flutes and Harp

E. WOLF-FERRARI . . . . Sinfonia da Camera (Op. 8)
For Piano, Two Violins, Viola, 'Cello, Bass, Flute, Oboe, Clarinet, Horn, and Bassoon
  I. Allegro moderato.
  II. Adagio.
  III. Allegretto.
  IV. Finale.

ASSISTING ARTISTS

Mr. H. SCHUECKER, Harp   Mr. K. KELLER, Bass

AND

THE THEODOROWICZ QUARTET

Mr. J. THEODOROWICZ, First Violin   Mr. A. GIETZEN, Viola
Mr. A. RIBARSCH, Second Violin   Mr. J. KELLER, 'Cello

PIANO, MASON & HAMLIN

Two newspapers had little to say of this work, the *Journal* merely mentioning it as 'extremely modern,'[7] and the *Advertiser* expressing thanks that the composer led the symphonic poem into 'pleasanter and less exciting paths' than other nature oriented compositions such as 'the Mazeppas, the Amphales, the Hercules, and the Macabre Dances.[8]

Only the critic of the *Transcript* was moved to discuss the Bumcke work in detail.

[7] 'Longy Club Delights Very Large Audience,' *Boston Journal*, Dec. 31, 1907.

[8] Louis C. Elson, 'The Longy Club Concert,' *Boston Advertiser*, Dec. 31, 1907.

[9] 'Potter Hall: The Longy Club,' *Boston Transcript*, Dec. 31, 1907.

> It is evident that Mr. Longy has to go farafield in his search for novelties, for the name of Gustav Bumcke has apparently eluded the makers of musical dictionaries. 'The Walk' would seem to have a programme that is replete with incident and emotion, for it is in five movements with a title for each. At first thought it appears hazardous to attempt a symphonic poem for eight wind instruments and harp, for this constitutes after all rather a limited medium for the descriptive painting of even emotion in the abstract, not to mention possible realistic details. From the technical point of view, this poem attracts decidedly. It is made with uncommon cleverness in the writing for the instruments, each has abundant chance to show its capabilities, the harp is especially prominent and gratefully so. In perception of tone contrast and skilful writing up to each of the groups, the composer has shown a dexterity that is wholly admirable. As regards musical sentiment and in imaginative treatment he is less happy. The first movement, 'Morning Wandering,' is decidedly prosaic, there is little distinction in the musical thought. 'Rest,' the second section, is not without its touches of poetry in the weaving of figures for clarinets and flute, although there are disquieting moments singularly at variance with the title. 'Dreams in the Forest,' is not without forebodings that suggest fear of kobolds and gnomes of uncanny appearance. The 'Intermezzo' pleases by its touches of humor, although there is much that is commonplace; the fifth movement, 'Evening,' is the most pleasing as regards musical expression of the lot. This poem called forth abundant technical resources and its performance was a delight in its constant exhibition of virtuosity and skillful ensemble.[9]

Next on the program was a brief excerpt from Berlioz' *L'Enfance du Christ*, for two flutes and harp, which drew little attention from the critics: 'delightfully simple and melodic,' said the *Journal*; 'quaint and archaic,' said the *Advertiser*.

It was the final work on this concert that aroused the most interest from the critics, a real chamber symphony, conducted by Longy. Their interest came in part from their often hinted at belief that without strings one could hardly make music, and because of their interest in hearing contemporary music which was not French. This last perspective was addressed in particular by Louis Elson in the *Advertiser*.

> It is pleasant to notice how the new Italian composers are tending towards orchestral forms ... and avoiding the ascetic style planted in the new French school by Cesar Franck. It is possible that Italy and Russia may yet lead us back to pleasant paths in classical instrumental forms.

The composition in question was the *Sinfonia da Camera*, op. 8, by Ermanno Wolf-Ferrari (1876–1948), with Longy conducting his club together with the visiting strings of the Theodorowicz Quartet. Although Elson introduces this work to his readers with the above praise of the Italian school, he admits hearing in the first movement, 'something of the Liszt vein of dramatic contrasts,' while Philip Hale, in the *Herald*, heard some German characteristics.

> The music is original, it is individual, both in conception and expression. It has warmth and emotion; there is both southern sensuousness and German thoughtfulness.

Hale also notes that Longy conducted with 'marked elasticity in the interpretation and with great spirit.'

In contrast to his colleagues's discoveries of various stylistic sources, the critic of the *Transcript* found the work completely original.

> As a whole it impresses at the outset as the work of a man who has something to say, and is not content to follow slavishly the accepted traditions of chamber music. It is singularly free from obvious influence of composer or school.

The Third Concert

The final concert of the eighth season was given on the evening of 10 February 1908. The concert began with a repeat performance ('by request,' the program reads) of the Magnard Quintet, which had been performed on the first concert of this season and which the critics had reacted to with very negative reviews. Perhaps it appears again because the players believed in the work, or perhaps they (especially the pianist Mr. de Voto) wanted another chance to try to perform it better.

What did the critics think on second hearing? Philip Hale, of the *Herald*, rather pointedly failed to even acknowledge that he heard it, but the other two major critics seem, at least, to have tried hard to give the work a fair reconsideration.

> The concert was as enjoyable as any of the series. Yet the first number was not what one might call 'enjoyable.' We are beginning to believe that in music it is as in dietetic matters, whatever tastes badly, whatever one does not desire to eat is just what is best for the health. It can be only upon this principle that we have been fed upon ugly dissonances, weird progressions, and other musical bitters. We heard this work some months ago and were very much puzzled by it. We were not altogether sorry to hear it again ... for there must be some 'raison d'etre' for these very bad sounding modern works and if we condemn them at least we ought to be willing to faithfully study them.
>
> It was an advantage to hear the quintette while quite fresh—at the beginning of the programme. We again found some points of skill in the first movement, the beginning of the five-voiced fugue, much ingenious treatment of the figures, but again we could not solve the reason for the many unusual progressions, or for the disjointed style of treatment. Yet, on the whole, the first movement gained somewhat on a second hearing ...
>
> Mr. De Voto showed to good advantage in a very difficult piano part ... Mr. De Voto ... became a rock and a support in many of the trying passages of the finale.
>
> But there is no danger, in this instance that we shall 'first endure, then pity, then embrace,' for M. Magnard's work still seems to us fragmentary and ugly, and unnecessarily incoherent.[10]

[10] Louis C. Elson, 'The Longy Club Concert,' *Boston Advertiser*, Feb. 11, 1908.

> The repetition of the Magnard quintet served on the whole chiefly to confirm the original estimate of its qualities. Nevertheless there were episodes that gained undeniably upon a second hearing ... On the other hand, there are many passages of a tentative, experimental nature which seem still more elusive on a second hearing; there are incoherences, awkward developments of ideas that seem but to emphasize the composer's inexperience ... At the same time it is evident that there is more good music in this quintet than was at first apparent, for in its unevenness the less successful parts obscured the virtues of the better. The performance was uniformly excellent, even remarkable, and Mr. de Voto in particular made a markedly more favorable impression than on the first performance of this quintet.[11]

[11] E. B. H., 'Potter Hall: The Longy Club,' *Boston Transcript*, Feb. 11, 1908.

After being required to hear this work again, one can understand how delighted the critics were to hear a composition by Mozart—even a a minor work by Mozart.

> It was a remarkable contrast to go from this musical jungle to the clear progressions of Mozart. It means much to lead three simple voices through a whole three-movement sonata-form without becoming tiresome. Yet, perhaps Mozart's lengthy simplicity was the opposite extreme of Magnard's constant complexity and 'bizarerie'—and gained by its proximity to modern formlessness. It certainly was an exhibition of wood-wind playing worth traveling miles to hear, for Messrs. Longy, Grisez and Sadony performed the composition as only artists of the highest rank could do. We do not remember anything of this kind so perfectly done. The enthusiasm which followed was entirely deserved. [*Advertiser*]

> The Mozart trio, originally written for two clarinets or basset-horns and bassoon, is placed by the learned Dr. Kochel among the compositions of doubtful authenticity. Nevertheless this detracts from its intrinsic charm in no way in the present arrangement … It was indeed an object lessons to hear what sonority and variety of effect could be produced with this combination, what skillful interweaving of phrase, and command of part-writing. If these pieces were not by Mozart himself, they show a remarkable skill which no composer need be ashamed to own as his. [*Transcript*]

> The trio aroused enthusiasm. The music is characteristically Mozartian in its flowing line; in its gaiety tinged with melancholy; in the cadences that are as so many 'Yours truly, W. A. Mozart.' Only Mozart could have written a triffle that is so simply beautiful. [*Herald*] [12]

[12] Philip Hale, 'Longy Club Gives its Last Concert,' *Boston Herald*, Feb. 11, 1908.

The final work performed on this concert was the Arthur Bird Suite in D Major for pairs of flutes, oboes, clarinets, horns and bassoons in its Boston premiere. The Boston critics heard this work much in the vein of his earlier Serenade: pleasing, but not much musical significance was apparent.

> He is modern enough in what he has to say, but he does not indulge in extremes and his musical effects are attained without any very evident straining and without insulting all the harmony teachers. [*Advertiser*]

> Its musical sentiment is pleasing and unostentatiously fluent throughout. It does not display very pronounced individuality, neither is it reminiscent of any particular school or composer. While it does not attain either intensity or depth of expression, it nevertheless pleases by virtue of the simplicity, directness and unaffected manner in which the

> .. POTTER HALL ..
>
> EIGHTH SEASON, 1907-1908
>
> Monday, February 10, at 8.15 o'clock
>
> **Chamber Music for Wind Instruments**
>
> ... BY ...
>
> **The Longy Club**
>
> ### Members
>
> Flutes: Messrs. D. MAQUARRE and A. BROOKE
> Oboes: Messrs. G. LONGY and C. LENOM
> Clarinets: Messrs. G. GRISEZ and P. MIMART
> Horns: Messrs. F. HAIN and H. LORBEER
> Bassoons: Messrs. P. SADONY and J. HELLEBERG
> Piano: Mr. A. DE VOTO
>
> ### Programme
>
> ALBERIC MAGNARD — Quintet (Op. 8) for Flute, Oboe, Clarinet, Bassoon, and Piano
> (BY REQUEST)
>   I. Sombre
> II. Tendre
> III. Leger
> IV. Joyeux
>
> MOZART — Trio for Oboe, Clarinet, and Bassoon
>   I. Allegretto
> II. Larghetto
> III. Menuetto
>
> ARTHUR BIRD — Suite in D major for two Flutes, two Oboes, two Clarinets, two Horns, and two Bassoons
>   I. Allegro Moderato
> II. Andante Moderato
> III. Allegretto quasi Allegro
> IV. Allegro con fuoco
> (FIRST TIME)
>
> MASON & HAMLIN PIANOFORTES

musical thought is unfolded. Altogether a creditable, if not remarkable composition, which displays considerable scholarship and control of resources ... On the whole this suite is an agreeable addition to the repertory (all too slight) of effective work for wind instruments, and as such invites repetition. [*Transcript*]

His output has not answered the promise of his younger years ... The suite played last night is cheerful, amiable music, well put together, the work of a musician that uses easily his tools. It is fresh and spontaneous in an old-fashioned way. As far as harmonic progressions are concerned, the suite might have been written in the fifties. In fact there are progressions in the organ works of Buxtehude in the 18th century that are more modern.

> The melodies are of the square-toed variety. There is no doubt after hearing the first few measures how each tune will go on and end. The composer has no tricks, no surprises. His music is that of a prosperous man. Yet there is something pleasing about it. The unblushing frankness with which Mr. Bird adheres to orthodox forms and obvious expression is in its way admirable. [*Herald*]

The critic, Hale, concluded his review, as he often did, with an attack on the Boston public for not supporting this fine ensemble.

> The performance of the members of the club throughout the concert was most excellent. Mr. Longy, always the rare artist, played, especially in the trio by Mozart, with inimitable grace of phrasing and brilliance, while Mr. Grisez in the long solo in the second movement of the opening piece, Mr. Sadony in both florid passages and in recitative, and Mr. D. Maquarre in the rapid passages written by Mr. Bird where alike worthy of high praise.
>
> This was the last concert of the season. The concerts of this season and those preceding should have filled the hall. That they have not been appreciated by more is a serious blow to the reputation of this city as the favorite home of the muse, a reputation that is becoming more and more fictitious.

Season Nine, 1908–1909

An article in the *Transcript*, published a month before the beginning of the Longy Club's ninth season, advertised the coming concerts and mentions that the personnel was again unchanged. The writer again reminds the readers of the almost unique nature of this wind ensemble and offers some interesting insights into similar attempts by members of other major orchestras.

> For a ninth year, Mr. Longy and his associates of the Longy Club will renew their chamber concerts of music for wind instruments. No association of the kind in America has been so long-lived, and there is none indeed with which to compare it. The virtuosi of the wind choir of the New York Symphony Orchestra attempted, a few years ago, to give similar concerts, but they found no public. Next winter a quartet from the Thomas Orchestra [Chicago Symphony Orchestra] will hazard a similar venture. Here in Boston, however, the concerts of the Longy Club have become an established part of the scheme of the musical year; they have an assured, though necessarily a limited, public of connoisseurs in the music that they play; and they have steadfastly maintained the interest of their programmes and the quality of their performance. Thus the concerts have become unique in their kind in the artistry of the ten virtuosi who, with Mr. de Voto, make the club; in the obscure and rather exotic music that they make known, and in the rare pleasure that they give to those who have instinctively the taste for the timbres, the charm and the elegance of wind instruments or who have acquired it.[1]

[1] 'The Longy Club,' *Boston Transcript*, Oct. 17, 1908.

The First Concert

The first concert of the ninth season was given on the evening of 23 November 1908, and all the newspapers speak of a large audience—the *Herald* adding that it was a 'most applausive audience.'[2] Two critics began their review by echoing the earlier comments in the *Transcript* on the novelty of these concerts.

[2] Philip Hale, 'First Concert of the Longy Club,' *Boston Herald*, Nov. 24, 1908.

The programmes of this club, thanks to the tact of M. Longy, are models in their way. Never too long, they always present some novelty, something of interest, even with the scant repertoire of wind-wind music as the chief list to draw from.[3]

Mr. Longy's programs only appeal to a small circle of concert-goers, but they are very interesting to the musical expert and admirer of compositions for wind instruments. The little band of players are artists of great ability, their close association for years enable them to give authoritative interpretations, and in their sphere there is no club in America, and but one or two abroad, that rank with them.[4]

One very unusual aspect of this concert was mentioned by almost every reviewer—the first flute, Daniel Maquarre, failed to appear for the concert! As Philip Hale explains,

> Mr. Brooke, a few minutes after the hour appointed for beginning the concert, told the audience that Mr. D. Maquarre, the first flute, had not arrived and that he (Mr. Brooke) would play the flute part in Falconi's sextet, although he had not seen it. Mr. Brooke is an excellent musician, so the audience was not seriously disturbed; but Caplet's suite calls for two flutes, one of them interchangeable with piccolo, and no flutist, however skillful he may be, can play two flutes or even one flute and a piccolo at the same time. Mr. Longy, no doubt, looked out at a window like the mother of Sisera and cried through the lattice: 'Why is Mr. Maquarre's chariot so long in coming? Why tarry the wheels of his chariot?' But Mr. Maquarre did not come, and the suite was played with nine wind instruments instead of the decreed ten.

The November concert began with the first performance of a Sextet by Alfonso Falconi (1859–1920), for woodwind quintet and piano. The critic of the *Journal* did not reveal his personal opinion of this work, but noticed, 'a slight seeming incoherence in the first movement,' and added that the audience enjoyed the 'curious involved phrasing and surprising nuances of the Italian.'[5] Elson, in the *Advertiser*, found the work acceptable and even enjoyed the final movement.

> Falconi did not attempt a falcon's flight at the beginning and the first three movements might have been a conservatory student's prize composition, but the finale was very much better. It contained a bit of fugal work (six-voices we believe) that was finely worked out. At no time did the composition become radical, and at all times it was well worth hearing, but, as intimated, its power, like that of a wasp, was in its end.

[3] Louis C. Elson, 'Fiedler Conducted Handel Concerto,' *Boston Advertiser*, Nov. 24, 1908.

[4] 'First Longy Concert,' *Boston Globe*, Nov. 24, 1908.

[5] 'Longy Club Plays Two Novelties,' *Boston Journal*, Nov. 24, 1908.

Members of the Club

Flutes: Messrs. D. MAQUARRE and A. BROOKE.
Oboes: Messrs. G. LONGY and C. LENOM.
Clarinets: Messrs. G. GRISEZ and P. MIMART.
Horns: Messrs. F. HAIN and H. LORBEER.
Bassoons: Messrs. P. SADONY and J. HELLEBERG.
Piano: Mr. A. DE VOTO.

Assisting Artists

Mr. MAX FIEDLER, Conductor

Violins.
J. THEODOROWICZ.
A. BAK.
W. KRAFFT.
E. FIEDLER.
A. RIBARSCH.
P. FIUMARA.
S. GOLDSTEIN.
H. GOLDSTEIN.

Violas.
H. HEINDL.
A. GIETZEN.

Cellos.
J. KELLER.
L. NAST.

Basses.
K. KELLER.
T. SEYDEL.

Programme

No. 1. Alfonso Falconi   Sextet in E-flat for Piano, Flute, Oboe, Clarinet, Horn and Bassoon, (Op. 60)
    I. Allegro
    II. Adagio } without interruption
    III. Scherzo }
    IV. Con Vita
    (First Time)

No. 2. G. F. Haëndel . . Concerto for Oboe
(Composed at Hamburg in 1703)
With strings accompaniment, Mr. MAX FIEDLER, Conductor
    I. Grave — Allegro
    II. Sarabande — Largo
    III. Allegro
    (First time at these concerts)

No. 3. André Caplet   Suite Persane for two Flutes, two Oboes, two Clarinets, two Horns and two Bassoons
(With Piccolo interchangeable in third movement)
    I. Scharki (Allegretto quasi andante)
    II. Nihawend (Andantino)
    III. Takia Samaïal (Vivace)

The second concert will take place on December 21

THE PIANO IS A MASON AND HAMLIN

On the other hand, two critics took pains to object to this composition.

> For eight years the Longy Club has given concerts here of chamber music for wind instruments. It has been diligent in the searching of the elder composers for suitable pieces. It has been as zealous to bring to hearing new pieces of our own immediate time and unfamiliar music of the preceding generation. Such researches, however, cannot always be fruitful, and if a contemporary composer dabbles at all in music for a wind choir, he is apt to be only pretty and trifling.
>
> For some such reasons, perhaps, Mr. Longy had to be content with the sextet…that began the concert last night. A certain Alfonso Falconi, a minor Italian composer of the last generation, wrote it—wrote it with a perceptible sensitiveness to the contrasting or the blended timbres of his little choir and with, now and then, a pretty skill in the attaining of them. Once and again, too, he asked no little virtuosity—

that strange and subtle virtuosity of breath and touch that is peculiar to wind instruments—of his players. The sextet however, wants grace and elegance of form, fertility and charm of idea, and Mr. Longy and his companions could not save it from its own tedium.[6]

Perhaps the Longy Club was a little depressed last evening by the absence of the first flute; perhaps the fault was in the music of the sextet itself; whatever the cause, this sextet as performed had little distinction except in the ingenious use of the instruments for the purpose of obtaining effects of color. The themes have little profile and there is the thought of laborious construction rather than of spontaneous ideas with consequent and flowing development. [*Herald*]

Following the sextet, Mr. Max Fiedler, the current conductor of the Boston Symphony Orchestra, appeared with fourteen of his strings to accompany Mr. Longy in a performance of a Handel Oboe Concerto. All newspapers agreed this was the musical highlight of the evening, not only for the substance of the music itself but for the interpretation given it by conductor and soloist. The comments of Philip Hale, speak for them all.

The feature of the evening was the performance of Handel's concerto by Mr. Longy and his assistants. The exquisite art of Mr. Longy has long been recognized. It is always a cause for rejoicing, whether it be displayed in the orchestra or on the too rare occasions when he plays solos at the concerts of his club. It was a great pleasure to hear last night the stately and tender music of Handel, one of the few great melodists, a man to be ranked in this respect with Mozart, Rossini, Schubert, Verdi and Wagner. Both in the florid passages and in the beautiful sarabande Mr. Longy was always the poetic master of his instrument. By the way, what a pity it is that the word oboe ever drove out hautboy.

The final composition on this concert was the *Suite Persane*, by André Caplet, for pairs of flutes, oboes, clarinets, horns and bassoons. Only two critics discussed this work in detail, but both seem to basically like its unusual style.

Mr. Caplet has wrought his music of what presumably are Persian folk-tunes and folk-dances. He is plentiful in Oriental rhythms, harmonies and iterations. The suite compasses the exotic flavor that it would gain, and saturates the hearer with it. The essential monotony of its Oriental coloring becomes a fascination, and the listener takes joy of the sustained imagination and the susceptible fancy of it. [*Transcript*]

[6] 'The Longy Club …,' *Boston Transcript*, Nov. 24, 1908.

Max Fiedler, ca. 1900

Caplet's suite has been heard here before and it gains by repeated hearings. The first two movements are the best. The opening of the first movement is singularly impressive and the whole of this movement and the second are interesting melodically and harmonically. It matters not whether any theme be strictly Persian or not; the orientalism of a westerner is often more exotic than is the simon pure folk song of the East. Caplet's exoticism is not merely something unexpected, bizarre. It is apparently natural to him, as though the roses of Ispahan bloomed and were fragrant in his back garden. The third movement is not so euphonious, not so imaginative. [*Herald*]

The Second Concert

The second concert of the ninth season, given on the evening of 21 December 1908, was billed by one newspaper as 'Christmas Music,'[7] a reference to some of the songs sung on the program by guest soprano, Mrs. Marie Sundelius. For other critics, the fascination was still the medium itself.

[7] 'Christmas Music by Longy Club,' *Boston Journal*, Dec. 22, 1908.

> The Longy Club achieves such unique effects and of so much greater breath and richness than we are accustomed to associate with the idea of chamber music that expectations are likely to err on the maximum rather than on the minimum side; it is easier, that is, to take the volume and variety of sound in the orchestral sense than on the plane of chamber music.[8]

[8] 'A Second Concert by the Longy Club....' *Boston Transcript*, Dec. 22, 1908.

> There is an air of quaintness about the compositions written for the woodwinds that makes this class of music sound rather strange to the general auditor, and so the appeal is limited. To the adept and the student there is much that is interesting and instructive, and especially when interpreted by skilled performers like the Longy group.[9]

[9] 'Longy Club Concert,' *Boston Globe*, Dec. 22, 1908.

For the *Herald*, the concert was notable for the instrumentation of the particular compositions, because, 'the wind instruments did not in any part of the program get together in pairs and discuss their exclusive interests,' and for the French content (never mind the appearance of Bach and several other Northern composers!).

> For the most part it was a concert of the French, by the French, and, to judge by some conversation heard in the corridors after the entertainment, it was to a small extent a concert for the French.[10]

[10] 'Second Concert by the Longy Club,' *Boston Herald*, Dec. 22, 1908.

The critics all agreed that the highlight of this concert was, nevertheless, a French work, the Henry Woollett Suite for piano, two flutes, clarinet and horn—the review of the *Herald* even exclaiming in large type, 'Woollett's Suite Best Number on Program.'

> The best number on the program, the one best keeping the character of chamber music for wind instruments with no suggestion of the orchestra about it, was Woollett's Suite … When all the instruments played together there was a simplicity and clearness of form which because it was French was subtle and not to be lightly analysed. In the Nocturne there was scene-painting by the piano, there was acting of a human part by the horn. In the romance for clarinet there was philosophizing as though Voltaire talked in somber mood. The scherzo for the flutes was the banter of two shepherds in Arcadia. [*Herald*]

> Of the most interest was the suite by Woollett, not alone for the elasticity with which the somewhat rigid from was treated, but for its vivid and telling combinations and the variety and contrasts which played about in the interchange of voices … Without doubt the suite aims at a highly individual utterance; it is equally without doubt that it achieves this in its own language—which is that of a translation, from just what tongue would have been less definitely understood had we not, during the past few seasons, had such liberal programmes of the modern French composers. Translation or not, however, both Nocturne and Scherzo were movements of rare beauty. The long horn and piano dialogue which composes most of the structure of the former had that haunting contrast of the near and the far, the real and the unreal, which is the essence of the romance, the fairy tale and the legend—now here, now there, and gone. The Scherzo, a trio for piano and two flutes, was a piece of sheer rhapsody, flutes in league against the piano which declared itself in the lightest ripple and shimmer. [*Transcript*]

Next, as mentioned, the audience heard a guest vocalist with an aria from the *St. Matthew Passion* of Bach, apparently a work which was prepared for an approaching Bach festival in Boston.

Following the Bach was the Jules Mouquet *Rapsodie* op. 26, for solo English horn with flute, clarinet, horn and bassoon and five strings. The *Herald* complained that a new *Symphonietta* by this composer had been promised in the season's advertisement, and not the work which was performed. Otherwise, the only critic to mention this composition was the writer for the *Transcript*, who describes the path of this work as a 'gypsywise

Programme

Henri Wollett . . . . Suite
    I. Prélude (moderato) for Piano, Two Flutes, Clarinet and Horn.
    II. Romance (andante) for Piano and Clarinet.
    III. Scherzo for Piano and Two Flutes.
    IV. Nocturne (poco adagio) for Piano and Horn.
    V. Finale (allegro) for Piano, Two Flutes, Clarinet and Horn.
    (First Time)

J. S. Bach .   Aria from "Mathew's Passion" for Soprano, with Flute and Two English Horns Accompaniment

Jules Mouquet   Rapsodie (Op. 26) for English Horn Solo, with Flute, Clarinet, Horn, Bassoon and String Quintet Accompaniment
    (First time)

Sjögren   a. Two Songs from Julius Wolff's "Tannhauser"
Corner (1649)   b. An Old Sacred Lullaby

Jean Huré   Pastorale for Three Flutes, Oboe, English Horn, Two Clarinets, Horn, Two Bassoons and Piano

THE PIANO IS A MASON AND HAMLIN

career, but rather that of the gypsy who knows the values of a certain decorum, and who has suited her rhythmic frenzies to the town.'

The final work on this program was the *Pastorale* by Jean Huré for three flutes, oboe, English horn, two clarinets, horn, two bassoons and piano. None of the critics mentioned this work in their reviews.

An Extra Concert in Chickering Hall

On the afternoon of 24 January 1909, the Longy Club performed on the Tucker series of chamber concerts given in Chickering Hall. There are no known extant reviews of this concert, but a surviving program indicates the wind ensemble repeated the Woollett Suite and the *Pastorale* by Huré, together with four brief arrangements of the music of Grieg for flute, oboe, two clarinets and two bassoons, and a Trio by Edouard Destenay (1850–1924) for oboe, clarinet and piano.

Program

Suite. For Pianoforte, two Flutes, Clarinet and Horn. *Henri Woollett*
    I. Prélude (moderato)
    II. Scherzo
    III. Finale (Allegro)

Songs.
    La Danse, (Mazurka). . . . *Chopin-Viardot*
    Thy Beaming Eyes. . . . *MacDowell*
    Comment disaient-ils? . . . *Liszt*
    My Sweetheart and I. . . . *Mrs. Beach*

Trio. For Oboë, Clarinet and Pianoforte. . *E. Destenay*
    I. Allegro vivacio
    II. Andante non troppo
    III. Presto

Songs.
    Romance. . . . . . . *Debussy*
    Canzonetta. . . . . *Meyer-Helmund*
    (From "Margitta")

Four Small Pieces. For Flute, Oboë, two Clarinets, and two Bassoons. . . *Grieg*
    I. In My Country Land
    II. Young Bird
    III. Solitary Wanderer
    IV. Elves' Dance

Pastorale. For three Flutes, Oboë, English Horn, two Clarinets, Horn, two Bassoons, and Pianoforte. *J. Huré*

THE PIANOFORTE IS A MASON & HAMLIN

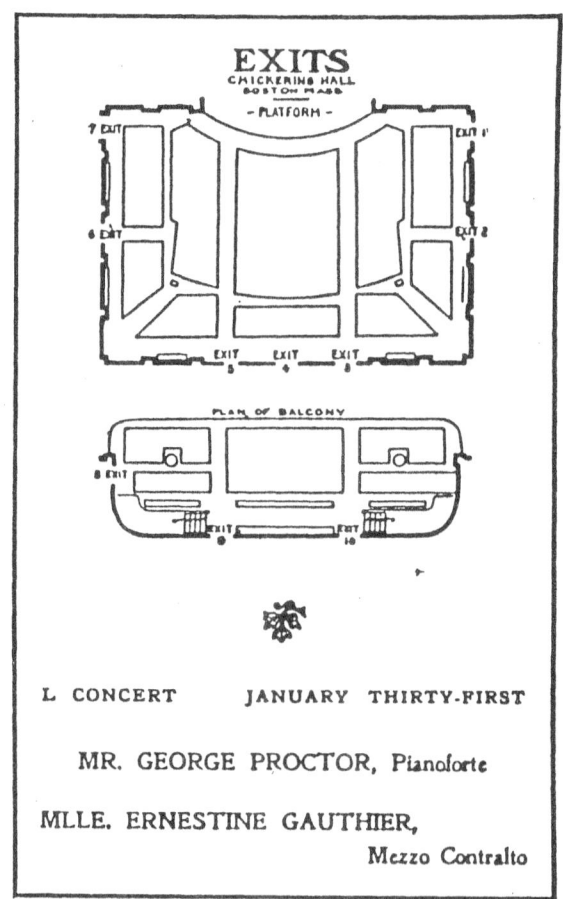

L CONCERT   JANUARY THIRTY-FIRST

MR. GEORGE PROCTOR, Pianoforte

MLLE. ERNESTINE GAUTHIER, Mezzo Contralto

The Third Concert

The final concert of the ninth season was given on the evening of 8 February 1909, and began with the American premiere of the Symphonie by the young Georges Enesco (1881–1955) for flutes, oboe, English horn, two clarinets, two horns and two bassoons. The *Globe* was the only newspaper to give a generally positive reaction to this work, calling it 'pleasing to the general ear,' and the only newspaper to mention that the audience erupted in applause after the first movement. The other critics clearly took sides against this work, although it is interesting to find them writing more extensively, and more interestingly, about it than would usually be the case for a work which they liked!

Georges Enesco at the piano, by E. Joaillier, Paris, 1930

> How many new names are appearing in Music! Each programme of the Longy Club sends us to our biographical dictionaries—in this case fruitlessly, except that we discovered Enesco to be a Roumanian of the present.
>
> His composition presented English horn in addition to the regular wood wind forces and managed to avoid the monotony which often results from the absence of the string tones. Yet any long work for wind instruments also is heavily handicapped. It was a three movement symphony. We shall not mention to M. Enesco that symphonies are generally of four movements—for he might write the additional movement.
>
> The first movement was not very striking, but had some fair counterpoint. The second was quaintly pastoral and attractive, giving the English horn some effective work, and the symphony grew steadily in interest to the end.[11]

[11] Louis C. Elson, 'Longy Club Ends Season Successfully,' *Boston Advertiser*, Feb. 9, 1909.

> During nine seasons this band of players on wind instruments, the men who furnish the rich hues of tone color that make the symphony concerts a delight, have maintained an aristocracy, a house of lords, in which they have discussed the interests of the musical realm. Wind players are clannish even in their regular place in the orchestra; as a rule they go in twos; and they admit new members into their ranks only for most important considerations. Their music has to be written for them in a large measure independently of the other instruments; they acknowledge the brasses as a sort of inferior aristocracy, but when they associate with the stringed instruments they invariably assert their aristocratic pretensions.
>
> When a critic hears flutes, oboes and clarinets giving out the leading melodies of a symphony or when he discerns their tones making some telling color combination in an operatic score, he feels that his musical wisdom is equal to appreciating them; but when he hears these peers of the orchestra discuss music in separate session his wisdom forsakes him. In making up his mind about such a matter as the Enesco sym-

phony, which stood as a new piece on the Longy program, he may compare it with some former performance by the same players; or, better than that, he may simply describe it. The symphony is short, as the music books say such a thing should be; for the ear soon tires of the tone of wind instruments and the players themselves must not be kept at work too long. The first movement of the little symphony is much given to developments of the themes on which it is based, and, while the composer has treated them as only a scholarly musician could treat them, it seemed more than once while the music was being played that the instruments were undertaking work that would more appropriately be done by a string quartet. In the slow movement, which is divided between romantic and playful subjects, flute, oboe and bassoon spoke with individuality, and so the restraint of the string quartet manner was removed. On the whole Enesco's symphony is musicians' music, agreeable to the ordinary listener because of his interest in the players, not because of anything the composer has to say.[12]

[12] *Moniter*, Feb. 9, 1909.

POTTER HALL
MONDAY, FEBRUARY 8, 1909, AT 8.15 O'CLOCK

CHAMBER MUSIC FOR
WIND INSTRUMENTS

BY

The Longy Club

THIRD AND LAST CONCERT

1908 — NINTH SEASON — 1909

Programme

No. 1. GEORGES ENESCO — Symphonie for Two Flutes, Oboe, English Horn, Two Clarinets, Two Horns, and Two Bassoons

   I. Allegro Tranquillo
   II. Lento Expressivo — Vivo — Lento Expressivo
   III. Allegro Assai

(First performance in America)

No. 2. Ch. M. LOEFFLER — Deux Rapsodies for Oboe, Viola, and Piano

   I. L'Etang (The Pool)
   II. La Cornemuse (The Bagpipe)

No. 3. GABRIEL PIERNÉ — Pastorale Variée dans le style ancien (Op. 30) for One Flute, One Oboe, One Clarinet, One Trumpet, One Horn, and Two Bassoons

Andantino
Elms in Canone
First Double (Scherzosamente)
Second Double (Tourbillon)
Third Double (Tempo di minuetto)
Fourth Double (Alla Siciliana)
Fifth Double (Final) Allegro Maestoso

THE PIANO IS A MASON & HAMLIN

> Judged by the opening number, Enesco is a young prophet of ultra-impressionism whose utterance flows in constantly reiterated phrases, glowing now in this color and now transformed in that, weaving on persistently through a maze of subtle evanescent harmonies which scarcely grant one clear vision until the pattern has changed again, but in the new design the same threads of color reappear—reminiscent, alluring, yet ever baffling …
>
> The allegro tranquillo of his new symphonie was frankly disappointing at this first hearing. It advances several themes of no particular beauty or significance. The development is most free, and does not always appear logical or conclusive; indeed, in several instances this movement narrowly missed being chaotic. The vivo of the second part brought a rhythmic, fantastic theme of oriental flavor upon the flute. It is pleasantly developed until the whole choir shared it. The grotesque bassoon, unwilling to let it pass, carries a snatch of it over in the lento with droll insistence. The closing movement had more unity of design and reassembled the preceding themes.[13]

[13] 'Longy Concert,' *Boston Herald*, Feb. 9, 1909.

> The Symphony of Enesco … was fortunate in leading the programme, for had it followed the rhapsodies it would have seemed to have less feature than it really had. Its melodies are short-lived, and its ideas patter on as birds run. The lively tune of the 'Vivo' in the second movement descends to flippancy. In the final allegro, however, the flute spins a theme through many windings which employ the serene beauties of the instrument to their utmost. The melody then as suddenly fades.[14]

[14] 'Mr. Loeffler's Rhapsodies,' *Boston Transcript*, Feb. 9, 1909.

The second portion of this final concert was given over to two Rapsodies for oboe, viola and piano by Charles Loeffler, who also played the viola part in his own composition. These works, which are inspired by the poems, 'The Pool' and 'The Bagpipe,' by Maurice Rollinat (1846–1903) also inspired rather interesting commentary by the critics.

> That Mr. Loeffler's playing on the viola was most expressive goes without saying. The void which he left in the orchestra has never been filled and it is always a keen pleasure to hear him in solo work. Mr. Gabhard is known as a poetic pianist in the most modern school and M. Longy is the greatest oboist in this century and the equal of any artist on this instrument that we have ever heard; therefore, the interpretation of the two numbers cold not have been bettered.
>
> As regards the contents of the compositions we cannot speak with quite as much enthusiasm. Mr. Loeffler is a modern of moderns and is often morbid. Why this amiable gentleman should produce such charnel-house rhapsodies passes all comprehension. Let us confess at once that both numbers were impressive, the first especially so, but the pic-

ture of a foul pond, which the board of health ought to drain at once, is not an inspiring topic to dwell upon. Nevertheless, the players were called out four times at the end of the Loeffler compositions. [*Advertiser*]

If Mr. Loeffler had not himself played the viola part in his two little tone poems, it would be easy to say that he made a miscalculation in putting the viola's weak voice against the oboe's twang. There is some resemblance in the tone color of the two instruments and there was a time during the playing of the second of Mr. Loeffler's pieces when the viola played an accompaniment to the oboe that sounded faintly like a droning bag pipe. The little pieces are refinements of musical expression too subtle even for a program of subtleties; yet they succeed in putting a hearer into a distinct mood, if not into an exalted one, and keeping him there as long as the music lasts. [*Moniter*]

Mr. Loeffler's contribution to the program was unquestionably the more enjoyable. He is harrowingly effective in depicting the gruesome in idea or circumstance, but he does not forget its analogy to the central figure. Kollinat's poems present a noticable trait of the romanticists in poetry. The misery of the human subject is enforced and intensified by surrounding nature. The dank pool, the blind fish, the dull thunder, the impish goblins, the croaking frogs, the ghastly reflection of the pale moon, the weird notes of the mocking bagpipe were all pregnant with brooding horror as the instruments portrayed them, but they were not mere interpretative tricks—they made the pathos of the old dead piper the more poignant. [*Herald*]

The charm of novelty belonged to Mr. Loeffler's two rhapsodies, to the spectral 'bagpipe' which went wailing down the lonely glens, but more especially to the first of the pair, 'The Pool.' The intimate strangeness of the scene which inspired the poem is the first link; the second is the odd vividness of the verses which inspired the rhapsody, and the music, in its turn, conjures a scene no less phantasmagoric. Some essayist, perhaps it was Walter Pater, defines romanticism as the element of strangeness in beauty. But when that strangeness is knit with the elements of familiarity and even of the common, it acquires an altogether new force, as a common word turns strange when thought on intently, or as the colorings of the impressionists look unfamiliar when they do but render the truth of details observed unthinkingly by most. There is nothing strange in the scene described in Maurice Rollinat's verses except the intensity of the description. He sees an old pool full of fish that have lived there countless years and gone blind in its opaque waters a generation since—brown, shuddering pool under a sky full of storm clouds which mutter dull thunder, but withhold the splashing drops. On its splashy margin among the purple osiers summer halts and red autumn waits. There is chill in the air, a plaint of dismal frogs high priests of the marshy sanctuary. Or, as night bends of the lowlands and presses on the morass the goblin fires burn eerily, and a sickly moon, flat-faced, peers into this leaden mirror to scan her spectral visage—her 'death's head lighted from within.'

To this haunt of imagination someone has applied the word morbid. Nature knows not the meaning of the word, and this dank, lonely pool is Nature. Even more intensely than the versifier, the composer has caught the pathos of one of her forgotten works. The pool has a neglected beauty which fills the beholder with a nameless and passionate regret. He comes upon it at the margin of a morass, or it may gather its green mantling at the spot of his own garden; it is a pool of no importance in nature's scale, and therein lies it pathos. It is such a pool as Hilda mocks at in Ibsen's 'The Lady from the Sea.' Of some such sense of a dumb and wistful spirit animating the inanimate were born both pieces, poem and rhapsody. The neglect is expressed in the timbre of a forgotten instrument, the viola, most musical and most melancholy. Little less foreign to the average trio is the oboe, winding its bouts of linked sweetness; while the figures of the piano are so subtilized as to make even that instrument something vague and rich. The rhapsody is thus a certain intense mood in the presence of something small, desolate and lonely, all in a cloudy autumnal twilight. It pictures one of those spots which take the fancy not by the assault of beauty, but by the insinuation of unique charm; there is nothing else like it in the whole world; nature could spare it, but fortunately she has not; it music be revisited again and yet again, and born away on the inward eye which is the bliss of solitude. The music in minor details is aptly pictorial, and, as the composer and his brother artists played it last night, the whole secret charm of the scene with its weird fascinations unfolded, in deep sighs of strings and wind, piano playing in the neutral tints or dark background masses, through to the pensive modulations of its last measures and the close, with a pair of whole notes double-stopped n the viola, the very smoothing away of flat pond water untroubled by a ripple. The sound ceased; the pool was still. Its waters were opaque, but they were pure. The pool was Wordsworthian. [*Transcript*]

Given these challenges, one can understand how the critics were peacefully relieved to hear the final work on this concert, Gabriel Pierné's (1863–1937) *Pastorale Variée* ('dans le style ancien'), op. 30, for flute, oboe, clarinet, trumpet, horn and two bassoons. Indeed, Elson, of the *Advertiser*, declared this work, 'the best of the entire concert.' Other views were equally happy.

Pierne's little variations were played and were over with almost as soon as they began. Of the rest of the program proved the books are right in saying that the ear soon wearies of the tone of wind instruments, this music of Pierne proved them to be greatly mistaken. [*Moniter*]

The closing composition shows Pierne a modern, but less of an impressionist. He has altogether disavowed dignified imitation, but he has added color and striking rhythmic effect to form. [*Herald*]

Pierne's pastoral was a delicious bit of grotesquerie off a piece of old tapestry. The pompous 'Selah!' of the bassoon at the terminations of its doubles stirred to laughter. And if its tunes are pasty to the memory, they have one of the virtues of good paste. The stick. [*Transcript*]

In general this was a very successful concert. As a footnote, the *Journal* mentions both the frequent applause and the efforts of one audience member, Max Fiedler, Conductor of the Boston Symphony Orchestra, 'who took a leading part in attempting to get encore numbers. Every attempt, however, failed completely.' [15]

[15] 'Longy Club in Final Concert,' *Boston Journal*, Feb. 9, 1909.

Season Ten, 1909–1910

THE LONGY CLUB WIND ENSEMBLE began their tenth season without a change in personnel, however, they did change the location of their concert series from Potter Hall to Chickering Hall, Boston.

The First Concert

The *Herald* reported a 'small but interested audience,'[1] for the first concert of this season, which was given on the evening of 23 December 1909. The program began with the *Sextuor*, by Malherbe, for flute, oboe, English horn, clarinet, horn and bassoon. Of the three extant reviews of this concert, the *Globe*

[1] 'Season Opened by Longy Club,' *Boston Herald*, Dec. 24, 1909.

Members of the Club

Flutes	Messrs. A. MAQUARRE and A. BROOKE
Oboes	Messrs. G. LONGY and C. LENOM
Clarinets	Messrs. G. GRISEZ and P. MIMART
Horns	Messrs. F. HAIN and H. LORBEER
Bassoons	Messrs. P. SADONY and J. HELLEBERG
Piano	Mr. A. DE VOTO

Assisting Artist
Mr. H. SCHUËCKER, Harp

.. Programme ..

No. 1. Ed. Malherbe   Sextuor for Flute, Oboe, English Horn, Clarinet, Horn and Fagott
   I. Allegro Moderato
   II. Andantino
   III. Presto

No. 2. Max Reger   Sonata in As dur (Op. 49) No. 1, for Clarinet and Piano
   I. Allegro
   II. Vivace
   III. Larghetto
   IV. Prestissimo Assai
   (First time)
Messrs. G. GRISEZ and A. DE VOTO

No. 3. Leland A. Cossart   Suite (Op. 19) for two Flutes, two Oboes (with English Horn interchangeable), two Clarinets, two Horns, two Bassoons, and Harp
(First time)
   I. Introida
   II. Élégie
   III. Theme with Variations

The Second Concert will take place on February Eighth

THE PIANO IS A MASON AND HAMLIN

did not comment on this composition and the critic of the *Post* admitted he arrived late and did not hear it.² The *Herald*, on the other hand, liked the work.

² 'Longy Club,' *Boston Post*, Dec. 24, 1909.

> Malherbe's sextet is a gracious, fluent work. The first two movements have long, singing phrases, which gave the instruments an opportunity to appear at their best. The third movement, a frisky little presto, captivated the audience by its daintiness.

The second work on this concert was the Max Reger (1873–1916) Sonata op. 49, no. 1, for clarinet, performed by Mr. Grisez and de Voto. The newspapers found this work not so interesting as Reger's later works. The *Herald* heard it as, 'remarkably simple in its harmonic progressions and its form,' and the *Post*, somewhat in search for a metaphor, noted,

> It can only be said that the music sounded like good 'paper work'—and very little else. The Reger of the big orchestral pieces is a far more individual figure, it seems, than the man who strings off opus numbers one after another, as though it was as necessary for him to spin notes as it is nature for a spider, whatever the time or circumstance, to construct a web from his intervals.

The final work on this concert, the Leland A. Cossart (1877–1965) Suite op. 19, for pairs of flutes, oboes, clarinets, horns, bassoons and harp, being new attracted more attention from the press.

> Nor was the Cossart's suite of a very serious nature, so as to cause the listener fatigue. It is a pleasant composition, and showed the skill and quality of each player. There is a rich network of close harmony, and in the variations the composer runs the gamut of style, from a choral to a sentimental serenade. [*Herald*]

> The suite by Cossart is not unique, but it is a happy and unforced invention. The 'Introida' is built on a rapid figure of no particular significance and is pleasantly brief. The 'Elegie' is the most interesting movement, and very well adapted to display the moving tone qualities of the various wind instruments. The theme, with variations, is like too many other themes with variations. [*Post*]

> Cossart has used this wind band and harp with excellent effect in a short first movement, styled, by the program, 'Introida.' A melodic theme of much beauty, given out in the opening measures is developed in the returning passage against a lovely counter melody in the horn and flowing arpeggios in the harp.

The 'Elegie' employs individually by turns, English horn, clarinet, oboe and horn in phrases of grave and tender beauty. The treatment of the truly elegiac English horn, as evidenced in Mr. Lenom's sympathetic tone, was admirable.

The third and closing movement of the suite is a set of six variations upon a theme of the simplicity of a folk-tune. These embellishments, while tolerably well contrasted in rhythm and in melodic and harmonious structure to give variety, gained most distinctly last night in the fifth by reason of the pure tone, expressive phrasing and remarkably flexible legato of the horn playing of Mr. Hain in its songful share of the number.[3]

[3] 'Longy Club Concert,' *Boston Globe*, Dec. 24, 1909.

The Second Concert

The second concert was given on the evening of 8 February 1910, and began with the only real wind ensemble composition of the entire program, the Mozart *Symphonie Concertante*

CHICKERING HALL

FEBRUARY 8, 1910, at 8.15 O'CLOCK

Chamber Music for Wind Instruments

— BY —

The Longy Club

SECOND CONCERT

1909 — TENTH SEASON — 1910

.. Programme ..

No. 1. Mozart . . Quartette for Oboe, Clarinet, Horn, Bassoon, with Piano Accompaniment
    I. Allegro
    II. Adagio
    III. Andantino con Variazioni
    (First time)

No. 2. Songs
    Louis Aubert . . Melancholia / Hélène
    Rhené Bâton . . Apporte les cristaux dorés / Lune de Cuivre / Frêle comme un harmonica

No. 3. Haendel . . Sonate for Oboe and Piano
    I. Adagio — Allegro
    II. Adagio — Allegro

No. 4. Songs . Gustave Charpentier . Prière / Parfum exotique / Complainte

No. 5. Maurice Ravel. Introduction and Allegro for Harp with String Quartette, Flute and Clarinet Accompaniment
    (First time)

The Piano is a Mason & Hamlin

The Third and Last Concert of the Season will take place on March 10, at 8.15 o'clock, with Mr. Max Fiedler assisting.

(called 'Quartet' on this occasion) for oboe, clarinet, horn, bassoon and piano performing an orchestral reduction. The only reviewer to mention this work was Philip Hale of the *Herald*.

> Mozart wrote the music in haste, in four days, he said, and while it is fluent and well made, it has little real charm or distinction. If it were not signed by Mozart it is doubtful whether this quartet would be played.[4]

4 Philip Hale, 'Longy Club Gives Second Concert,' *Boston Herald*, Feb. 9, 1910. As is generally known, a complete form of this work does not in fact exist in Mozart's hand and there is some doubt as to it being genuine.

The Mozart was followed by a guest soprano, Marie Sundelius, and a Handel Sonata for oboe. The remaining ensemble work on this concert was the Ravel *Introduction and Allegro* for harp, flute, clarinet and strings, conducted by Longy. This work also failed to make a strong impression on the critics.

> Simplicity is one of the characteristics of this latter piece of Ravel's, but it is that kind of French simplicity which is reached only through much refinement of artistry.[5]

5 'Longy Club Concert,' *Moniter*, Feb. 9, 1910.

> There are charming effects of color, effects of the moment that leave no lasting impression. Neither structure, contents, or rhythms are of real interest. [*Herald*]

The Third Concert

The final concert of this season was given on the evening of 10 March 1910, and an extant review in the *Herald* reports a 'good size' audience that was especially enthusiastic after the Fried composition.

The program began with the Beethoven Octet op. 103, of which the *Herald* laments, 'One listens with resignation to the Allegro and Andante of Beethoven, and with pleasure to his Minuet and Finale.'

Following a Bach flute sonata, the wind ensemble, with Boston Symphony Orchestra Conductor, Max Fiedler, performed a new work, the Oskar Fried (1871–1941), *Adagio and Scherzo*, op. 2, for three flutes, two oboes, English horn, two clarinets, bass clarinet, three horns, two bassoons, contrabassoon, two harps and timpani. This work the critic of the *Herald* heard as being a better composition than the Beethoven!

Oskar Fried, 1906

The harmonically adventurous spirit and fuller knowledge of color possibilities for wind instruments characteristic of today gives such a work as that of Fried precedence over Beethoven's Octet in interest and beauty …

    He seems in his writing to have sifted out what is best in the modern German manner; he distinctly has something to say, and it is said without exaggeration, without padding, without straining for effect. His combination of instruments is extremely happy. Upon the mellow foundation of bassoons and softly accenting tympani he builds exquisite melodies taken up first by clarinet and then by oboe, until all are blended in a climax of rich power. Throughout flashes the clear shower of the harp or the sweet high tone of the flute. The two parts of the work are in great contrast, yet both have extreme freshness and originality.

The wind ensemble closed the program with a standard work in their repertoire, the Huré *Pastorale* for three flutes, oboe, English horn, two clarinets, horn, two bassoons and piano. The *Herald* calls this work, 'less ambitious,' but, 'so genuinely pretty that it comes as a relief.'

Programme

Members of the Club

Flutes	Messrs. A. Maquarre and A. Brooke
Oboes	Messrs. G. Longy and C. Lenom
Clarinets	Messrs. G. Grisez and P. Mimart
Horns	Messrs. F. Hain and H. Lorbeer
Bassoons	Messrs. P. Sadony and J. Helleberg
Piano	Mr. A. de Voto

Assisting Artists

Mr. MAX FIEDLER, Conductor
Miss SHAW and Mr. SCHUECKER, Harps
Mr. A. BATTLES, Flute   Mr. J. PHAIR, Horn
Mr. F. MUELLER, Oboe   Mr. E. MUELLER, Bassoon
Mr. K. STUMPF, Bass Clarinet
Mr. A. RETTBERG, Tympani

No. 1. Beethoven . . Octet (Op. 103) in E-flat major, for two Oboes, two Clarinets, two Horns, and two Bassoons
    I. Allegro
    II. Andante
    III. Menuetto
    IV. Finale

No. 2. Bach . . Sonate in B minor, for Flute and Piano
    Messrs. A. Maquarre and A. de Voto
    I. Andante
    II. Largo e dolce
    III. Presto — Allegro Moderato

No. 3. O. Fried . Adagio and Scherzo (Op. 2), for three Flutes (with Piccolo interchangeable), two Oboes, English Horn, two Clarinets, Bass Clarinet, three Horns, two Bassoons, Contra Bassoon, two Harps and Tympani
    (First time)
    Mr. Max Fiedler, Conductor

No. 4. Jean Huré . Pastorale for three Flutes, Oboe, English Horn, two Clarinets, Horn, two Bassoons and Piano
    (By request)

The Piano is a Mason & Hamlin

Season Eleven, 1910–1911

With the addition of the second bassoonist, Joseph Mosbach, the Longy Club began this season with a new member for the first time since the season of 1905–1906. There would be no further changes until the season of 1914–1915. The consistency of the personnel over so long a time undoubtedly made a fundamental contribution to the high artistic level of which the music critics speak.

The First Concert

The first concert of the Longy Club's eleventh season was given on the evening of 26 December 1910. While Louis Elson, of the *Advertiser*, grumbled over the proximity with Christmas Day, he reports a 'very good-sized and very applausive audience.'[1]

The program began with the Mouquet Suite for flute, oboe, horn, two clarinets and two bassoons, which the *Globe* found rather unimpressive.

[1] Louis Elson, 'Longy Club Opens its Season Well,' *Boston Advertiser*, Dec. 27, 1910.

> The composer lives in Paris where he teaches piano and composition, and composes in the smaller forms.
>
> The suite is in three movements. The adagio is devoid of color, and needlessly bare in scoring. The first section of the aubade lacks the lightness and zest for a piece of morning music. The horn introduces a more melodic passage in the second.
>
> The Scherzo develops a sprightly figure with both ingenuity and charm.[2]

[2] 'The Longy Club,' *Boston Globe*, Dec. 27, 1910.

The other critics had rather higher opinions of this composition.

> If Dvorak's work was the largest of the concert, Mouquet's little Suite was by all odds the best.
>
> The suite was the gem of the concert. Its performance was superb. A better ensemble could not be imagined. The work is tuneful too, which is something to be grateful for in this 20th century. The charm of the Morning-son, the second movement, was ineffable, and the piquancy

of the Scherzo was also very effective. In this latter there was some striking counterpoint and figure treatment, and the bassoons did some especially commendable work. [*Advertiser*]

CHICKERING HALL   **SEASON 1910–1911**

Chamber Music for Wind Instruments
BY
The Longy Club
(ELEVENTH SEASON)

MEMBERS

Flutes: Messrs. A. MAQUARRE AND A. BROOKE
Oboes: Messrs. G. LONGY AND C. LENOM
Clarinets: Messrs. G. GRISEZ AND P. MIMART
Horns: Messrs. F. HAIN AND H. LORBEER
Bassoons: Messrs. P. SADONY AND J. MOSBACH
Piano: Mr. A. DE VOTO

FIRST CONCERT
Monday Evening, December 26th, at 8.15 o'clock

PROGRAMME

J. Mouquet . Suite for Flute, Oboe, Horn, 2 Clarinets, and 2 Bassoons

H. Woollett . . . . . . Sonate for Flute and Piano
Messrs. A. Maquarre and A. de Voto
(First time at these Concerts)

A. Dvořák . Serenade (Op. 44) for 2 Oboes, 2 Clarinets, 2 Bassoons, 3 Horns, 'Cello, and Double Basse
(First time at these Concerts)

Assisting Artists

Messrs. PHAIR (Horn)   J. KELLER ('Cello)
E. HUBER (Double Basse)

MASON AND HAMLIN PIANO

Mouquet's suite is very pleasant music. Is it an early work? Because it is written very much on traditional lines and in spite of the real freshness of invention, of melody and harmony, there are often perceptible the nails which join the structure together, the passages which are empty in themselves, serving only to connect material of more importance. Yet this music is youthful and charmingly melodic.[3]

The suite by Mouquet cannot justly be considered music of great depth or breadth of score, but it is skillfully written for a restricted combination with no little ingenuity, it is undeniably pleasing and affords much opportunity for agreeable solo effect. The adagio is not lacking in sentiment, the aubade is graceful, while the scherzo is unusually vivacious.

[3] Olin Downes, 'Longy Club in Novelties,' *Boston Post*, Dec. 27, 1910.

Throughout the suite one's attention is constantly attracted to the skill of workmanship, by its spontaneous freedom of tonality, and its effective rhythmical treatment. There is avoidance of the commonplace, and there is distinctive individuality in the music.[4]

4 E. B. H. 'Chickering Hall: The Longy Club,' *Boston Transcript*, Dec. 27, 1910.

Following the performance of a sonata for solo flute by Woollett, the wind ensemble performed for the first time the now famous Antonín Dvořák (1841–1904) Serenade op. 44. As hard as it is to believe, none of the critics heard this work for the masterpiece that it is. Although Elson, of the *Advertiser*, thought the Dvořák ranked below the Mouquet, as the reader has seen above, he nevertheless was the only critic to praise the work without qualification.

Antonín Dvořák, by Jan and Joseph Mulač, Prague, 1901

Dvorak has something to say with this unusual combination of instruments, and he is always fluent. Perhaps he had the fatal facility which caused Raff to fade out so suddenly after his demise. The work was a full-toned and almost symphonic end of a remarkably interesting concert.

It is astonishing, today, to understand how the other critics could be so unimpressed with the Dvořák, considering it shared a concert with Woollett and Mouquet and followed some ten years of rather minor French repertoire.

The Serenade by Dvorak, also, was worth bringing to a hearing, although it is decidedly unequal in musical value. There is quaint humor in the first march-like movement, the minuet has the suggestion of peasant merry-making, which is an insistent note in Dvorak's music, and to which he reverts upon the slightest excuse. The slow movement seems long and somewhat over-elaborated; it is not without a perfunctory element of gravity because occasion demanded it, rather than as a spontaneous expression of mood. The finale, again, seems more casually put together, nor does the episodic reference to the first movement seem inevitable. But as a whole the serenade contains interesting if not invariably beautiful music, whose distinguishing characteristic is the artlessness and refreshing absence of pose. Dvorak's innate sense of color has led him to take every opportunity for contrast of tonal effect, and his skill in opposing combinations of instruments in a telling manner was one of the most conspicuous impressions of the work. [*Transcript*]

The two middle movements, the sprightly minuet and the songful andante, are the most interesting of the four. [*Globe*]

The *Transcript* closed its review with the kind of lament so often found in various Boston newspapers, a gentle rebuke of the public for not supporting the Longy Club in greater numbers.

> The audience, while responsively appreciative, should have been larger. The individual skill of the members of this club and their painstaking and brilliant ensemble should have a more attentive response from a supposedly discriminating public. Such concerts as these should attract music lovers in far greater numbers, if only for the remarkable artistry displayed therein. Furthermore students, whether of orchestration of not, should recognize their value from an educational standpoint. They would find ample cause for reflection and assimilation.

An Extra Concert in Boston

A brief notice in the *Transcript* indicates that on 29 December 1910, the Longy Club wind ensemble performed a concert for a small, but enthusiastic audience of visitors to the city, who were attending a conference.[5] Again, it is a tribute to the high level of performance maintained by this ensemble that this concert, given only three days after the previous one, consisted of nearly entirely different compositions. This concert included the Beethoven Quintet op. 16; two movements of the Mouquet Suite; the *Introduction and Rondo* for clarinet by Widor and the Gouvy Octet op. 21.

[5] 'Longy Club Entertains Visitors,' *Boston Transcript*, Dec. 30, 1910.

The Second Concert

The second concert of the eleventh season was given on the evening of 13 February 1911. The first horn, Mr. Hain, was ill at the last moment and missed this concert, being replaced by a Mr. Windler, who was also a member of the Boston Symphony Orchestra, being described as the 'first chair of the second quartet.'

The first work on this program was the Nocturne by Léon Moreau (1870–1946) for pairs of flutes, oboes, clarinets, horns and bassoons. This work was appreciated by the critics, although Philip Hale, of the *Herald*, makes a very rare observation that in this work the members of the Longy Club 'were not always precise in attack.'[6]

[6] Philip Hale, 'Second Longy Concert,' *Boston Herald*, Feb. 14, 1911.

His nocturne tends pleasantly toward seriousness. There are too well-contrasted divisions, the first built upon a syncopated theme, melodious, not of troubled harmony, and for the greater part homophonic. The second division is more vivacious.[7]

Moreau's Nocturne, somber at the beginning, is warmly colored and has character. It also is well knit together and is not so vague and rambling as some of the compositions for wind instruments by the younger French composers that have been heard here. [*Herald*]

This was followed by transcriptions of two Domenico Scarlatti keyboard pieces, also for ten winds, by Louis Hasselmans (1878–1957), a conductor at the Opera Comique in Paris. Hale thought these were effectively done and the *Globe* was moved to describe them as, 'music graven as a frieze upon a Greek temple.'

[7] 'Longy Club Concert,' *Boston Globe*, Feb. 14, 1911.

CHICKERING HALL

Monday Evening, February 13, 1911
At 8.15 o'clock

CHAMBER MUSIC FOR
WIND INSTRUMENTS
.. BY ..

The Longy Club

SECOND CONCERT

1910 ———— ELEVENTH SEASON ———— 1911

.. Programme ..

LÉON MOREAU — a. Nocturne
(First time)

D. SCARLATTI — b. Pastorale and Capriccio, for 2 Flutes, 2 Oboes, 2 Clarinets, 2 Horns, 2 Bassoons
(Transcription by L. Hasselmans)
(First time)

~~P. DUKAS~~ Woollett. — ~~Villanelle for Horn and Piano~~ Trio for flutes and piano from suite.
(First time)
Messrs. F. Hain and A. de Voto

HAENDEL — Sonate in form of Trio, for 2 Oboes and Bassoon
 I. Adagio
 II. Allegro
 III. Affettuoso
 IV. Allegro

C. DEBUSSY — Première Rapsodie, for Clarinet and Piano
(First time)
Messrs. G. Grisez and A. de Voto

GOUVY — Octet for Flute, Oboe, 2 Clarinets, 2 Horns, 2 Bassoons
 I. Larghetto—Allegretto Moderato
 II. Danse Suédoise
 III. Romance
 IV. Rondo

The Third Concert will take place on March Sixth

At this point in the concert the indisposed Mr. Hain was to perform the Dukas *Villanelle*; instead a movement from the Woollett Suite was substituted. Next the ensemble presented a 'Sonate in form of Trio,' by Handel for oboes and bassoon.

The critics were especially interested to hear the next performance, the first Boston performance of Debussy's *Premiere Rapsodie*, for clarinet and piano. Two extant reviews have lengthy and very interesting first reactions to this now familiar work.

> There was particular interest in Debussy's rhapsodie for clarinet, composed last year for a test piece for graduates at the Paris conservatory. It is no sinecure, although it sounds as though the composer were trying to write for an instrument the secrets of whose voice he did not know intimately. Else why the marked neglect of the chalumeau register and its deep tones of noble beauty?
>
> There is an opening melodic passage of pronounced and ingratiating simplicity. The use of extremely rapid and florid arpegggi demands and exploits the performer's facility, but does not denote any particular design or musical idea.
>
> Mr. Grisez's performance was masterly. His tone is of unqualified beauty. It retains its richness and poise in the hazardous notes on the lower half of the staff; it attains purity without shrillness above, and organ-like breadth below. He phrases with taste and with exquisite graduation of nuances. He played the embellishment fluently. [*Globe*]

> Mr. Grisez ... gave a remarkable performance ..., remarkable as an exhibition of technic and of dramatic and poetic feeling. I am informed that the Rhapsody was composed for the competition for the clarinet prize at the Paris Conservatory last season. It bristles with difficulties, but the virtuoso passages are written with such art that they do not seem as though they were prepared as pitfall for competing students.
>
> These passages to test technical proficiency are wildly rhapsodic, at times highly poetic. There is in this music the Debussy of the later period with a reminiscence here and there. 'The Afternoon of a Faun,' the elusive Debussy of haunting hints a melodic figures, of rhythms that are suspected rather than felt, of subdued and exquisite nuances. There is also the Debussy of the earlier years who had a tendency to obvious tunes after the manner of Massanet. [*Herald*]

The concert concluded with a performance of the Gouvy Octet for flute, oboe, and pairs of clarinets, horns and bassoons. The *Globe* thought, 'The second and last movements gave particular pleasure by the graceful melody and exhilarating rhythm.' The *Herald* added some interesting details about the composer.

> With the Octet of Gouvy there was a return to orthodoxy and music that belies the composer's nationality. Gouvy lived so long in Germany that he could not escape its influence. He had his reward. Three years before he died he was made an associate member of the Berlin Academy.

The *Globe* concluded its review of this concert with the following reflection.

> Mr. Longy and his fellow artists deserve unstinted praise for affording this opportunity of hearing these instruments which pall upon the average ear.

The Third Concert

The final concert of this season was given on the evening of 6 March 1911. Two reviews seem to disagree in their report of the size of the audience, the *Globe* calling it 'an audience of moderate size,'[8] and the *Herald* describing it as, 'an audience of a size that bespeaks the high esteem in which are held the performances of this club.'[9]

The critics were also quite divided in their reaction to the first work, a Suite by Ernest Wagner (1870–1954) for piano, two flutes, oboe, clarinet and bassoon.

> The suite by E. Wagner, whom biographical dictionaries avoid is simple unpretentious music. The first movement suffers from persistent recurrence of the same rhythmical pattern, with regular distribution of solos, although aside from this the musical ideas are pleasing. The second movement has some depth of expression, and not a little of poetic beauty. Its thoughtful sentiment and artistic workmanship attract more than a passing attention. The third movement, although brisk and animated suffers from the same faults as the first.[10]

> The Wagner suite was short, clear and intelligible … The first movement of the suite was clear and concise. The second longer and more ambitious, but the best movement of the three, the finale, though short, was full of originality.[11]

[8] 'Longy Club Concert,' *Boston Globe*, March 7, 1911.

[9] 'Longy Club Concert,' *Boston Herald*, March 7, 1911.

[10] 'An Interesting Concert by the Longy Club,' *Boston Transcript*, March 7, 1911.

[11] Louis C. Elson, 'Longy Club Gives a Delightful Concert,' *Boston Advertiser*, March 7, 1911.

> The suite by E. Wagner … has marked simplicity in tonality and in the choice and development of musical ideas. The themes of the three movements show a family resemblance. Those of the first are worked over with much repetition, yet there is freshness and spontaneity. The second is monotonous by reason of its lack of harmonic color. The principal theme is a bald arpeggio in the minor mode, and is unsuited to the style of the movement. The last movement has a certain restless animation and more elasticity in development. [*Globe*]

Next, Mr. Hain performed the Dukas solo work which had been scheduled originally for the previous concert. The *Transcript* reports he played with, 'brilliant effect, and appropriately romantic sentiment.'

The final work on this concert was the first Boston performance of the great Mozart *Gran Partita*, K. 370a, for twelve winds and string bass. Two critics wrote extended and interesting commentary and it is interesting, if extraordinary, that neither fully appreciated this work as music.

> The Mozart serenade excited interest first of all by the employment of two basset-horns, the first of which was played by Mr. Grisez on an alto clarinet, an instrument of almost identical quality, the second by Mr. Stumpf. The tone of these unusual instruments, simply continuing the clarinet range, made possible a variety of passages all in clarinet tone with singular beauty of effect. As an example of skillfully contrasted instrumental timbres, this serenade was invaluable to the student, and should attract the layman by its individuality and solidity of tone. As music it sometimes suggests too strongly the perfunctory manner of the 18th century, although the actual style is impeccably pure. But there are many moments which give pleasure, or even impress deeply by their beauty as both trios of the first minuet, the second trio of the second, the poetic melody of the Adagio, the characteristic vivacity of the variations, and the sprightly if brief rondo. All in all, a work of unusual interest, and moments of great beauty. It was played exceedingly well, with a few pardonable slips of intonation in clarinet and horn. For the problems in intonation of so large a group are vexatious in the extreme. To have solved them so well was little short of a triumph. [*Transcript*]

> The Mozart serenade was chiefly interesting because of its use of the Basset horns. This instrument deserves to be resuscitated because of it peculiar tone quality. It is a rather twangy-toned clarinette of deeper register. It transposes down a fifth, like the English horn, and it is related to the clarinette exactly as the English horn is related to the oboe. In Mozart's day it was made in a different shape from the modern instrument used yesterday. In the old days it had several sharp angles

in its tube which must have had a peculiar effect upon its tone, making it peculiarly hollow-toned and sometimes dull, like the bassoon in its middle register. Those who have heard it in Mr. Converse's 'Pipe of Desire' may recall the weird melancholy of even the modern instrument. Mozart used it in funeral music, in both his requiem and in his Masonic funeral music, as well as in some operas.

But we ought not to forget that when this serenade was written the clarinette was a stranger instrument than the Basset horn, and it was Mozart who really introduced the clarinette into the symphonic orchestra. Nevertheless it is plain that he did not fully comprehend its spectral tone-color in the lower register, nor did Beethoven for that matter. The first composers to comprehend the true worth of the Chalumeau register of the clarinettes were Weber and Mendelssohn.

The serenade as music is somewhat antiquated. It was, in the 18th century, a suite of rather small proportions, and Mozart here extends it to its largest proportions—seven movements. But each of these movements is melodious and they are in contrast with each other … There were 12 performers—'abeit omen!' [*Advertiser*]

Mozart, *Gran Partita*, manuscript

Season Twelve, 1911–1912

The First Concert

BEGINNING WITH THIS SEASON THE LONGY CLUB moved their concert series to Jordon Hall. The first concert was given on the evening of 20 November 1911, and the *Herald* reports, 'a large audience was present and gave enthusiastic evidence of its appreciation. The performance was marked by its accustomed finish in the matter of detail, finesse in tone gradations and generally admirable ensemble playing.'[1]

The first work on the November concert was the Mozart Partita K. 375, for eight winds. Of the three extant reviews, only the critic of the *Globe* seemed to appreciate the true value of this music.

Jordan Hall, New England Conservatory of Music, Boston.

> The serenade is thoroughly Mozartean in flavor, the flourish of playful pomposity in the opening measures of the allegro, the archness of the minuets, the tenderness and grace of the contrasting and songful passages, and the spontaneity with which each measure flowers into its successor, now to satisfy anticipation with a sequence, not to pique it by the surprise of some new caprice.
>
> Here observance of form implies no labor. It is much to afford refreshment, and did so last night, for Mr. Longy and his colleagues played it with appreciation. The first movement and the minuet in particular were in this vein.[2]

[1] 'Season Opened by Longy Club,' *Boston Herald*, Nov. 21, 1911.

[2] 'First Longy Concert,' *Boston Globe*, Nov. 21, 1911.

Next Mr. Longy performed two pieces for solo oboe with piano by Louis-Joseph Diémer (1843–1919). The *Herald* said of this distinguished oboist, 'The exquisite delicacy of phrasing and unerring sense of proportion displayed by M. Longy might well serve as a valuable lesson to many singers.' The *Transcript* makes an especially interesting observation.

> Diemer's pieces for the oboe were salon music, which to a modern concert audience is a priori under the obligation of justifying itself. Nowadays we are too busy, or at least too occupied, to be willing to sit down and pass away the time with polite jeux d'esprit. Like the newspaper article, the musical composition must enter into competition with everything else that might claim our attention, and must convince us from the start that it deserves consideration. So it is always damning

Louis-Joseph Diémer, 1896

praise to call a piece of music pleasing. Diemer's romance was pleasing; the intermezzo was really stimulating; while both are graceful and well written. The second, with its suggestion of goblins dancing on their heels, suited the character of the oboe far better than did the lyric sweetness of the first.[3]

The final work on this concert was the Rimsky-Korsakov Quintet for piano, flute, clarinet, horn and bassoon. The two critics who discussed this work disagreed dramatically as to its worth. First, the critic of the *Globe*, who did not like this composition.

> There are posthumous pieces that might better repose in the grave with their creators than be revived to bear their name. The Rimsky-Korsakow is tediously prolix and given to endless and idle repetitions in attempted development of themes which are dry and without significance. There is meager suggestion of the brilliant Russian of fertile invention of the 'Sheherazade' suite. The andante contains a songful theme for horn of possibilities when properly phrased and the rondo betrays some imagination, but is needlessly long.

The reviewer of the *Transcript*, on the other hand, was quite taken by this work and makes a lengthy case why it is more successful than the Mozart Partita.

> For several reasons the Russian was most interesting. In the first place he chose his instruments and used them with an attention to their individualities which for the most part has been cultivated since Mozart's time. Any composer working with a band of wood-winds must spend much of his attention overcoming the natural difficulties of the combination, which, at best, is likely to tire the hearer very soon; he must often achieve beauty in spite of his instruments rather than by means of them. The ensemble is very apt to be muddy, and the rasp of the reed from which the ear soon shrinks, can be relieved only by the horns, as in Mozart's combination, and then not for long. There are two ways of using a wood-wind band—as a self-sustaining ensemble, which demands that most of the instruments play most of the time, or as a group of solo instruments supported by the piano. In the first method it is impossible to get the full effect of contrast and relief, because there must always be similar tones in the accompaniment. In the second the instruments can be used for their full solo individuality, and there is no need of thickening tone with tone, and scraping reed on reed. Besides, Mozart rejected the flute in his combination—the flute which alone lightens up the wood winds, and like some particular tone on the painter's palette can give verve and character to the color combination in almost endless variety. Mozart used the first method, and even then

[3] H.K.M., 'Jordan Hall: The Longy Club,' *Boston Transcript*, Nov. 21, 1911.

did not do what a modern would have done to individualize the instruments. Rimsky used the second method, with a fine feeling for shade and tonal balance. Further, Mozart's serenade is in no way remarkable, although the minuets and the adagio are in themselves very lovely. Rimsky, on the other hand, did a distinguished piece of work, one that easily deserves to go into the Longy programmes in future seasons.

The Russian's quintet, in its first movement, might have been written by Beethoven. It has a masculine energy, an omnipresent sense of a controlling will and many striking similarities of phrasing and sequence, to remind one of the sonatas of Beethoven's best period. The chief theme, indeed, is very similar to the subject of the Emperor concerto; the lovely contrasting theme, dwells affectionately on its cadence and draws out its linked sweetness without a note of banality. The form is strict and cogent, and the coda inevitably recalls the way Beethoven summons his forces for a final overwhelming assertion at the end. The second movement, the most original and probably the most popular of the three, has a Russian phrase which sets its character. It has the brooding, reflective mood which, if you choose, suggests the Siberian steppes or the melancholy Slavic temperament. In this movement the individualization of the instruments is most finely achieved. The searching theme of the horn, the slow runs of the clarinet and the oboe, the gently echoing of the flute, are all placed so as to gain their full effect. The folk-song phrase, which enters as a sort of reflective interlude between the sections, is finally stated by all instruments in unison, after each has given it as a solo. The effect is powerful. It is not an ensemble of five instruments, it is the combined assertion of five individual voices—the sort of thing which Mozart did not think of doing. The final rondo is delightful, though not of the musical caliber of the other sections. The quintet as a whole is completely satisfying—not a commonplace phrase from beginning to end, hardly a note which one would willingly have sacrificed.

The Second Concert

The second concert of the Long Club's twelfth season was given on New Year's Day, 1912, with a program which the *Transcript* called

> a remarkably consistent and stimulating programme … The variety of the programme in point of color and its unusual interest in a purely musical way made it one of the most interesting Longy programmes we have heard.[4]

[4] H. K. M., 'Jordan Hall: The Longy Club,' *Boston Transcript*, Jan. 2, 1912.

The concert began with the Henry Woollett *Octuor* for saxophone, oboe, clarinet and string quintet, a composition one critic failed to appreciate.

> The ... octuor ... by Henry Woollett, was for the most part disappointing, of slovenly construction and colorless, save for certain passages in the second movement. Mrs. Hall played the music allotted to the saxophone with taste.[5]

5 'Longy Club Gives Second Concert of the Season,' *Boston Herald*, Jan. 2, 1912.

On the other hand, two critics liked this work which featured the famous amateur saxophonist of Boston, Mrs. Richard Hall.

JORDAN HALL
Monday Evening, January 1, 1912, at 8.15 o'clock

Chamber Music for Wind Instruments
..BY..
THE LONGY CLUB
(*Twelfth Season*)

SECOND CONCERT
..PROGRAMME..

HENRY WOOLLETT . . Octuor for Saxophone, Oboe, Clarinet, and String Quintette
(First Performance)

MAX BRUCH . Five Pieces (Op. 83) for Clarinet, Viola, and Piano
(First time)

CHRISTIAAN KRIENS . 3 Aquarelles Hollandaises for 2 Flutes, 2 Oboes, 2 Clarinets, 2 Horns, 2 Bassoons, and Bells
(First time)

Assisting Artists:
Mrs. R. J. HALL, Saxophone

Messrs. S. NOACK / A. BAK } Violins   Messrs. E. FERIR, Viola / J. KELLER, 'Cello

Mr. E. HUBER, Double Bass

The Piano is a MASON AND HAMLIN

Tickets, 50c., $1.00, and $1.50   On sale at Symphony Hall

The Woollett octet is remarkable, chiefly for its original yet natural melodic procedure. There is nothing 'ultra' in it, but it has a way of avoiding the commonplace, which is at once stimulating and restful. The last movement, an andantino, is done in masterly fashion, with a strange rhythmic modal melody supported on a weird harmonic foundation and sustained almost entirely in the one strain. [*Transcript*]

The octet heard last night is in three movements. The second, an adagio, is the most coherent and pleasing. The strings announce a theme of a certain illusive character by reason of its insistence upon secondary degrees of the scale. The saxophone repeats … pleasurably in the ensuing dialogue. Mrs. Hall's playing is always to be enjoyed, as it was last night, for the purity and sympathy of her tone and for her excellent style.[6]

6 'Longy Club Concert,' *Boston Globe*, Jan. 2, 1912.

Second on the concert, the traditional place for a solo number in the Longy Club concerts, the audience heard a performance of the Max Bruch (1838–1920) *Five Pieces*, op. 83, for clarinet, viola, and piano, in their first Boston performance. While the *Herald* called these pieces, 'commonplace,' the *Transcript* recognized that the, 'individuality was evident … These Bruch pieces are distinctly of the kind which one hopes to hear again.'

The final work on this concert was the 3 *Aquarelles Hollandaises*, by Christiaan Kriens (1881–1934), for pairs of flutes, oboes, clarinets, horns, bassoons with bells. This composer was born in The Netherlands (his father was an orchestral conductor in Haarlem) and was at this time a violinist in the New York Symphony. His composition received its American premiere by the Georges Barrère wind ensemble in New York in February 1911, and its first performance in Paris the previous February. Of this work the *Transcript* observed,

Max Bruch, ca. 1913

Krien's 'Aquarelles Hollandaises' did not show the finished musicianship of the Woollett octet. They are of the 'atmosphere' genre, and often get their effect through the tonal qualities of the instruments used, with music which on the piano would sound commonplace. The first of the pieces picturing presumably a cathedral by the waterside deeply shrouded with fog while the bells clang from somewhere above, is undoubtedly an experiment worth while, stressing as it does the peculiar individualities of each of the ten instruments used (not to mention the bells). The last piece, a set of variations on a rollicking Dutch tune, 'Piet Hein,' hardly showed the originality that might have been expected, but at least set off an eminently healthy melody in brilliant fashion.[7]

7 This traditional Dutch folk-tune celebrates a cobbler who left his bench to join in the wars for the Dutch Republic and who, through deeds of bravery, became an admiral.

The Third Concert

The final regular concert of the twelfth season was given on the evening of 12 February 1912. The critic of the *Advertiser*,[8] writing of the good-sized audience, gets interestingly off the subject and compares the Longy Club wind ensemble with the Barrère wind ensemble in New York City.

[8] 'Longy Club Concert,' *Boston Advertiser*, Feb. 13, 1912.

> Last night, as a counter-attraction to 'Tristan,' the Longy Club gave their third and last concert of the season at Jordan hall. This unique organization, composed as it is of artists of the highest type, stands unexcelled in this country. New York boasts of a club somewhat similar to it, but the Gotham men cannot approach the Longy club in richness and flexibility of tone, or in the polish of their playing. Good works are seldom written for such a wood-wind band as this; they range of selection is necessarily very limited; and the music of this stamp can appeal only to the select few. But these few (despite 'Tristan') were many.

This concert began with the d'Indy masterpiece, the *Chanson et Danses*. While earlier reviews were only respectful, now the Boston critics seemed to genuinely like this work—if one can accept the *Advertiser*'s comment that this work, 'has lost none of its weird fascination,' as a compliment.

> The 'Chanson' is poetic and melodious; the instrumental colors are effectively displayed. The sharply marked rhythms of the main theme of the 'Danses' have the most character of any portion of the piece. The quiet ending is a grateful surprise, as those who started to applaud too early should be able to testify.[9]

[9] *Boston Transcript*, Feb. 13, 1912.

> It is an exquisitely wrought piece of musical workmanship, bucolic in character, with charming passages for single instruments, while the Danses are pervaded with a spirit of pagan revelry suggestive of nymphs and fauns at play.[10]

[10] 'Concert by Longy Club,' *Boston Herald*, Feb. 13, 1912.

In the traditional place for a solo composition, this concert presented a violin sonata by Enesco. The reviewer of the *Transcript* took this opportunity to make a nasty little reference to the cultural level of Boston audiences.

> Enesco is well 'backed' in musical Boston: the right people are his sponsors. His music reaches us by way of France and thus he may be said to have been properly introduced. The only apparent reason why there

has not long since been here an Enesco cult is his seriousness and artistic sincerity, which tends to result in demands, reasonable to be sure, but unwelcome, on the hearer's intelligence.

The final composition on this concert was one which appeared frequently on the programs of the Longy Club, the Raff *Sinfonietta*. On this occasion two of the critics contributed quite interesting commentary.

> Raff's Sinfonietta does not sound very modern, after the other works on the program, but one is tempted to ask, why should we care if the matter is somewhat too plainly cut from the good old Teutonic stock, which has inexhaustibly incited the Kapellmeister's pot to boil for the past century, at least the manner excels in one typically modern particular – skilful and delicate use of the tone-color of the several instruments. As to the actual themes, the less said the better; had they been signed with any other name—let us say, Rheinberger—they would have sounded as sickish sweet, all but one broad melody in the slow movement, of genuine character and power, which occurs almost note for note, and with the same harmony, in the slow movement of Bruckner's ninth symphony. [*Transcript*]

> Joachim Raff has fallen into unmerited oblivion. He is known to the younger generation as the composer of the over-worked 'La Fileuse'; but his 'Im Walde' symphony, his piano concerto and numerous of his other works show him as a composer of rare ability, and they deserve at least an occasional performance. The 'Sinfonietta' gives ample evidence of his mastery over the polyphonic forces, the freshness of his melodic output, and his vigorous and interesting style. Even though his tunes are often mere 'potboilers' and his treatment of themes bombastic and trivial, his thoughts are at least comprehensible and agreeable. The 'Scherzo' gave the club a fine chance to display their brilliant virtuosity. Mr. Maquarre's flute come in for some taxing passages, the clarinet work of Mr. Grisez was unapproachable, and the snoring bassoons covered themselves with honor. [*Advertiser*]

An Extra Concert

On Friday 15 March 1912, the Longy Club performed a concert in the Franklin Union, Boston, in an appearance sponsored by the city Department of Music. The extant program lists another five concerts (including two by high school orchestras) sponsored by the city during the same month and also mentions that these were presented free to the public. The program also carries two notes to the audience which offer interesting insight into the audiences of that era. They read, 'Ladies in the audience will confer a favor by removing their hats,' and 'The audience is requested to refrain from conversation during the performance.'

The Longy Club wind ensemble performed as a sextet on this occasion, playing the Thuille Sextet, the Quef Suite op. 4, as well as solo, duets and trios by Kriens, Mozart, Gouvy and Klughardt.

MUSIC DEPARTMENT—CITY OF BOSTON

FRANKLIN UNION,

Friday Evening, March 15, 1912,

AT EIGHT O'CLOCK.

Chamber Music for Wind Instruments

BY THE

LONGY CLUB SEXTET.

Members of the Sextet.

FLUTE.—Mr. A. Brooke.	HORN.—Mr. F. Hain.
OBOE.—Mr. G. Longy.	BASSOON.—Mr. P. Sadony.
CLARINET.—Mr. G. Grisez.	PIANO.—Mr. A. de Voto.

The audience is requested to refrain from conversation during the performance of the following

Program

THUILLE	Sextet.
	a. Allegro Moderato.
	b. Larghetto.
	c. Gavotte.
	d. Vivace.
C. KRIENS	"La Nymphe Bocagere," for Flute and Piano.

Messrs. A. Brooke and A. de Voto.

MOZART	Trio for Oboe, Clarinet and Bassoon.
	a. Allegretto.
	b. Larghetto.
	c. Minuetto.

Messrs. G. Longy, G. Grisez and P. Sadony.

GOUVY	Piece in F major for Horn and Piano.

Messrs. F. Hain and A. de Voto.

A. KLUGHARDT	Three pieces for Oboe, Clarinet and Piano.
	a. Allegro.
	b. Andantino.
	c. Allegro furioso.

Messrs. G. Longy, G. Grisez and A. de Voto.

C. QUEF	Suite, op. 4.
	a. Allegro.
	b. Andantino.
	c. Rondo Final.

Ladies in the audience will confer a favor by removing their hats.

Concerts have been arranged as follows for the month of March, 1912:

March 19. West Roxbury High School, Orchestral Concert.
March 21. Charlestown High School, Orchestral Concert.
March 26. Faneuil Hall, Orchestral Concert.
March 28. Dorchester High School, Trio Concert.
March 29. Ford Hall, Orchestral Concert.

Tickets are free and may be had by applying at the office of the Music Department, 43 Tremont Street, Room 908, Carney Building.

Season Thirteen, 1912–1913

The First Concert

THE FIRST CONCERT OF THE LONGY CLUB'S THIRTEENTH SEASON was given on the evening of 17 December 1912.[1] This concert seems to have drawn a larger than usual audience, large enough to call attention to itself to the press.

> In a thirteenth series of concerts—in spite of the foreboding number—the Longy Club seems at last to be entering into its just reward. There was actually a numerous audience for it in Jordan Hall last evening and an audience that seemed not to consist too largely of bidden guests.[2]

> Judging from the large audience last night and its enthusiastic reaction to Mr. Longy and his associates, it would appear that justly enough there is an increasing public for these unique and admirable concerts.[3]

The *Journal*, alone, was not quite satisfied, grumbling that Jordan Hall should have been 'crowded,' but acknowledged that, 'it would tax the imagination to conceive a finer performance than these pieces had last night. It kept a good-sized audience in a state of enthusiasm.'[4]

For years, various critics had mentioned in passing how difficult it must be to find music for such an ensemble, not only because so little must exist but because the ear tires of winds so quickly, etc. Struck by the large audience on this occasion, the critic of the *Transcript* turned his attention to the question of programming and, in particular, to Longy's success in this.

> Admittedly, liking for concerts of music for a wind choir is an exotic and fragile taste. Some devoted listeners to music never acquire it. Those that have it must nurture it carefully and must not indulge it too often nor for too long on any single occasion. The blended or the contrasted timbres of flutes, oboes, and clarinets, of horns and bassoons are singular, piquant—and speedily cloying. Composers who write for them are inevitably hampered by the limitations that the quality and the capacities of the chosen instruments lay upon them. To play a wind instrument as the members of the Longy Club play theirs, seems to the listening layman an adroit and delicate virtuosity. To write for such a choir music that shall unite beauty and diversity of sound with

[1] An article in the *New York Times* from 6 October 1912 states that the Longy Club were scheduled for a performance at the Northampton Academy of Music on 11 December 1912 and that they had also played there 'several years ago'.

[2] 'The Longy Club and Strauss,' *Boston Transcript*, Dec. 18, 1912.

[3] 'Longy Club Concert,' *Boston Globe*, Dec. 18, 1912.

[4] 'Longy Club Gives its First Concert of Fall Season,' *Boston Journal*, Dec. 18, 1912.

fertile and happy play of fancy seems yet more a feat of ingenuity and imagination to that same layman. He takes his pleasure of both with a few grains of wonder to spice his delight.

Mr. Longy and his companions of the wind choir of the Symphony Orchestra are astute in these things. They do not undertake too many concerts—only three, at long intervals, through each season. These concerts are wisely short, so that the virtuosi on the stage shall not be wearied or the listeners in the auditorium cloyed. Three, or at most four, pieces usually make the programme and varying combinations of instruments diversify them as much as may be; while more and more in recent years the piano for a contrasting voice has had its part in these combinations. Wisely, too, Mr. Longy's choice of music has ranged widely. He has searched the classical composers—especially the masters of the 18th century—when writing for wind choir was more the fashion than it is nowadays and when 'noble patrons' even commanded such music. He has turned the dull and manifold pages of the secondary and tertiary composers of the last century on the chance, usually fulfilled, that he might find one or another piece for wind instruments that deserved performance. And he has been open-eyed and open-eared for music from contemporary hands, returning to old fashions, ventur-

---

JORDAN HALL
Tuesday Evening, December 17, 1912
AT 8.15 O'CLOCK

CHAMBER MUSIC FOR WIND INSTRUMENTS
BY
The Longy Club

FIRST CONCERT

1912—THIRTEENTH SEASON—1913

PROGRAMME

MOZART . Quintett in E-flat major, Op. 452, for Oboe, Clarinet, Horn, Bassoon, and Piano
    I. Largo — Allegro moderato
    II. Larghetto
    III. Rondo (Allegretto)

CARL REINECKE. Undine, Op. 167, Sonate for Flute and Piano
    Messrs. A. Maquarre and A. de Voto
    I. Allegro
    II. Allegretto vivace
    III. Finale (allegro molto agitato)

RICHARD STRAUSS. Suite in B-flat major, for 2 Flutes, 2 Oboes, 2 Clarinets, 4 Horns, 2 Bassoons, and Contra-bassoon
    (First time)
    I. Allegretto
    II. Andante
    III. Allegro
    IV. Introduction and Fugue

The second concert will take place on **Thursday** evening, January 23, 1913.

ing new experiments for writing with some individual predilection and aptitude for wind choir. More than one Frenchman and here and there a German does so.

This concert began with the Mozart Quintet K. 452, for piano, oboe, clarinet, horn and bassoon. Although, as Philip Hale, of the *Herald*, pointed out, Mozart himself once wrote his father that this was the best music he had written,[5] the *Globe* was unimpressed, finding the work, 'not equally interesting in its selection of material.' For the critic of the *Transcript*, the Mozart was—shall we say, Mozartean.

[5] Philip Hale, 'Strauss Music by Longy Club,' *Boston Herald*, Dec. 18, 1912.

> Pleasurable to hear for the ingenuity of fancy that kept the music weaving gracefully lined patterns in tone, while oboe or piano multiplied the Mozartean brightness; horn or bassoon mellowed the Mozartean suavity; or the clarinet bore light or melancholy Mozartean song.

Next came the Reinecke *Undine* Sonate, op. 167, for flute and piano, a work which critics in the past never liked. On this occasion only the *Transcript* devoted space to this composition.

> Reinecke was no inventor of remarkable melodies, but he had an endless fertility and a happy adaptive skill with them. Accordingly he could make his flute ripple through bravura passages or sing in warm or melancholy song. All of which was the more appropriate since Undine was a water sylph, who loved a mortal and was grievously betrayed. No more was she human than is the flute quite a human-voiced instrument.

The new work, for Boston, on this concert was the Suite in B♭ by Richard Strauss for thirteen winds. It was, of course, this work which most attracted the attention of the critics and drew the larger than usual crowd as well. The scholar-critic, Philip Hale, supplies the now well-known background of this composition.

> It was composed when Strauss was about 20 years old and known as a reverer of the classics. He had already composed a Serende for wind instruments—the Serenade in E♭ and in one movement, Op. 7, which was published in 1881. It was produced at Dresden, Nov. 27, 1882 and Buelow brought it out in Meiningen in 1882 and played it on a concert tour, describing Strauss as a 'young Munich composer, classical school' and adding that the music displayed the brilliant virtuosity of the wind instrument players of his orchestra.

Richard Strauss, ca. 1910

Buelow was so pleased with the Serenade Op. 7 that he asked Strauss to write another work for 13 players, and mapped out a plan for him; but Strauss had already sketched the first movements and could follow Buelow's suggestions only in the Gavote and Finale with Fugue. The work was completed in Munich. Strauss's father, Franz, a celebrated horn player, begged Buelow, who was coming to Munich with the Meiningen orchestra, to rehearse the new work. Buelow agreed to the plan, but insisted that Strauss should conduct. There was no rehearsal. The first performance, then, of this suite was by players of the Meiningen orchestra in the Odeon, Munich, Nov. 13, 1884, and Strauss for the first time held a baton. The father went into the artist's room to thank Buelow, who was smoking cigarettes, nervous, and n a fiendish temper. As the son relates, 'He fell like a raging lion on my father and screamed out: 'I have not forgotten all that you have done against me here in this cursed Munich. What I did today, I did because your son and talent, not for you.'

The suite was not published until the fall of 1911. In some way Mr. Barrere, flute player in New York, obtained a manuscript copy and produced the suite at a concert of the Barrere Ensemble of that city on Feb. 6, 1911.

There are these movements: Prelude, Romanze, Govotte, Introduction and Fugue. The instruments are used with fine appreciation of their respective capabilities and limitations, and there are effective combinations and contrasts of timbres. The stately Prelude has not so much individuality as the Romanze, which is thematically beautiful and rich in color. The Gavotte is interesting, especially in the section beginning with the drone-bass. The Introduction is impressively somber, but the Fugue is disappointing. The exposition, as heard last night, seemed clumsy, and it was surely not euphonious, nor was the counterpoint at the beginning much better than ordinary student's work. There was greater mastery shown in the final pages.

To this history, the *Transcript* adds the interesting note that,

as some say, Strauss retouched this Suite when it was published. Perhaps; but it is hard to believe that such a revising Strauss would have left unrepaired the limping fugue that makes the finale. On the other hand, the mature Strauss might read or hear without shame the warmly imagined, richly expanding, largely modulated sound of the slow movement, feel anew the full, strong, propulsive march of the prelude, smile with a touch of gratification over the quirking humor with which he decorated the scherzo, or the assembled skill with which he makes the large-voiced introduction to the finale both summary and anticipation.

The critic of the *Globe* adds still another interesting note, although this time with reference to the earlier Serenade.

> The distinction between this suite and the serenade, Op. 7 ... has been clearly made by Max Smith, the New York critic, who is an assiduous statistician. According to Mr. Smith, the Serenade had its first performance Nov. 27, 1882, in the banquet room of the 'Three Ravens' restaurant in Dresden, conducted by Franz Wueliner, father of the lieder singer ...
>
> There is [in this Suite] a lithe and muscular fiber in this music, a note of appreciable, though not dominating personality, and an evidence of surprising knowledge of what material is suitable to the various instruments. As Ernest Newman pointed out in the sonata for cello and piano, the impetuous young Strauss of that day was not happiest in the tranquility of the andante, nor is the slow movement here inspired by deep lyric feeling. The allegro which stands for the scherzo, was most enjoyable for the rhythmic vivacity, general alertness and humor, well presented by alternating groups of instruments as though engaged in repartee. The fugal subject in the last movement is not a likely one for development.

The Second Concert

The second concert of the thirteenth season was given on the evening of 23 January 1913, in Jordan Hall, and for the second time this season there was a large audience.[6] The first and last compositions on this program, the Saint-Saëns *Caprice sur des Airs Danois et Russes*, op. 79, and the Piernè *Pastorale Variee (dans le style ancient)*, op. 30, had previously been performed in these concerts and were enjoyed by the press.

> The pieces by Saint Saens and Pierne were familiar. Their inherent charm has not grown old and stale.[7]

> So much for the newer fashions of 'chamber music for wind instruments' as the programme officially labeled the concert. Saint-Saens 'Caprice on Danish Airs' and Pierne's variations in the olden form and style upon a pastoral melody were of another sort. In them, the composers, after the manner of most of those who have written for wind choirs, were content to charm. They devised fanciful melodies, made fanciful play with them; and left the rest to the exotic timbres of the instruments and the virtuosity of the players. The thin-voiced, wistful, penetrating Danish folk-tunes of Saint-Saens's 'Caprice' were born for the timbres of flute, oboe and clarinet, and the polished skill of Mr.

[6] 'The Longy Club,' *Boston Globe*, Jan. 24, 1913.

[7] Philip Hale, 'New Works in Longy Recital,' *Boston Herald*, Jan. 24, 1913.

Maquarre, Mr. Longy and Mr. Grisez is meet for the little deft turns and the little elegances of accent that Saint-Saens gave them in his study in Paris. Pierne was not so modestly content. He must add a trumpet for the brilliant flares of color that the 18th century composers like to draw from it as a solo instrument before their successors began to bury it in the orchestras. And he must have bassoons for the homely background 18th century fashion again—to this pastoral tune ... The oboe is the shepherd's pipe of the orchestra—and for Parisian composers pretending to pastoral song. It is penetrating, it is melancholy, it sounds as simply as Mr Longy's playing seems easy. While as for the flute—and at Mr. Maquarre's hands—it could make Pierne's fancies sound like bright arabesques on the air.[8]

[8] H. T. P. 'Music and Musicians,' *Boston Transcript*, Jan. 24, 1913.

MEMBERS OF THE CLUB

Flutes:
Messrs. A. MAQUARRE and A. BROOKE

Oboes:
Messrs. G. LONGY and C. LENOM

Clarinets:
Messrs. G. GRISEZ and P. MIMART

Horns:
Messrs. F. HAIN and H. LORBEER

Bassoons:
Messrs. P. SADONY and J. MOSBACH

Piano:
Mr. A. DE VOTO

Assisting Artists:
Messrs. S. NOACK, Violin; A. GIETZEN, Viola
Messrs. H. WARNKE, 'Cello; G. HEIM, Trumpet

THE PIANO IS A MASON AND HAMLIN

PROGRAMME

C. SAINT-SAËNS . Caprice sur des Airs Danois et Russes (Op. 79), for Flute, Oboe, Clarinet, and Piano

FLORENT SCHMITT . Lied and Scherzo (Op. 54), for Horn principal, Piccolo, Flute, Oboe, English Horn, 2 Clarinets, Horn, and 2 Bassoons.
(First Time)

F. WEINGARTNER . Quintet in G minor, Op. 50, for Clarinet, Violin, Viola, 'Cello, and Piano
  I. Allegro non troppo (ma con brio)
  II. Tempo di Minuetto (Molto Moderato)
  III. Adagio
  IV. Allegro Molto
(First Time)

GABRIEL PIERNÉ . Pastorale Variée dans le style ancien (Op. 30), for Flute, Oboe, Clarinet, Trumpet, Horn, and 2 Bassoons
  Andantino—Tema in Canone
  1st Double (Scherzosamente)
  2d Double (Tourbillon)
  3d Double (Tempo di Minuetto)
  4th Double (Alla siciliana)
  5th Double (Allegro Maestoso)

The third and last concert of the season will take place on Thursday evening, March 6th.

The critics were most interested, of course, in the works being heard for the first time in Boston and the first of these was the Florent Schmitt (1870–1958), *Lied and Scherzo*, op. 54, for solo horn, piccolo, flute, oboe, English horn, two clarinets, horn and two bassoons. Although Philip Hale heard this work as 'ultra-modern' a synonym among Boston critics for the modern French school, most of the reviewers liked the Schmitt particularly because it seemed to have more traditional values than the music of most of his contemporaries.

> Florent Schmitt, from whom came the other new piece of the concert, has also this habit of musical industry. Three pages of fine type are necessary to list his 'works' in a Parisian record of contemporary music and the 'Song and Scherzo' played yesterday, is the 50th piece—and more—of a composer who is hardly middle-aged. That same record finds Schmitt hard to classify—an unforgivable offending in a 'French composer. He is no follower of Saint-Saens, nor yet of Massenet. He derives not from Franck, and he is not walking in the ways of d'Indy. He does not imitate Debussy; he might have never heard the music of Ravel. He is the stout-bodied independent of contemporary French music, going his own way and quite ready to justify it in its results. If he descends at all he may descend from Chabrier.
>
> For this 'Song and Scherzo' for horn and wind choir is tout, highly colored music that sounds very much alive. There is not much suggestion of shading it in the delicate Gallic fashion. There is an abundance of deep-voiced song, full-bodied harmonics, restless rhythms and very bright or very shadowed instrumental color. Schmitt lays on his hues gaily, racily, exuberantly, for the pure joy of their brightness, as in those runs for flute and piccolo. When he makes his song for his dominant horn he will make it as intensely as he can … A curious temperament and imagination, as they seem, all intensity and vitality—German rather than French in the liking for big breathe of expression and large glows of color. Yet French none the less in the control of these energies and in the balancing and the blending of all these hues. It was good music to hear – antidote, maybe to the sublimated d'Indy, the aerated Debussy, the subtilized Ravel. The old New Englanders, translated to the Paris of music in 1913, might call Scmitt a 'come-outer.' [*Transcript*]

Florent Schmitt, by Eugène Pirou, ca. 1900

> Florent Schmitt … is a striking figure. Here is no mere experimenter searching for some new or fantastic thing to say. His use of rhythm in the scherzo appears restless if not chaotic, but it has virility and imagination. In the lied the individuality of his style is the more easily apparent. There was a polyphonic passage across which streamed a light of mystic and seraphic beauty. The blended tints of these wood winds and horns were perfect for it. [*Globe*]

The other work on this program which was new to Boston was the Quintet for clarinet, piano and strings by Felix Weingartner (1863–1942), who was at this time one of the leading conductors in Europe. Because this composer's name was so well-known, each reviewer gave an extended analysis of this quintet. As to its general worth, they could not, however, agree.

> The Quintet is a work that increases respect for Weingartner as a composer. Here and there the reminiscence hunter may point a finger and say: 'Ha!,' but the music as a whole is original and ingenious, with many pages of genuine beauty and emotion. [*Herald*]

> Operas he cuts after the manner of conductors from the earliest times; but when he writes himself he is prone to lengths. His symphony of last winter was not short; and the quintet of last evening nowhere suffers from a compressed brevity. The slow movement is interestingly long; the final movement runs in less interesting prolixities. Always … Mr. Weingartner's workmanship is careful and thorough, often imaginative—out of experience with much music and the instruments that give it voice, if not invariably out of fertile fancy or large inspiration. [*Transcript*]

> It is peculiarly disappointing music. It is too long and it is unequal in merit. Here and there will be ingenious, effective and even beautiful thoughts, while again it will be weak in invention, incoherent in structure, mistaking flurry for intensity and sound for sonority. [*Globe*]

Felix Weingartner, by Julius Cornelius Schaarwächter, ca. 1900

The Third Concert

The final concert of this season was given on the evening of 6 March 1913, and began with the Quintet for piano, flute, oboe, clarinet and bassoon by Andrè Caplet. In earlier years relatively little was said of his music, but by this date Caplet was an important opera conductor in Boston and so the critics gave him his due.

> It was composed when he was very young, and perhaps today he speaks slightingly of it as a youthful offence, but he has no cause to be ashamed of the second movement, an Adagio, and the third, a Scherzo.
>   The first movement is tuneful and constructed according to approved rules. It shows little individuality. There is too often the suggestion of the first movement of Schumann's quintet, and not only is the suggestion one of the prevailing mood, but there is a curious thematic resemblance, or reminder. The thematic development is at the expense of fancy in digressions, and the music reminds one of the earnest, painstaking student.

The Adagio, contemplative, at times somber, is poetic and the Scherzo trips gaily with agreeable rhythmic contrasts. In the last movement the hearer is again conscious of the faithful student mindful of academic instruction.[9]

Mr. Caplet's quintet … was interesting as coming from a man not widely known as a composer, and proved itself in the course of its performance music of a very high order indeed. It clearly possesses that fine French contour which may be recognized in much ultra-modern music, though in spite of many imaginative passages it reveals little wealth of sheer melodic ingenuity. The principal theme of the first movement, for example, is a simple, attractive and somewhat academic melody, like the exercise of a clever student, but it curves outward in the transitional passages into music of no little imaginative liveliness. Of the four movements, the adagio is the most remarkable, a rich tonal piece of work at once sensuous and severe. The Scherzo, very spiritual and charming, brought much pleasure and was warmly applauded. It is too little to say of the whole work that it reveals the same qualities of imaginative sympathy and the strong sense of beauty which distinguish Mr. Caplet as a conductor.[10]

The performance of the Caplet was followed by a guest soprano, Marie Sundelius, of whom the *Transcript* notes with pleasure, 'she has no apparent use for those silly tricks of facial expression which most of our sopranos so love to exercise in characteristic music.'

The final work on this program was one regularly played by the Longy Club, the Bernard *Divertissement* op. 36 for ten winds.

[9] Philip Hale, 'Last Concert by Longy Club,' *Boston Herald*, March 7, 1913.

[10] C. V. W., 'The Longy Concert,' *Boston Transcript*, March 7, 1913.

Season Fourteen, 1913–1914

DURING THE SEASON OF 1913–1914 GEORGES LONGY attempted to begin a new series of chamber music concerts in New York City. This experiment seems not to have continued beyond the first concert in November 1913, in part, perhaps, as the *Boston Transcript* pointed out, it was a 'city already overcrowded with concerts.'[1] The *New York Times* wrote of this initial concert,

> Mr. Longy and his associates have, of course, long been playing this kind of music in Boston, and they bring with them to New York consummate skill and a perfection of ensemble attained through long experience and intimate mutual understanding. Consequently, the new organization made an admirable impression, so far as its playing was concerned. But it may be hoped that the literature of modern chamber music for wind and strings has something more interesting to offer than the octet by Paul Juon, Op. 27, which was the principal number on this first programme.
>
> Although Juon has composed a good deal of music, especially chamber music, he is better known in New York as the translator of Modeste Tschaikowsky's life of his brother Peter than as a composer. This octet is by no means a favorable specimen of his musical inspiration. It is singularly lacking in significant thematic invention, and is prolix in its development of ideas unimportant in themselves. The most interesting passages are furnished by themes of the Russian folk-song character in the first and last movements.[2]

The First Concert

The first regular concert of the fourteenth season of the Longy Club in Boston was given on the evening of 27 November 1913. This concert featured works created by composers born in America, a gesture Philip Hale, of the *Herald*, supposed, 'was probably an act of courtesy rather than of rapt musical appreciation.'[3] The *Globe* was more appreciative.

> If the offerings of these gentlemen proved to be nothing of the epoch-making importance in the literature of American composition, the discredit will not lie with Mr. Longy and his colleagues for their performance of the music was one of characteristic painstaking and artistry.[4]

[1] *Boston Transcript*, Nov. 10, 1913.

[2] *New York Times*, quoted in the *Boston Transcript*, ibid.

[3] Philip Hale, 'Longy Club in American Music,' *Boston Herald*, Nov. 28, 1913.

[4] 'First Longy Concert,' *Boston Globe*, Nov. 28, 1913.

The first composer on this concert was Arne Oldberg (1874–1962), who was represented by his Quintet op. 18, for piano, oboe, clarinet, horn and bassoon. Neither extant review offered praise for this work.

> Oldberg's quintet was disappointing because they make much of this composer in Chicago. Mr. Stock has conducted his symphony and his overture, 'Paolo and Francesca,' possibly other works. Born in 1874 at Youngstown, O., Oldberg studied in this country, then at Vienna and afterwards at Munich. In 1899 he became professor of composition and the piano at the Northwestern University. In spite of his years of study, Mr. Oldberg's quintet is amateurish in the treatment of wind instruments and in the structure of his movements.
>
> The most pleasing of the four is the Menuetto, which begins in a distinctly Brahmsian manner. In the other movements, the themes have not a decided profile and instead of true development, there is futile and annoying repetition. Nor is the music often euphonious. In the first movement, there are brilliant passages for the piano and the wind instruments enter and retreat without purpose. A disjointed work, in which the composer is seen stopping for breath and saying: 'I wonder what should come next!' [*Herald*]

> This apparently is the first representation of Mr. Oldberg in Boston as a composer. It would be preferable not to believe it his best. There are promising thematic ideas here of an ingratiating melodic character. They have fecundity, and the hearer awaits their germination only to hear them repeated by the various instruments without leading to new thoughts or the surprise of the known in a new guise.
>
> Voices are to be heard that may show conventional respect for the pitch, and yet be flat in quality. This music by Mr. Oldberg betokens neat workmanship—the scoring is cleverly done except in the finale, where the composer seems to have heard stringed instruments—but it lacks emotional perspective. A movement progresses, but does not lead the mind or stimulate feeling. [*Globe*]

The next American composer was Howard Brockway (1870–1951), of whom the Longy Club performed *At Twlight* and *An Idyl of Murmuring Water*, for ten winds. The two extant reviews of this concert read quite differently from this point on. The *Herald* found the Brockway music interesting, but the *Globe* did not.

> Mr. Brockway, born in Brooklyn in 1870, is not unknown here. His 'Sylvan Suite' and Symphony in D Major have been performed at Symphony concerts and I believe chamber music by him has been heard.

The two pieces performed last night are of an impressionistic character, modern in sentiment, and they show a poetic spirit even when it is not always happily expressed. The ideas in this instance have significance, and the treatment of them, especially in the Idyl, is often interesting. [*Herald*]

His 'twilight' was disturbed last night by an early fog arising from the whole tone scale. The low lying marshes where dwelt the bassoons were filled with restive croakings. The idyl contained some purling passages for flute and clarinet that were pictorial. Again, there were plausible and inviting themes, but the development was constrained and mannered; the instruments were not employed in the happiest manner, and there was no apparent reason in either number for the marked hiatus to be heard between the upper and lower voices. [*Globe*]

The *Pastorale*, op. 8, by Daniel Gregory Mason (1873–1953) drew the reverse opinions: the *Globe* liked this music and the *Herald* did not.

> Mr. Mason's pastorale is grateful and quietly engaging music. Tranquil in character, it flows peacefully through a graceful melodic vein, in which now one and now the other of the instruments announces an idea, while its fellow continues the dialogue. There is development here worthy of the name, and there is sufficient contrast of lyric with sterner moods to make variety. [*Globe*]

> Mr. Mason's Pastorale is amiable music, easily heard and immediately forgotten. [*Herald*]

The final work on this concert was the Bird Serenade for ten winds, although neither reviewer mentioned it. The *Globe* did, in summary, comment on the artistry of the club's first clarinetist.

> While the performance was a carefully considered and well-balanced one, there is reason for a word of appreciation of the extraordinary subtlety of shading and for the beauty and control of soft and sustained tone in Mr. Grisez's playing. There was a cordial audience of good size.

The Second Concert

The second regular concert of the fourteenth season was given on the evening of 22 January 1914. The first work on the program was new to Boston, the Édouard Flament (1880–1958) *Fantasia con Fuga*, op. 28 for flute, oboe, English horn, two clarinets, bassoon and horn. The reviews of this work were mixed; the *Transcript* rather liked the work.

> Flament's fantasia, played for the first time here, was solid and workmanlike writing, brief, felicitous and effective.[5]

The *Globe*[6] and the *Herald*,[7] on the other hand, were not so generous.

> The piece was remarkable, chiefly for the paucity of ideas and roughness in scoring. The fugal subject with its repeated notes upon the same degree would suit brass instruments in articulation if not in range

[5] 'Novel Music From the Longy Club,' *Boston Transcript*, Jan. 23, 1914.

[6] 'The Longy Club,' *Boston Globe*, Jan. 23, 1914.

[7] 'Concert by the Longy Club,' *Boston Herald*, Jan. 23, 1914.

Members of the Club

Messrs. A. Maquarre and A. Brooke	Flutes
Messrs. G. Longy and C. Lenom	Oboes
Messrs. G. Grisez and P. Mimart	Clarinets
Messrs. F. Hain and H. Lorbeer	Horns
Messrs. P. Sadony and J. Mosbach	Bassoons
Mr. A. de Voto	Piano

Assisting Artists

Mr. J. Keller, 'Cello
Mr. E. Huber, Bass
Mr. E. Miersch, Horn

THE PIANO IS A MASON & HAMLIN

Programme

E. Flament — Fantasia con Fuga (Op. 28), for Flute, Oboe, English Horn, two Clarinets, Bassoon, and Horn
(First time)

A. Maquarre — Three Romantic Numbers, for Flute, Oboe, two Clarinets, and two Bassoons
   I. In the Woods (Andante)
   II. Near the Spring (Scherzo)
   III. Frolics of the Stags (Allegro vivo)

V. d'Indy — Fantaisie sur des Thèmes populaires Français, for Oboe and Piano

A. Dvorák — Serenade (Op. 44), for two Oboes, two Clarinets, two Bassoons, three Horns, 'Cello, and Bass
   I. Moderato quasi marcia
   II. Menueto
   III. Andante con moto
   IV. Finale (Allegro molto)

The THIRD CONCERT will take place on MARCH 4

---

better than wood-wind. There is evident attempt at modernity in treatment, but for bold or arresting originality there is mere crudeness and commonplace disorder. Attempting an authoritative or striking statement the composer has stopped at incongruity. In neither melodic nor harmonic scheme has the piece anything of interest to say. Certain measures were engaging more for the manner in which they were played than for their inherent value.

Edouard Flament's name is not known here to the great majority of music lovers. Born in Douai, Aug. 27, 1880, he studied at the Paris Conservatory and in 1898 took the first prize for bassoon playing.[8] He then became a member of the Lamoureaux orchestra. As a man he is not without a sense of humor, for the lately eulogized his instrument in this manner: 'The bassoon is the cello of proud, homesick, souls and these that have the modesty of their sadness. By reason of its deep tones it plunges to the unexplored depths of melancholy; it moves us as a distant echo of Proserpine's sighs. The cello in comparison has only an insipid beauty. One burning tear is of more value than a whole rainbow. The bassoon, like Shakespeare, runs through the gamut of human emotions.'

[8] In the National Library in Paris there are a number of his original compositions for large ensembles of bassoons.

And in like manner, when the bassoon player in the negro minstrel show was asked by his associate what he was going to play, he answered: 'Anything that comes out.' A man may be a skilful bassoonist, fantastical in his praise of the beloved instrument, and yet be prosaic in his own musical thought. How is it with Mr. Flament? What has come out of him?

It would be unfair to dispose of Mr. Flament's merits as a composer by commenting upon this one piece. The Fantasia is short. After a few introductory measures of a pensive nature the chief theme of the fugue is given out. This theme is commonplace and its working out displays little originality on the part of the composer.

The next work on this concert was composed by one of the ensemble's own members, first flutist, André Maquarre. This composition, *Three Romantic Numbers*, for flute, oboe, two clarinets and two bassoons also attracted mixed reviews.

> Mr. Maquarre's pieces have decided character and gave much pleasure to the audience. 'Frolics of the Stags,' the third, newest, and most interesting, is original in character and treatment. It is fluent, well made, and there are charming effects of color. The composer was warmly applauded. [*Herald*]

> Mr. Maquarre's 'Romantic Numbers' showed many beauties and were roundly applauded in the presence of the composer who played the first flute part and acknowledged the applause. Thou they showed any amount of skill in writing for, of rather writing 'to,' the instruments, their beauties were mostly of an easy going, old-fashioned sort, sometimes reminding one of good old romanticism in the person of Weber, and sometimes of a popular ballad. Sometimes there were touches of something more modern and sometimes the desire for certain tone effects seemed to change the musical style. But though no individual or synthesized style was noticeable there was constant felicity in the creation of pleasing effects. The chief fault in the pieces was their great length; repetitions were frequent, and each number was carried out to two or even three times the length justified by the thematic material and the general scheme. [*Transcript*]

> Its tone is that of bucotic gayety, with the suggestion of a rollicking country dance. Rhythmic vivacity is the feature of the second, although with an element of abruptness in treatment; a more sustained contrasting section might have made the principal subject matter more effective, for the average ear will not thrill long to the staccato chirpings of a flock of wood-wind instruments. [*Globe*]

Mr. Longy next performed a solo oboe work by d'Indy, the *Fantasie sur des Themes populaires Francais*. This work surprised the critic of the *Transcript* because, contrary to the suggestion of its title, it has nothing in common with popular music.

> The d'Indy fantasia is longer and more pretentious [than Flament]. It is the farthest possible removed from the sort of piece we usually associate with such a name; it is symphonic in character, and so closely knit that one forgets that it is solo and accompaniment and remembers only that it is music. In this treatment of the themes (they have none of the graces of the more familiar French songs) d'Indy is his most personal self, intense and willful, 'rather brain than emotions.' [*Transcript*]

The final work on this concert was the Dvořák Serenade op. 44. When the Longy Club last played this work the critics were somewhat unenthusiastic for this work, an attitude no longer apparent after this performance.

> The Bohemian's obvious, homely and comprehensible melodies must have been grateful to many. [*Globe*]

> The Dvorak 'serenade' might better be called a symphony for small orchestra. It is not chamber music; for in chamber music the various instruments are solo instruments even in ensemble, while in this, as in orchestral music they are essentially ensemble instruments even when they play solos. The selection of instruments, alone … whets the curiosity. Omitting all that makes the orchestral ensemble light in tone and movement, the composer would seem sure to become heavy and monotonous. But this was not the result. Dvorak's treatment of the various voices—his ability to carry the oboe part through the solid accompaniment of horns, to make the cello obligato effective beneath the heavy ensemble of wood winds, to give the bassoons tonal independence from the bass strings—were an achievement no less in its way than the ability to write a good symphony. [*Transcript*]

The Third Concert

The final regular concert of the fourteenth season was given on the evening of 4 March 1914, and was an evening which pleased the critics. Not only was every work being heard for the first time in Boston, but every composition was warmly appreciated. As the *Advertiser* summarized the concert,

> The club holds a place wholly its own in our musical life; individual in its composition (of wind instruments); in its singleness of purpose (perfection of ensemble); in its presentation of rare and unique works, and in the acme of their interpretation. These results are the natural outcome of such leadership as Mr. Longy's. This, their last concert of the season, was made memorable by presenting three new fruits from the garden of music, and, though of differing flavors and thus not calculated in each instance to please every musical palate, the fine gold of their art was impartially lavished in the serving. Each one was marked by some special beauty of skilful presentation.[9]

9 F. J. F., 'Longy Club Concert at Jordan Hall,' *Boston Advertiser*, March 5, 1914.

The first work on this final concert was the woodwind Quintet by Gustav Strube (1867–1953), a former member of the Boston Symphony Orchestra. As mentioned all the critics were delighted with this program.

> Mr. Strube's quintet evidently gave much pleasure to the audience, which was of good size.[10]

10 'Third and Last Concert Given by Longy Club,' *Boston Herald*, March 5, 1914.

> One can easily believe that Mr. Strube saves his best ideas for such chamber music as this. Always facile, he has not always convinced his hearers that every note he wrote was written from inner necessity. But in this quintet there seemed to be no passages which had not passed a second revision before being set to paper. The work maintained its romantic charm in unusual degree. Mr. Strube treats his little group of wind instruments much as he might treat a full orchestra; he does not seem to limit his ideas in the feeling that he is working with a severe limitation of means. Rather, he lays out his canvas on something like a heroic scale, with pretentious preparation, and long foreseen climaxes. And his skill with the instruments is such that he is able to gain a variety and richness of effect sufficient to carry through his large ideas without seeming inappropriateness. The charm of his writing is the romantic charm; it is as far as possible removed from that other charm of chamber music, the charm of pattern, of joyous technical exercise with limited means. The quintet last night had always great beauty of idea. The intermezzo which made the third movement was an andantino so delightful that if it were written for a more usual combination

of instruments it would surely gain wide popularity. And throughout the work Mr. Strube had so chosen from his best ideas that there were no waste stretches.[11]

> The Strube 'Quintet' – written especially for the Longys and played from manuscript – was rather a surprise, in these strenuous days, by its restraint and lack of bizarre or striving for effect at all costs. There is hardly a unison part in the first three movements, though not lacking in novelty. It has many fresh, delightful color harmonics and the tone qualities of instruments are beautifully used to sustain with quiet power the Elegiac sentiment of the work; this sentiment changes to one of the gentle gaiety in the 'Intermezzo' and becomes stirring, though not boisterous in the 'Finale'—a strong climax. Mr. Strube's great orchestral experience has made him familiar with the possibilities of all the instruments, and their characteristic beauties were shown not only separately but in ensemble. [*Advertiser*]

The traditional solo work came next, in this case a Sonata for flute and oboe by Jean-Baptiste Loeillet (1653–1728). This was a time when not as much older music was performed as is the case today (and there were not yet recordings) and the *Transcript* appreciated this, noting, 'Nothing which the Longy Club can do can be more acceptable than such occasional reviving of old pieces which could never be heard otherwise.'

The final work on this concert was the Chamber Symphony op. 27, by Paul Juon (1872–1940). This was the work featured in the New York City concert in the beginning of the season and which the New York Times disliked. The Boston critics heard the work in quite a different spirit.

> His chamber symphony is interesting and of marked originality. The four movements are sharply rhythmed and generally romantic in color. In each case the chief theme at first given out by one instrument is taken up in turn by the others. There are themes of secondary importance, variations and elaborations. The second movement, Andante Elegiaco, is perhaps the most beautiful. The third is singularly effective and the fourth rises to a stirring climax. [*Herald*]

> By far the most important thing in last night's concert, and the most important in many Longy concerts within memory, was the chamber symphony, Op. 27 … by Paul Juon, whose 'Wachterweise' has recently been heard at the Symphony Concerts. Juon lives quietly pursuing his own way and writing what pleases him, without self-advertisement. His music is solidly based on the classics, and is perfectly intelligible in every note. The feeling of honesty that it gains by the avoiding of

[11] 'Longy Club Concert,' *Boston Transcript*, March 5, 1914.

anything esoteric captures the sympathy of the hearer from the start. The chamber symphony heard last night is a minor composition only in its limited number of instruments. Musically it is creative work of the highest order. Though technically it contains little that might not be heard in Brahms, it never for a moment shines with reflected glory. Every measure of it is personal utterance.

Programme

Members of the Club

Messrs. A. Maquarre and A. Brooke	Flutes
Messrs. G. Longy and C. Lenom	Oboes
Messrs. G. Grisez and P. Mimart	Clarinets
Messrs. F. Hain and H. Lorbeer	Horns
Messrs. P. Sadony and J. Mosbach	Bassoons
Mr. A. de Voto	Piano

Assisting Artists

Mr. J. Theodorowicz, Violin
Mr. K. Rissland, Viola
Mr. J. Keller, 'Cello

Gustav Strube — Quintet (M.S.) for Flute, Oboe, Clarinet, Horn, and Bassoon
   I. Quasi Adagio—Allegro Commodo
  II. Pastorale (Molto Adagio)
 III. Intermezzo (Allegro Moderato)
 IV. Finale (Rondo) Allegro giocoso
     (First time)

Jean-Baptiste Loeillet (1653-1728) — Sonate in D minor for Flute, Oboe, and Piano
   I. Largo
  II. Allegro con fuoco
 III. Adagio—Allegro
     (First time)

Paul Juon — Chamber Symphony (Op. 27) for Violin, Viola, 'Cello, Oboe, Clarinet, Horn, Bassoon, and Piano
   I. Allegro non troppo
  II. Andante Elegiaco
 III. Allegro non troppo quasi Moderato
 IV. Moderato
     (First time)

THE PIANO IS A MASON & HAMLIN

It is not simple music in the sense that any fool with a smattering of Brahms could reproduce it. The opening theme awakens the ear to a peculiar and personal interest; its full meaning is not understood until it has been fully developed. No composer dares announce such a theme unless he also understands how to use it. Nowhere in the symphony is there any suggestion of 'padding'; any transitional passage, selected at random, will show musical beauties worth listening to. In such a work as this the phrase 'development of thematic material' gains a new meaning. The word 'development' in these days, too often means a mere repetition and variation of the theme until the ear is sufficiently tired of it. With Juon the development is structural, in no simple fashion, but so clearly and eloquently that at the close of the movement the whole scheme of it, and the relations of the parts to the whole, lie plainly in hand. The themes, too, are without exception melodies of distinction and beauty; usually they show at their first entrance that they are made for extended development, not because they are good enough to have repeated, but because their beauty is of that fundamental sort that demands personal sympathy and implies a large super-structure. The chief phrase of the Andante Elegiaco was repeated endlessly, but the ear seemed to be thirsty for it, and with each repetition it became more satisfying. The structure of the movements is the frankest sonata form, or trio and da capo, but only because the composer knows he can speak most freely in this strict form. The statement of the themes is always unmistakable; the 'Durchfuhrung' is full of romantic color; the coda never fails to raise the emotional pitch and give a satisfying finality to the movement. Throughout all the restrained expression of the symphony there is a deep nobility and dignity which only the sincerest of composers can achieve. [*Transcript*]

Juon's 'Chamber Symphony,' the latest of his works, is orthodox in form, though he uses fully the resources of modern contrapuntal science; curious modulations; free Russian rhythms in five-four and seven-four time, and the Russian scheme of figuration winding around a few notes. In the presentation of his material—Russian folk themes—these are woven together with a Teutonic thoroughness somewhat conventionalizing their original Slavic form.

Juon has lived for many years in Germany, but it is dangerous in most cases for a composer to sever himself from his native land. Better to express your feelings in the native idiom, rough though it be, than in the more polished language of a foreign tongue. The accents will strike the ear with more truth and originality, and leave a more lasting impression on the mind and heart.

In the Op. 27, his latest work, he is in touch with his native land, and accordingly his music makes a strong impression. [*Advertiser*]

In closing, the *Globe* summarized this concert as follows:

Admirers of musical literature of the higher forms were given a very enjoyable evening. The unusual abilities of the club in ensemble playing have always been in the line of artistic interpretations of music unfamiliar to many, and the program of novelties made the performance unusually interesting to an audience of goodly proportions.[12]

[12] 'Longy Club Evening,' *Boston Globe*, March 5, 1914.

An Extra Concert

On the evening of 21 April 1914, the Longy Club appeared on the Steinert Series of chamber music concerts in Boston, with a substitute flutist, August Battles, among its members. The program included the Gounod *Petite Symphonie*, the Strube Quintet, and the Bernard *Divertissement*, alternating with a soprano, Miss Lucy Marsh.

FOURTH CONCERT
OF THE
STEINERT · SERIES
TUESDAY EVENING, APRIL 21, 1914, AT 8.15 O'CLOCK

LONGY WIND CHOIR
(Ten Musicians from the Boston Symphony Orchestra)
Messrs. A. Brooke and A. Battles, Flutes
Messrs. G. Longy and C. Lenom, Oboes
Messrs. G. Grisez and P. Mimart, Clarinets
Messrs. F. Hain and H. Lorbeer, Horns
Messrs. P. Sadony and J. Mosbach, Bassoons
MISS LUCY MARSH, Soprano
Mrs. Jennie M. Case, Accompanist for Miss Lucy Marsh

Program

1. Petite Symphonie in B flat . . . . *Gounod*
    a. Adagio — Allegretto
    b. Andante Cantabile
    c. Scherzo
    d. Finale
    LONGY CHOIR

2. a. Prelude No. 1 . . . . *Landon Ronald*
   b. Dearest Night . . . . *Bachelet*
   MISS LUCY MARSH

3. Quintet for Flute, Oboe, Clarinet, Horn and Bassoon . . *G. Strube*
    a. Quasi Adagio — Allegro commodo
    b. Pastorale (molto adagio)
    c. Intermezzo (allegro moderato)
    d. Finale (Rondo) Allegro giocoso
    LONGY CHOIR

4. a. Le Baiser . . . . *Thomas*
   b. Le Printemps . . . . *Stern*
   MISS LUCY MARSH

5. Divertissement, op. 36 . . . . *Bernard*
    a. Andante Sostenuto — Allegro molto moderato
    b. Allegro vivace
    c. Andante — Allegro non troppo
    LONGY CHOIR

STEINWAY PIANO USED
M. STEINERT & SONS CO., 509 Westminster Street, New England Representatives

Boston Symphony Orchestra wind section, 1914, showing many members of the Longy Club

Standing: August Battles, flute; Albert Chevrot, flute; Max Fuhrmann, bassoon; Edmond Mueller, bassoon; Paul Mimart, clarinet; Arthur Brooke, flute; Augusto Vannini, clarinet; Pierre Fossé, oboe; Clement Lenom, oboe

Seated: André Maquarre, principal flute; Joseph Mosbach, principal bassoon; Peter Sadony, bassoon; Georges Longy, principal oboe; F. C. Mueller, oboe; Karl Stumpf, bass clarinet; Georges Grisez, principal clarinet

Season Fifteen, 1914–1915

ALTHOUGH IT MIGHT NOT HAVE BEEN IMMEDIATELY APPARENT to the members of the Longy Club, this season marked a turning point in the fortunes of the ensemble. To begin with, World War I was a dominant influence. This war touched the wind ensemble not only in its personnel, who were primarily French, but in its literature, as the reader will discover below. Perhaps the war also affected the climate for this kind of music as well, for the first concert saw the hall only one-third full. One critic perceived these signals and wrote what might be considered a forecast of the end of the ensemble; indeed there would be only two more seasons after this one.

> A fair number of string quartets exist in the United States today; soloists, vocal and instrumental, differ from the seventeen-year locusts in that they sweep over the land annually instead of less often. So far as I am aware, there are only two or possibly three organizations of woodwind players in the whole country which perform serious chamber music. Boston is fortunate in being the home of the best of these organizations, and especially fortunate in retaining it today despite troubled times. If war has not disbanded this worthy society, old age sooner or later must, for not even great artists are immortal. It would be fitting as indicting that our much-vaunted 'musical public' has at least some slight interest in music apart from its association with famous personalities if this same public would fill Jordan Hall more than a third full at concerts of the Longy Club.[1]

[1] P. G. C. 'The Longy Club Plays Novel Pieces,' *Boston Transcript*, Nov. 27, 1914.

One very significant effect of the war on the Longy Club at this time was the departure of the very highly praised principal clarinet, Georges Grisez, who returned to France to defend his country. His replacement, both in the Longy Club and in the Boston Symphony Orchestra, was the Russian clarinetist, Mr. A. Sand. Judging by a comment in the *Globe*, he apparently did not find the shoes of Grisez easy to fill.

> Mr. Sand replaces Mr. Grisez as the principal clarinet. Whether or not he may have altered reed or mouthpiece, his tone last night and at the last two Symphony concerts has been more characteristic of his instruments.[2]

[2] 'First Longy Club Concert,' *Boston Globe*, Nov. 26, 1914.

The First Concert

The first concert of the fifteenth season was given on the evening of 25 November 1914, and began with an arrangement by four pieces by Bach for two flutes, oboe, English horn, two clarinets, bass clarinet, two horns and two bassoons by a Mr. Gibson. At a time when people had very few opportunities to hear Baroque music, the critics were delighted.

The Beethoven Horn Sonata was presented in the traditional spot for a soloist on these concerts. Philip Hale, of the *Herald*, who called this, 'music of the most part in the style of Mozart, but Mozart in a conventional and perfunctory vein,' offered his readers some interesting, if not entirely lucid, background.

PROGRAMME

BACH–GIBSON — Pastoral Suite for two Flutes, Oboe, English Horns, two Clarinets, Bass Clarinet, two Horns and two Bassoons
   (First time)
I. Pastorale
II. Musette
III. Aria
IV. Prelude and Fugue

BEETHOVEN — Horn Sonate (Op. 17)
   (First time)
I. Allegro
II. Adagio — Rondo

ALBÉRIC MAGNARD — Quintet for Flute, Oboe, Clarinet, Bassoon, and Piano
   (In Memoriam)
I. Sombre
II. Tendre
III. Léger
IV. Joyeux

MEMBERS OF THE CLUB

FLUTES . . . . . Messrs. A. MAQUARRE and A. BROOKE
OBOES . . . . . . Messrs. G. LONGY and C. LENOM
CLARINETS . . . . Messrs. A. SAND and P. MIMART
HORNS . . . . . . Messrs. F. HAIN and H. LORBEER
BASSOONS . . . . Messrs. P. SADONY and J. MOSBACH
PIANO . . . . Mr. A. DE VOTO

ASSISTING ARTIST

Mr. K. STUMPF (Bass Clarinet)

It was composed for Johann Stich, the greatest horn player of his day, who in Italy changed his name to Punto and thus made a pun. He led an adventurous life, played on a silver instrument because he thought thus to better the quality of tone, not knowing that the material of a wind instrument has little or nothing to do with the timbre; and now lies buried in Prague with a scurvy diptych in Latin on his tombstone. Beethoven in 1800 wrote this sonata for him on the day of his concert. The audience was so pleased that it insisted on a repetition, although there was an ordinance against recalls and applause in an imperial theater in Vienna.[3]

3 Philip Hale, 'Concert by Longy Club,' *Boston Herald*, Nov. 26, 1914.

If the initial public liked the composition, some of the Boston critics did not.

Beethoven's horn sonata is musically commonplace. [*Transcript*]

Beethoven's sonata for horn is not representative music, even of his youth. [*Globe*]

Beethoven's sonata for the horn, Op. 17, though admirably performed, will not be missed by the concert-goers for some seasons to come. It is very conventional music.[4]

4 'Longy Club,' *The Boston Post*, Nov. 26, 1914.

The final composition on this first concert again brought the war home to the Longy Club. The Albéric Magnard Quintet for piano and winds came from their regular repertoire but on this occasion was performed 'In Memoriam' for the composer. Apparently the composer was in his villa near Nanteuil when two German soldiers invaded his garden. He was armed and he killed them. More troops returned later, shot the composer, and set fire to his villa destroying everything, including a famous collection of porcelain. On this occasion the press was respectful, although not always agreeing in the characterization of Magnard's style. The *Transcript* described it as owing, 'a good deal to Franck,' while the *Post* called it 'ultra-modern music.'

Albéric Magnard, 1911

The Second Concert

The second concert of the fifteenth season was given on the evening of 20 January 1915, with tickets having been sold in Symphony Hall at prices ranging from 50 cents to $1.50.

The concert began with a composition new to Boston, the Fritz Volbach (1861–1940) Quintet op. 24, for oboe, clarinet, horn, bassoon and piano. While the *Post* simply mentions the work as being 'the work of a modern composer of orthodox music,'[5] the remaining critics were disappointed with this composition and even rude in their commentary.

[5] 'Longy Club Concert,' *Boston Post*, Jan. 21, 1915.

> This quintet for piano and wind instruments is a respectable composition by a respectable composer. We can easily think of its success at a Liedertafel concert, with beer drawn from the keg. The chief theme of the first movement is developed in orthodox fashion; the second movement is a sentimental romance with a melting theme announced by the horn; the third movement—we frankly confess that we have forgotten what it was. It sounded like many other finales for this combination of instruments.[6]

[6] Philip Hale, 'Second Concert of the Season by Longy Club,' *Boston Herald*, Jan. 21, 1915.

> Volbach's quintet is not an important work; there must be two hundred writers in Germany alone who can produce an infinite number of such compositions. The themes are without distinction, excepting the principal subject of the slow movement, which owes much to Handel's famous aria from 'Xerxes.' The horn part is difficult but fairly brilliant; the other instruments are used without color. The 'structure' might pass for admirable—that is, themes in themselves without character are exposed and developed without originality according to time-honored formula.[7]

[7] P. G. C., *Boston Transcript*, Nov. 21, 1915.

> The quintet cannot be said to show distinction to its ideas. The horn appears to have an opening phrase that promises well, but the first movement lacks character. The song again for the horn in the slow movement is worthy of respect, and in the last there is a Spanish dance rhythm developed with some skill.[8]

[8] 'Longy Club Concert,' *Boston Globe*, Jan. 21, 1915.

> The quintet is a case of promise not fulfilled.[9]

[9] 'Longy Players Give Novelties,' *Boston Traveler*, Jan. 21, 1915.

For the moment usually reserved for soloists, the audience now heard for the first time a work by A. Wooters for four flutes, the Adagio and Scherzando, op. 77. This really was a novelty and considering the rather disrespectful remarks made

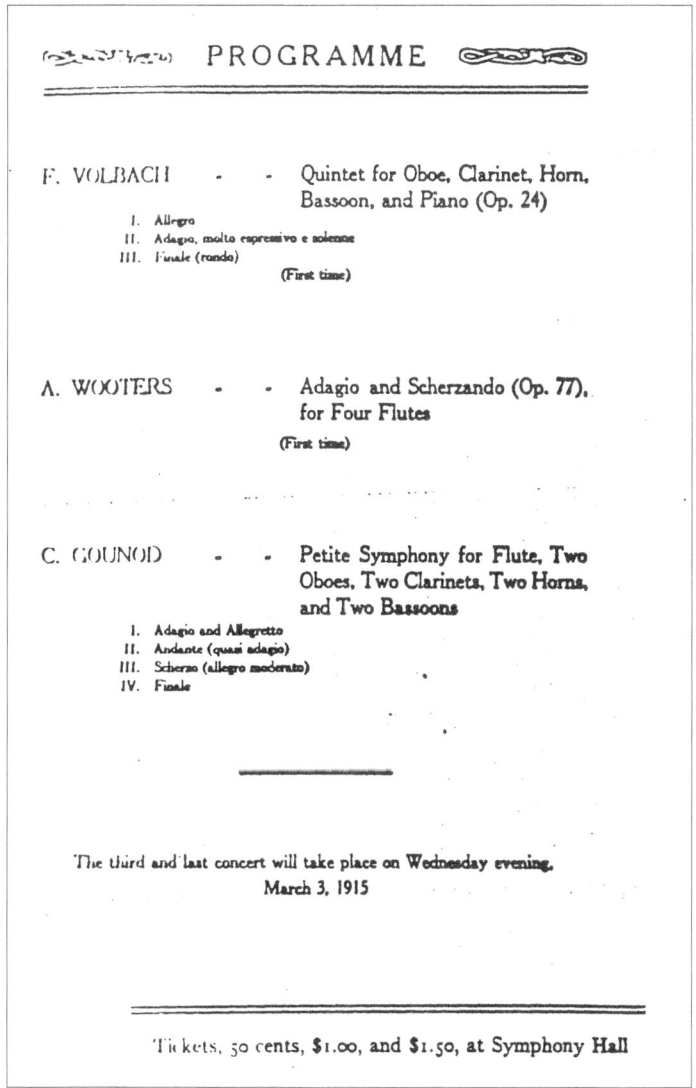

about this instrument in past years, it is almost astonishing to find all the Boston reviewers liking this composition. One of the more interesting discussions, in the *Herald*, reads,

> Those who look askew on the flute as a water logged instrument and compare the most accomplished virtuoso to a man eating with relish green corn on the cob after it has been thoughtfully buttered and salted, might well have shuddered at the thought of four flutes playing together. Kuhlau and Reicha have written such quartets, and possibly they are played in some barbaric city. The quartet by Wooters was an agreeable surprise. The Adagio was not too pretentious and the Scherzando was delightful by reason of its simplicity and graceful vivacity.

The final work on this concert was the *Petite Symphony* by Charles Gounod for flute, with pairs of oboes, clarinets, horns and bassoons. The critics justly appreciated this small masterpiece for wind ensemble.

> Gounod wrote his little symphony for wind instruments in 1888 for a club in Paris. It was practically the last of his compositions for orchestral instruments.
>
> The four movements are simple, melodious, and written with an intimate knowledge of horns, and wood-wind. How much clearer, how much more effective, is Gounod's treatment of this combination than that of many of our German laborers in the vineyard! The first movement recalls the Gounod of the first act of 'Faust.' The Andante is tuneful; the Scherzo, with its hunting calls and relieving trio, is effective – the whole work, in fact, is agreeable music. [*Herald*]

> Gounod's little symphony is already known here as an amiable and well-constructed work. Nothing remotely resembling depth of thought or feeling is discernible in it, but it is not dull and it possesses considerable grace. [*Transcript*]

> Gounod's little symphony suggests not only the classic vein but in certain details the melodic idioms of the Mozart whom Gounod adored. It is light but charming music, and it was performed with the most finished of art. [*Post*]

> Gounod's small symphony afforded a striking illustration of the established fact the old masters were masters in the truest sense. [Traveler]

The Third Concert

The final concert of the fifteenth season was given on the evening of 3 March 1915, before an audience which the *Transcript* called, 'somewhat larger than Boston usually offers to encourage resident musicians.'[10]

As was now almost a tradition, the concert began with a work unknown to Boston, the Johan Amberg (1846–1914) Suite for flute, oboe, clarinet and piano. On the whole the critics liked the work.

> The piece is modern in spirit. The Rondo is the most effective of the three movements.[11]

[10] P. G. C., 'Mr. Sand and Miss Fay,' *Boston Transcript*, March 4, 1915.

[11] 'Last Concert of Longy Club,' *Boston Herald*, March 4, 1915.

PROGRAMME

MEMBERS OF THE CLUB

FLUTES . . . . Messrs. A. MAQUARRE and A. BROOKE
OBOES . . . . . . Messrs. G. LONGY and C. LENOM
CLARINETS . . . . Messrs. A. SAND and P. MIMART
HORNS . . . . . Messrs. F. HAIN and H. LORBEER
BASSOONS . . . Messrs. P. SADONY and J. MOSBACH
PIANO . . . . Mr. A. DE VOTO

Assisting Artists
Miss MARY FAY
(SOPRANO)

Mrs. DUDLEY T. FITTS
(ACCOMPANIST)

The Piano is a Mason & Hamlin

J. AMBERG . . Suite for Flute, Oboe, Clarinet, and Piano
    I. Seguedille
    II. Devant la Cathédrale
    III. Ronde Villageoise
    (First time)

WEBER . . Concertino (Op. 26) for Clarinet and Piano

Songs
a. G. FAURÉ . . . . . Après un Rêve
b. A. GÉDALGE . . . . . Sérénade
c. H. BUSSER . . . Vénus, étoile du Soir

MOZART . Sérénade (No. 11) for Two Oboes, Two Clarinets, Two Horns, Two Bassoons

---

The first movement is rhythmic, full of color, and altogether charming. The second is rather too long and heavy. The last regains some of the charm of the first, but is wanting in thematic interest and lacks climax. [*Transcript*]

Amberg's suite is cheerful music, well composed, and idiomatic for the instruments.[12]

It is a tuneful, colorful, rhythmic composition deserving of a wider public than it will probably have through its restriction as woodwind music.[13]

After this work the new clarinetist, Mr. Sand, performed the Weber Concertino op. 126, with piano accompaniment. The critics were warming to his performance, the *Herald* mentioning his, 'consummate art and rare beauty of tone,' and the *Monitor* his, 'tone of unguessed softness and appeal.' The *Transcript* called him a 'master of technique,' but believed he held back his tone due to the acoustics of the hall.

[12] 'Singer with Longy Club,' *Boston Post*, March 5, 1915.

[13] 'Longy Club Gives its Last Concert of Present Season,' *Monitor*, March 4, 1915.

Following songs by guest soprano, Miss Mary Fay, the wind ensemble concluded the program with a performance of the Mozart Serenade K. 375 in the version for eight winds. The critic of the *Post* thought this one of the highlights of the entire season.

> The performance of Mozart's music was one of the bright particular triumphs of the Longy Club's present season, a season of interesting programmes and brilliant performances.

But Boston critics in the past had been slow to warm to Mozart and on this occasion there is again a lack of enthusiasm.

> The Mozart Serenade lost somewhat of its brilliancy by reason of the tempo. It was too slow. [*Monitor*]

> Mozart's serenade is full of pleasant bits. The opening is characteristic, and there are touches of 'color' which should annoy the academically inclined. The adagio is warmly melodious. The second minuet twinkles with the sly humor which one suspects often underlay the outwardly formal gallantry of Mozart's time. The finale is quaintly, sometimes drolly, good-natured, and there is a suggestion that its principal theme may have influenced Mendelssohn in the finale of the latter's 'Scotch' symphony. [*Transcript*]

The *Monitor* offered a nice summary for the season which this concert brought to a conclusion.

> Each year when the last concert of the Longy Club has been given a larger number of admirers are left to await the opening of the next season. At this, the last concert of the club's fifteenth season, there is more interest than ever before in the music that it plays. Some of the men have been with it since the start, others have come later. Under Mr. Longy's scholarly interpretation and skilful direction it seems to make little difference in the resultant tone whether a player has been for a long or a brief while in the organization.
>
> Pleasure in woodwind music with many has to be an acquired taste. Ears accustomed to the string tone in orchestra music or quartet, or to the sound of the brass in a band have to get used to the quality of woodwind instruments. There has been much music written for these instruments both by old and new writers. The only way to get acquainted

with it is through the efforts of an organization like this. The music will not bear transcription. And it rests with the leader of such a club to make his programs attractive, varied and stimulating, instructing by entertainment rather than by exposition. Such a leader Mr. Longy has proved himself. In the first rank of the oboe players of the world, he combines with his technical proficiency an excellent artistic sense that orders his program-making and conducting.

Season Sixteen, 1915–1916

The First Concert

THE FIRST CONCERT OF THE LONGY CLUB'S SIXTEENTH SEASON began with a concert on the evening of 18 November 1915, in Jordan Hall, Boston. The *Monitor*, in commenting on the first work on this program, gives a nice introduction of the season to its readers.

> Each year those who follow the work of Mr. Longy and his associates note with pleasure the increased attendance at the concerts of the club. The faithful have watched the evolution of the audiences from scattering few almost surrounded by empty seats to such an assembly as greeted the club last night, where the empty seats were scattered. A large part of these newcomers to the concert must be those who are finding for the first time the attractiveness of the wood wind instrument, when played by artists such as Mr. Longy and his confreres of the Boston Symphony Orchestra.
>
> A glance at the programs of former years will show a surprising number of 'first times' noted. Mr. Longy has done more than Boston yet appreciates in making new music known here. Rare is the concert that does not bring forward at least one new piece. Some of these, failing to find the approval of the public, go back on the shelves, but others, like the Raff sinfonietta that began the program last night, are placed in the repertoire of the club. The piece in question has been played twice before, the last time some five or six years ago, and it will no doubt delight other audiences in the future.[1]

[1] 'Longy Club in First Concert of the 16th Season,' *Boston Monitor*, Nov. 19, 1915.

The *Transcript* agreed with this evaluation of the Raff.

> Raff is always tuneful, always melodic; he writes for the ear rather than for the visual sense or the intellect, and his pleasing and happy music deserves occasional resurrection.[2]

[2] C. W., 'Familiar and Unfamiliar Music for Wind Choir from the Longy Club,' *Boston Transcript*, Nov. 19, 1915.

The second work on this concert was the Brahms Trio op. 114, for clarinet, cello and piano. It is difficult for readers today to understand why, but both the critics and the public of the early twentieth century did not yet fully appreciate Brahms.

> Mr. Longy introduced a trio of Brahms for the first time at these concerts which met with only a moderate degree of approval. [*Monitor*]

Brahms wrote his clarinet trio at Ischl in 1891, after a period of great mental depression, when he thought gloomily about death. This perhaps accounts somewhat for the elegiac tone of the composition.[3]

Brahms's Trio … is typical of the Brahms we all know, and, except in certain moods, some of us dread. [*Transcript*]

The final work on this concert was new to Boston, the Paul Juon Divertimento op. 51, for flute, oboe, clarinet, horn, bassoon and piano. Here was a work all the Boston critics were attracted to.

A 'Divertissement' by Paul Juon, that immediately took its rightful place as a welcome addition to the program stock of the club. Juon is the Russian who has built on his Moscow foundation a superstructure of

[3] 'Longy Club Gives First Concert of its Season,' *Boston Herald*, Nov. 19, 1915.

German musical ideas that has well night hidden underlying Slavic. So this sextet ... sounds more German than Russian and becomes at times almost an exercise in counterpoint.

Counterpoint, however, is Juon's delight, so each instrument in turn had its neat and delicate pattern to weave in the fabric of tone and in turn its theme of warmth and beauty to announce. [*Monitor*]

Paul Juon's divertissement is the sort of musical bonbon that owes its inspiration to things like Tschaikowsky's 'Nut Cracker Suite.' The motives are Slavic, or at moments distinctly oriental. The fourth of the five numbers ... is possibly the most original and charming. A waltz in groundwork, it is full of strange broken rhythms, presumably Russian, and is altogether fascinating.[4]

His music is to be respected for its solid workmanship, which is often lightened by a whimsical fancy, but it is not easy to trace in his music that we have heard any suggestion of his native country. [*Herald*]

The most interesting 'number' on the programme was the new 'Divertissement,' by Juon, played…with a keen appreciation of its sturdy workmanship, its occasional graces and vivacities and its pulsing, attractive rhythms. In it as in the whole programme, the club kept to its familiar standards. Its works are the reward of its faith. [*Transcript*]

The Second Concert

The second concert of the sixteenth season was given on the evening of 20 January 1916. The first work on this program was the Woollett Quintet for flute, oboe, clarinet, horn and bassoon, which the *Post* called, 'conventional and undistinguished,'[5] but which the *Advertiser* described as 'delightful and well worth a second hearing.'[6]

For the traditional solo work, Longy introduced his own daughter, Renee, joined by the club's accompanist, Alfred de Voto, in a work for two pianos by Enesco. Although this was her first appearance as a pianist, the *Advertiser* mentions that she had a local reputation as a 'successful exponent in another form of art—that of eurythmics.' As for her piano skills, the *Transcript* observes,

[4] 'Longy Club in First Concert,' *Boston Post*, Nov. 19, 1915.

[5] 'Concert by Longy Club,' *Boston Post*, Jan. 21, 1916.

[6] A. E. W., 'Longy Club, *Boston Advertiser*, Jan. 21, 1916.

The music, generally speaking, far more brilliant than inspired, gave Miss Longy little opportunity to make a very personal impression, but so far as one could gather she plays with surprising strength of wrist and finger, occasional sonority, still more surprising in so young a girl, the true French vivacity.[7]

After three songs by mezzo-soprano, Mrs. A. Roberts Barker, the wind ensemble concluded the program with the *Chanson et Danses* of d'Indy.

Although Vincent d'Indy is a serious and thoughtful composer with a reputation of not caring in the least to please the public ear, the Chanson et Danses deserve more than a passing mention. The first contains music of elevated beauty and poignancy, the second is exquisite in the simplicity of its style and the remarkable effects attained with a small group of instruments. [*Advertiser*]

[7] 'New Music by Enesco,' *Boston Transcript*, Jan. 21, 1916.

MEMBERS OF THE CLUB

FLUTES	Messrs. A. MAQUARRE and A. BROOKE
OBOES	Messrs. G. LONGY and C. LENOM
CLARINETS	Messrs. A. SAND and P. MIMART
HORNS	Messrs. F. HAIN and H. LORBEER
BASSOONS	Messrs. P. SADONY and J. MOSBACH
PIANO	Mr. A. DE VOTO

Assisting Artists
Mrs. A. ROBERTS BARKER
Mademoiselle RENÉE LONGY

Pianos, Mason & Hamlin

.. PROGRAMME ..

H. WOOLLETT . . Quintet in E major, on popular themes for Flute, Oboe, Clarinet, Horn and Bassoon
  I. Vif et Gai
  II. Andante Grazioso
  III. Scherzo vivace (ma non presto)
  IV. Moderato con Simplice

G. ENESCO . . . . Variations for Two Pianos (Op. 5)
  (First time)
  Mlle. RENÉE LONGY and Mr. A. DE VOTO

a. FLORENT SCHMITT . . . . Demande
b. MARC DELMAS . . . . . S'il revenait un jour
c. GUY ROPARTZ . . . . Berceuse
  (First time)
  Mrs. A. ROBERTS BARKER (Mezzo-Soprano)

V. D'INDY . . . . Chanson et Danses (Op. 50), Divertissement for Flute, Oboe, Two Clarinets, Horn and Two Bassoons
  I. Chanson
  II. Danses

The Third Concert

The final concert of this season was given on the evening of 9 March 1916, and began with a new work, the *Sextette* op. 33, no. 3, by the English composer, Joseph Holbrooke (1878–1958), for flute, oboe, clarinet, horn, bassoon and piano. The critics were unanimous in declaring this a poor work.

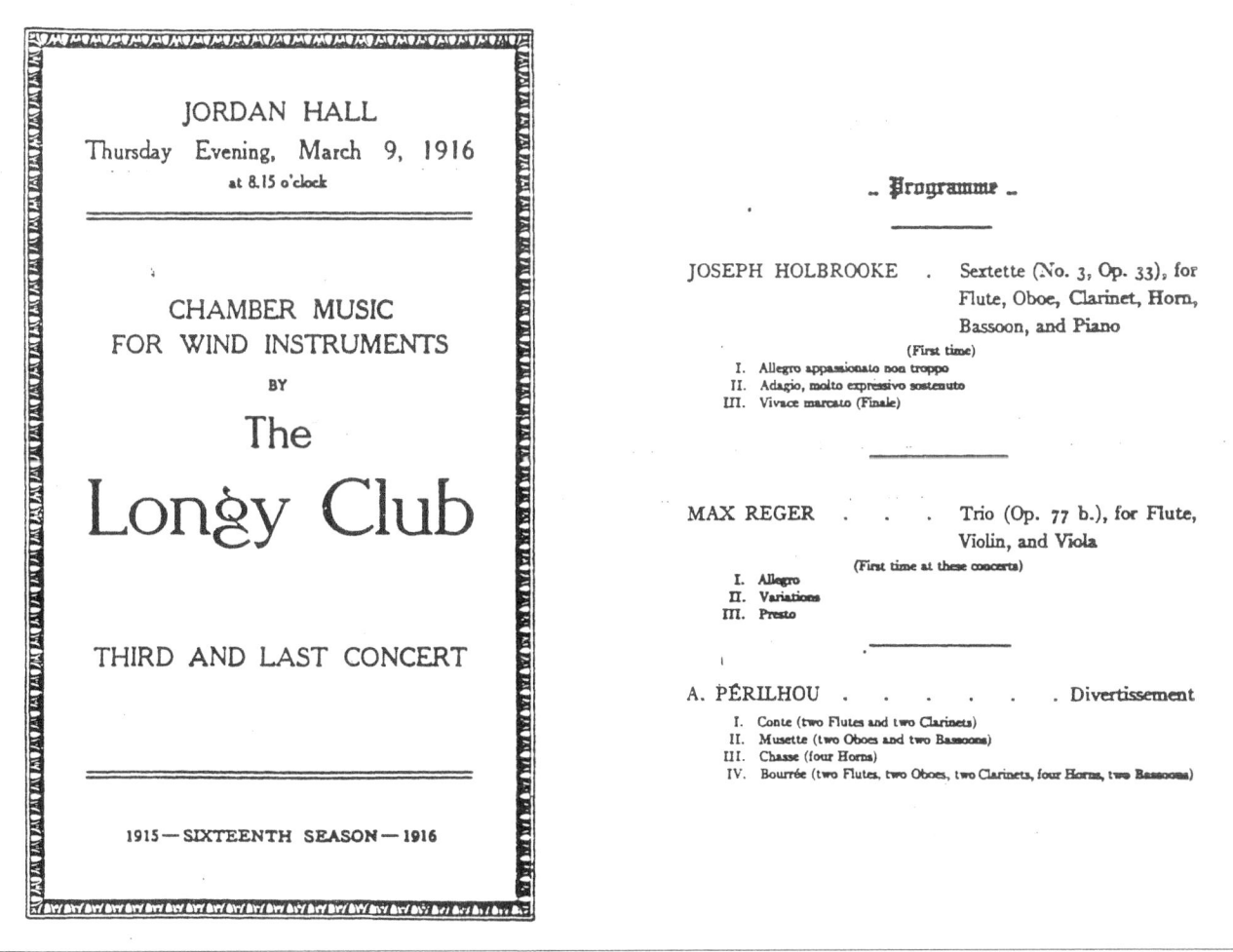

Themes not without possibilities are advanced, but the development is strangely desultory, scrappy, inconsequential. Most of it is boresome. There is bold play to make the audience sit up on the last movement, with a syncopated circus theme that should delight the heart of a comic opera maker.[8]

[8] 'Longy Club Recital,' *Boston Globe*, March 10, 1916.

Discursive and uninteresting ... Its chief fault is the disjointed feeling produced by unskilled blending of piano and other instruments ... The themes are clumsily developed and the ideas spread too thin.⁹

The sextet for wind instruments is a prize composition. Yet it is uninspired music. The three movements are all of generous length. The first is pastoral in character, the second is melancholy contemplative nature, in the third there is an attempt at playfulness, a display of obvious humor, reminiscent of Sir Edward Elgar in a facetious moment ... The work as a whole lacks distinction, originality, melodic richness.¹⁰

The second work performed was the Serenade op. 77 [incorrectly titled in the program given the audience!], for flute, violin and viola by Max Reger (1873–1916). All the critics liked this work, the *Monitor* calling it, 'a piece of writing of surpassing skill and pleasing invention.' The *Globe* heard

> a welcome relief from his usually turgid, pompous style. This miniature in the folk vein, with a slow movement with Mendelssohnish sentiment is gracefully pleasing, fresh with sweet buccolic airs.

The final composition on this concert was the Périlhou, *Divertissement* for twelve winds. The *Herald* called this work, 'agreeable, spontaneous.' Of this performance, the *Monitor* also mentions, 'horn playing of a quality like this is seldom heard anywhere.'

9 'Longy Club in Last Concert of the Season,' *Boston Herald*, March 10, 1916.

10 'Longy Club Gives its Final Concert of Season,' *Boston Herald*, March 10, 1916.

Max Reger, ca. 1910

Season Seventeen, 1916–1917

THE LONGY CLUB BEGAN ITS SEVENTEENTH, and what would turn out to be its final, season with a rare change in personnel. The bassoonist Sadony died and his place was taken by Joseph Mosbach, whom the *Monitor* testifies, 'gave evidence of a warm, romantic tone, for he, too, has the ability to play the bassoon so it does not sound like a comic instrument.'[1]

[1] 'Longy Club in First Concert of Season,' *Monitor*, Nov. 8, 1916.

The First Concert

The first regular concert of the Longy Club's seventeenth season was given on the evening of 7 November 1916, and began with a performance of the Beethoven Quintet op. 16, for piano and winds. The *Transcript* wrote of both the quality of the music and its performance.

> Beethoven's early quintet for oboe, clarinet, horn, bassoon and piano is no lesser work. It is delicate and graceful in the vein of the first two symphonies, and quietly inspired throughout. The Andante, tender and wistful, recalls the later and more intense Mozart. And there is singular beauty in the interlacing of instruments, each with its marked color, and the intimacy of the solo quality refreshingly novel to the ear accustomed to the more impersonal orchestra. The horn gave contrast of color, stability, size and warmth. The piano part kept the atmosphere of chamber music uppermost, and it blended with the other instruments in the happy way in which none has excelled Beethoven. It was always in prominence—it supplied new vistas of color and supple agility to the concentrated dulcet quality of the wood-wind choir. Each player made the voice of his instrument run smoothly, expressively and uncloyingly. They played one and all because the instinct for music is deeply imbedded in their natures, and they brought the master to new life by their devoted sympathy with his greatness.[2]

[2] J. N. B., 'More Novel Debussy,' *Boston Transcript*, Nov. 8, 1916.

The critics, and audience no doubt, were especially interested in the next composition on the program, a previously unknown work by Debussy, his Sonata for flute, viola and harp. The reaction of the critics, however, was by no means enthusiastic.

Debussy afforded variety and diversion in plenty to the more staid course of the concert ... Debussy is fond of the harp ... but he has always used it for exotic effect. His use of it has always been occasional—a sweeping dash to a color scheme. Thrown suddenly into exaggerated prominence, enriched by the discreetly interwoven tones of the viola in its lower, dark and mellow register, it droned or rustled its accompaniment to the wild and willful meanderings of the flute. The whole was almost Russian in its exoticism. But it was weird and fanciful rather than melodic ... The sonata is not likely to make a vivid or lasting impression upon the minds of man. [*Transcript*]

Members of the Club

FLUTES	Messrs. A. MAQUARRE and A. BROOKE
OBOES	Messrs. G. LONGY and C. LENOM
CLARINETS	Messrs. A. SAND and P. MIMART
HORNS	Messrs. F. HAIN and H. LORBEER
BASSOONS	Messrs. J. MOSBACH and E. MUELLER
PIANO	Mr. A. DE VOTO

Assisting Artists

Mr. F. WITTMANN, Viola

Mr. T. CELLA, Harp

The Piano is a Mason & Hamlin

PROGRAMME

BEETHOVEN . Quintet (Op. 16), for Oboe, Clarinet, Horn, Bassoon, and Piano

    I. Grave—Allegro, ma non troppo—
    II. Andante Cantabile.
    III. Rondo (Allegro, ma non troppo)

C. DEBUSSY . Sonate for Flute, Viola, and Harp

    I. Pastorale
    II. Interlude
    III. Finale

(First performance in America)

Messrs. A. BROOKE; F. WITTMAN; T. CELLA

TH. GOUVY . Ottetto (Op. 71), for Flute, Oboe, two Clarinets, two Horns, and two Bassoons

    I. Introduzione (Larghetto) Allegro Moderato
    II. Dansé Suedoise (Allegro)
    III. Romance (Larghetto)
    IV. Rondo (Allegretto)

The first movement ... is finely thought, and is more interesting than the Interlude and Finale that followed. Or may it not be that the peculiar combination of instruments in spite of Debussy's ingenuity in using them, necessarily engenders monotony of color unrelieved by contrasts or timbre?[3]

Was it Debussy we were listening to? Was it not rather Schonberg? Or Stravinsky? Or at times even Ornstein? Only at intervals could we touch bottom in a familiar progression based on the whole-tone scale ... At the end, indeed, is a succession of major chords, which even more than the strange harmonies and uneven rhythms that precede

[3] *Boston Herald*, Nov. 8, 1916.

it, reveal a Debussy who is adventuring into new and strange paths. Stravinsky, it would seem, holds the beacon whose light Debussy chooses. [*Monitor*]

The final work on this concert was the Octet op. 71, by Gouvy. As heard by the *Transcript*:

> With flute added, and clarinets, horns and bassoons doubled into an Octet by Gouvy, the assemblage lost its individual quality, and became a small orchestra, to be pushed to the furthest powers of the wood-wind. Gouvy as we heard him last night was interesting at all times, and though he had little or nothing to say that was new or ahead of convention, yet his music was always amiable, ably expressed and delightful in its frank unpretentiousness.

The Second Concert

The second concert of this season was given on the evening of 15 January 1917. A large audience is mentioned in the *Transcript*, as well as, 'the usual musical atmosphere on stage and off, and the usual friendly response to each part of the performance.'[4]

The *Monitor* begins its review with an interesting discussion of the general nature of the concerts given by the Longy Club over a span of time. The present writer believes the criticism given here is absolutely 'on target,' however the wrong target. It might well be argued that the root of the problems discussed here are not those of a wind ensemble, but are characteristics of the nineteenth and twentieth century French repertoire for winds—which, of course, formed the core of the repertoire of this French ensemble located in Boston.

[4] J. N. B., 'With the Longy Club,' *Boston Transcript*, Jan. 16, 1917.

> A Longy Club program gives an audience more indirect pleasure, perhaps, than direct. It has a greater analytical interest than structural. It is more valuable for the opportunity it gives hearers to study the wind section of the orchestra than it is for any message it can convey from the composer. It throws a backward rather than a forward light. It is mirrored music.
>
> Although what Mr. Longy and his associates present to the public is as far as possible from being the kind of entertainment known as light, still it is far less exacting to listeners than what a group of string quartet players presents. The thematic material of the Longy pieces is usually simple and the development of it is seldom elaborate. If people who attend a performance like that of Monday evening will make it an

exercise in distinguishing tone colors, in observing points of technique and in marking details in phrasing and shading, without inquiring too seriously about architectural outlines and otherwise hunting for large intellectual meanings, they get all the pleasure there is to be had.

One can certainly understand this viewpoint when one considers that the only two works on this program for wind ensemble were the Thuille *Sextet* and the Enesco *Dixtuor*. The extant reviews do not speak with enthusiasm for either work. Of the Thuille, one reads,

> Of the two ... the more satisfactory was the Thuille ... for the discussion of straightforward themes and for the presentation of four clearly defined moods. [*Monitor*]

> One felt that Thuille was tolerably well versed in his assemblage of five wind instruments and piano, without exactly possessing the instinct for such a combination (far rarer than the instances of its use), nor had he collected musical ideas by any means suited to it. He was in his first movement what is sometimes called 'sturdy,' and throughout he was always decent and well-behaved. [*Transcript*]

And of the Enesco:

> Less satisfactory, notwithstanding its greater sonority, was the music of Enesco, in which the entire orchestral wind section took part in pairs. No skill on the part of the players could keep this music from sounding turgid. [*Monitor*]

> Like Thuille, he succeeded better when he relapsed from the pretentious preliminaries of the first movement into more engaging frivolities. Like Thuille, also, he strove for variety and color beyond his fixed bounds, and he strove for the instinctive orchestral liveliness which we so much admire. His instruments seemed continually to hold him back and dampen his ardor. [*Transcript*]

The remainder of this program was given over to two vocalists, Mrs. Martha Atwood-Baker and Mrs. Mary Shaw-Swain.

An Extra Concert in Symphony Hall

On the evening of 21 January 1917, the Longy Club gave a concert in the famous hall familiar to them in their primary roles as members of the Boston Symphony Orchestra. Still, it must have been exciting for the members of the club to return here as chamber soloists. All the more odd, that on this occasion Longy selected for the wind ensemble numbers (the rest of the concert being given over to ladies of the voice and keyboard), only three movements of the Gounod Symphony (no final movement), one movement by Novacek, three movements of Gouvy, and the little arrangement of Saint-Saën's *Feuillet d'Album*. Is it any wonder that the *Advertiser* reports, 'The audience was not of the usual Symphony Hall size, nor was there the usual enthusiasm.'[5]

[5] B. S. T., 'Mme. Frisch Stars at Sunday Concert,' *Boston Advertiser*, Jan. 22, 1917.

SYMPHONY HALL, BOSTON
SUNDAY AFTERNOON, JANUARY 21, 1917

POVLA FRIJSH
WINIFRED CHRISTIE
The LONGY CLUB

Flute, Mr. A. Brooke
Oboes, Messrs. G. Longy and C. Lenom
Clarinets, Messrs. A. Sand and P. Mimart
Horns, Messrs. F. Hain and H. Lorbeer
Bassoons, Messrs. J. Mosbach and E. Mueller

JEAN VERD, Piano

L. H. MUDGETT, Manager

SUNDAY, JANUARY 21, 1917

Programme

I.
(a) Adagio and Allegretto
(b) Andante cantabile
(c) Scherzo
.... Ch. Gounod
Longy Club

II.
Barcarole .... Chopin
Miss Christie

III.
(a) Gloire à la Nature .... Beethoven
(b) Air de Poppée .... Handel
(c) Wohin .... Schubert
Mme. Frijsh

IV.
(a) Feuillet d'Album .... C. Saint-Saëns
(b) Presto .... R. Novacek
Longy Club

V.
(a) In's Freie
(b) Frühlingsnacht
(c) Viel Glück zur Reise Schwalben
.... Schumann
Mme. Frijsh

VI.
(a) Jeux d'Eau .... Ravel
(b) La Fille aux cheveux de lin .... Debussy
(c) Waldesrauschen .... Liszt
(d) Concert Etude in G-flat .... Moszkowski
Miss Christie

VII.
(a) La Steppe .... Gretchaninoff
(b) Les Papillons .... Chausson
(c) Pastorale .... Stravinsky
(d) Med en primula veris (With a Primrose) .... Grieg
(e) Hymne au Soleil .... Alex. Georges
Mme. Frijsh

VIII.
(a) Aubade
(b) Ronde de Nuit
(c) Rondo
.... Th. Gouvy

Mason and Hamlin Piano

It is also not surprising that the reviewers concentrated on the various ladies on the program and devoted hardly a full sentence to any of the wind ensemble's efforts. The *Monitor* mentions only in passing, 'some insipid compositions for woodwinds and horns by Gounod,'[6] the work which the *Transcript* calls, 'pleasant and conventional routine music.'[7] Only the *Transcript* mentioned the Novacek, and then that its theme sounded like a 'train-whistle.'

[6] 'Sunday Afternoon at Symphony Hall,' *Monitor*, Jan. 22, 1917.

[7] 'Mixed Matters and Outcome,' *Boston Transcript*, Jan. 22, 1917.

Two Special Concerts

During the month of February 1917, Georges Longy apparently decided to attempt personally sponsoring concerts with broader appeal. For this purpose he presented two special concerts, each consisting entirely of the music of a single composer. These were the Jean Huré concert of 7 February 1917, and the Charles Loeffler concert of 21 February 1917.

The only wind composition of interest on either program was the Huré Andante for the unusual combination of solo saxophone, strings, harp, timpani and organ, performed by the locally famous saxophonist, Mrs. Hall, with Longy conducting. The reviewers were not impressed—and perhaps not awake, for the *Monitor* calls the solo instrument a 'saxhorn!'

> Hure would probably not be willing to be judged by his Andante … It was written to order, and few compositions thus invented are of a high rank. The combination of instruments I not a happy one; at least it was not for Hure. The music as played was purposeless and ineffective.[8]

[8] Philip Hale, 'First Longy Concert Heard is Agreeable,' *Boston Herald*, Feb. 8, 1917.

> To listen to an 'Andante' set forth by a string orchestra, organ, harp, drums and alto saxophone is to ask a single question: 'Why?' The harp and drums were not needed; the organ, made prominent, refused obstinately to blend with anything; and the saxophone took up the melody as lamely as the work ended.[9]

[9] 'Jean Hure's Music,' *Boston Transcript*, Feb. 8, 1917.

> In his andante, the composer uses strings, harp and organ in such a way as to take off the stridency of the solo instrument while keeping its expressiveness. This conquest of a difficulty in tone combination might be set down as the greatest merit of the piece.[10]

[10] 'Mr. Longy Produces Hure Compositions,' *Monitor*, Feb. 8, 1917.

The Third Concert

On the evening of 7 March 1917, the Longy Club wind ensemble gave its final concert of this season. Judging by the extant reviews, on the night of this concert no one was aware, or could have guessed, that this would in fact be the final concert of this historic ensemble. One wishes it were a more distinguished repertoire, but on the other hand it might be fairly said to be representative.

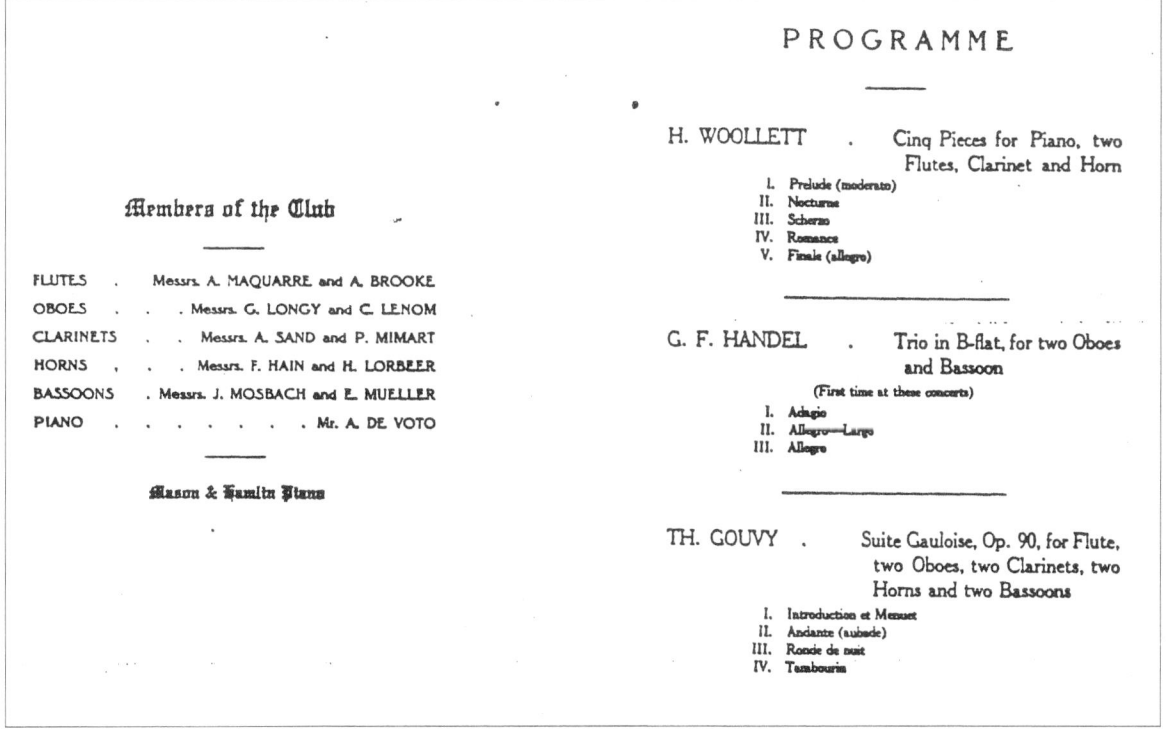

The concert began with the Woollett, *Five Pieces*, for piano two flutes, clarinet and horn. While the *Herald* heard these as, 'melodious, soothing,'[11] the *Advertiser* judged them, 'of slight importance.'[12]

For the solo portion of the concert, Longy found yet another Handel Trio for two oboes and bassoon. The *Advertiser*, in a town that loved its Handel, found praise for this small ensemble.

> The instrumental combination used in the trio by Handel … leaves much to be desired from the standpoint of sonority, and, at times, barely escapes being unintentionally grotesque. But, happily, this

[11] 'Longy Club Gives 3D Concert of Season,' *Boston Herald*, March 8, 1917.

[12] 'Longy Club in its Final Concert,' *Boston Advertiser*, March 8, 1917.

shortcoming is more than obviated by the spontaneous and happy resourcefulness of the great Handel, with his vigorous and dexterous polyphony, and we venture the guess that Handel's genius would have stood undaunted were he limited to two shawms and a sackbut.

The final work on this concert, the last to ever be heard by the Longy Club proper, was the Gouvy *Suite Gauloise*, a work which had long been part of the repertoire. The *Herald*, pointing to the influence of Mendelssohn, calls the work, 'simple, tuneful.' The *Advertiser* was somewhat more kind.

> It displays much mastery in true ensemble writing; the material being pregnant, well diversified and satisfyingly sonorous in handling.

The *Advertiser* closed its review with what seems an appropriate eulogy.

> Of the playing of this admirable organization nothing in the way of praise can be said which will add to their high artistic achievements.

The End of the Longy Club

It is probably no longer possible to point to a single factor which caused the demise of the Longy Club. Perhaps it was the aging of the members—the bassoonist, Sadony, had died the previous year. Perhaps with the end of World War I, some members wished to return to France. Perhaps it was related to a reorganization, mentioned in a review below, of the Boston Symphony Orchestra itself, of which the players were also members. Perhaps it was some loss of financial support. Perhaps it was all of these reasons and more. In any case, in November 1917, an article in the *Post* clearly informs us that a crisis had occurred in the life of this famous ensemble.

> It has been said, and the statement has not been contradicted from authoritative sources, that the Longy Club of players on wind instruments, one of the most representative musical organizations of Boston, may have to suspend its activities for the present season, lacking the necessary measure of support, in these war-ridden days, from the public. If this were so, it would be a deplorable loss to the city. The Longy Club is made up of leading members of the wind choirs of the Boston Symphony Orchestra. Frenchmen, for the greater part, who have, in

some instances, international reputations as masters of their instruments and as musical interpreters. Their performances have been every whit as finished and, from this standpoint, as creditable to the musical standing of the city as that of the orchestra from which the players are drawn. Furthermore, the Longy Club has been the means of introducing to this city a great many new and important works by modern composers. Mr. Longly is a passionate and curious student of his art, who leaves no stone unturned to do the utmost justice to its most recent developments as well as its long established standards. His concerts have attracted music lovers who have justly valued the opportunity given them of intimate contact with the work of present day composers of all nationalities—Russian, German, English, Italian, Bohemian, etc., who have written music which in Mr. Longy's opinion deserved a hearing. It is inconceivable that this measure of support required to have these concerts continue will be lacking. The many who know what it would mean to have the Longy Club even temporarily suspend its activities should register their support in a practical way.[13]

13 'The Longy Club,' *Boston Post*, Nov. 24, 1917.

It appears, in fact, that no concerts were given during the 1917–1918 season.

A brief notice in the *Transcript*, the following year, informs us that the Longy Club wind ensemble had been 'disbanded as a consequence of the recent reorganization of the Boston Symphony Orchestra.'[14] The article goes on to say that Longy would form a new ensemble from the faculty and students of his Longy School of Music.

14 'Items and Announcements,' *Boston Transcript*, Nov. 22, 1918.

Indeed, Longy seems to have organized one last concert in this manner, given the following 17 January 1919. Only one review is extant, that of the *Transcript*, which must be quoted to document the sad end of this great Boston wind ensemble tradition.

> As the signs say, Miss Terry's concert at the Copley Theatre on Monday afternoon, will afford the only opportunity to hear in Boston this season the reconstituted Longy Club. As now re-formed, it comprises Mr. Longy (oboe), Mr. de Mailly (flute), Mr. Stievenard (clarinet), Mr. Laus (bassoon), Mr. Tillois (violin), Mr. Miquelle (violoncellist)—all of the Symphony Orchestra—with Mr. Mason as pianist. They will be heard in light and ingratiating salon music.

Postlude

In 1925 Georges Longy retired from the Boston Symphony Orchestra and from the Music School he founded in 1915, to return to his native France. A 'Farewell Tribute' was given for him on 2 May 1925, in the form of a concert played by an orchestra consisting of members from all the institutions he had been so vital a part of: the old Longy Club, the Boston Orchestral Club, the Boston Musical Association, the Faculty of the Longy School, the MacDowell Club Orchestra and the Boston Symphony Orchestra.

On this concert there were no representatives of the repertoire of the Longy Club wind ensemble, with which he had so long been associated. There was, however, the performance of one composition by Longy himself, his Rapsodie for solo saxophone, two clarinets, bassoon, harp, string bass and three timpani. This work had been composed for Mrs. Hall, and performed on a MacDowell Club concert, but was performed on this occasion by Abdon Laus.[15]

[15] A native of Alger, but trained in the Paris Conservatory, Laus was a bassoonist in the Boston Symphony Orchestra, but was described in the program as 'founder and director of the Boston Saxophone Studio and the Boston Saxophone Orchestra.'

The Longy Club Repertoire

Amberg, Johan. Suite, for flute, oboe, clarinet and piano.
Beethoven, Ludwig van. Quintet op. 16, for piano and winds.
———. Octet op. 103, for pairs of oboes, clarinets, horns and bassoons.
Bernard, Emile. *Divertissement* op. 36, for 2 flutes, 2 oboes, 2 clarinets, 2 horns and 2 bassoons.
Bird, Arthur. Serenade op. 40 (1898).
———. Suite in D Major for pairs of flutes, oboes, clarinets, horns and bassoons.
Brahms, Johannes. Trio in A Minor, op. 114, for clarinet, cello and piano.
Brockway, Howard. *At Twilight*, and *An Idyl of Murmuring Water*, for pairs of flutes, oboes, clarinets, horns and bassoons.
Bumcke, Gustav. *Der Spaziergang*, op. 22, for flute, oboe, English horn, 2 clarinets, horn, 2 bassoons and harp..
Caplet, André. *Legende*, for saxophone, oboe, clarinet, bassoon and strings.
———. *Suite Persane*, for pairs of flutes, oboes, clarinets, horns and bassoons.
———. Quintet, for flute, oboe, clarinet, bassoon and piano.
Cossart, Leland. Suite op. 19, for pairs of flutes, oboes, clarinets, horns, bassoons and harp.
Destenay, Edouard. Trio, for oboe, clarinet and piano
Dvorak, Antonin. Serenade op. 44, for 2 oboes, 2 clarinets, 2 bassoons 3 horns, celli, string bass.
Enesco, Georges. Symphonie for 2 flutes, oboe, English horn, 2 clarinets, 2 horns and 2 bassoons.
Falconi, Alfonso. Sextet op. 60 for flute, oboe, clarinet, horn, bassoons and piano.
Fauré, Gabriel, trans., Gabriel Groview. Nocturne op. 33, for flute, 2 oboes, 2 clarinets, 2 horns and 2 bassoons.
Flament, Edouard. *Fantasia con Fuga*, op. 28 for flute, oboe, English horn, 2 clarinets, bassoon and horn.
Fried, Oskar. Adagio and Scherzo, op. 2, for 3 flutes, 2 oboes, English horn, 2 clarinets, bass clarinet, 3 horns, 2 bassoons, contrabsn, 2 harps, timpani.
Gounod, Charles. *Petite symphonie*, for flute, 2 oboes, 2 clarinets, 2 horns and 2 bassoons.
Gouvy, Theodore. *Ottetto* op. 71, for flute, oboe, 2 clarinets, 2 horns and 2 bassoons.
———., *Suite Gauloise*.
Hahn, Reynaldo. *Le Bal de Beatrice d'Este*, for oboe, 2 flutes, 2 clarinets, 2 horns, 2 bassoons, trumpet, timpani, piano, harps and percussion.
Herzogenberg, Heinrich von. *Quintette* op. 43, for piano, oboe, 2 clarinet, horn and bassoon.
Holbrooke, Joseph. *Sextette* op. 33, Nr. 3, for flute, oboe, clarinet, horn, bassoon and piano.
Huré, Jean. *Pastorale*, for 3 flutes, oboe, English horn, 2 clarinets, horn and 2 bassoons.
D'Indy, Vincent. *Chanson et Danses*.
———. Trio op. 29, for clarinet, cello and piano.
Juon, Paul. Chamber Symphony op. 27, for oboe, clarinet, horn, bassoon, piano, violin, viola and cello.
———. Divertissement op. 51, for flute, oboe, clarinet, horn, bassoon and piano.
Kauffmann, Fritz. Woodwind Quintet.
Klughardt, August. *Five Fantasies*, op. 28, for oboe, viola and piano.
Kriens, Christiaan. 3 *Aquarelles Hollandaises*, for 2 flutes, 2 oboes, 2 clarinets 2 horns, 2 bassoons and bells.
Lacroix. *Sextuor*, for flute, oboe, clarinet, horn, bassoon and piano.
———., *Variations Symphoniques* for flute, oboe, English horn, clarinet, bass clarinet, 2 horns and bassoon.
Lampe, Walther. Serenade op. 7 for pairs of flutes, oboes, clarinets, bassoons, 4 horns, bass clarinet and contrabassoon.
Lazzari, Sylvio. *Octuor* op. 20, for flute, oboe, clarinet, English horn, 2 horns and 2 bassoons.

Lefebvre, Charles-Édouard. Intermezzo-Scherzando, for flute, oboe, 2 clarinets, horn and bassoon.
Loeffler, Charles Martin. *Ballade Carnavalesque*, saxophone, flute, oboe, bassoon and piano.
Longy, Georges. *Impression*, saxophone, 3 horns, harp, strings, antique cymbals.
———. Lento, saxophone, 2 clarinets, bassoon, string bass, harp, 3 timpani.
Magnard, Albéric. Quintet op. 8, for flute, oboe, clarinet, bassoon and piano.
Malherbe, Edmond. Sextet, for flute oboe, English horn, clarinet, horn and bassoon.
Maquarre, André. *Three Romantic Numbers*, for flute, oboe, 2 clarinets and 2 bassoons.
Mason, Daniel G. *Pastorale*, op. 8, for clarinet, violin and piano.
Moreau, Leon. Nocturne for pairs of flutes, oboes, clarinets, horns and bassoons.
Mouquet, Jules. Suite for flute, oboe, 2 clarinets, horn and 2 bassoons.
———. *Rapsodie* op. 26, solo English horn, flute, clarinet, horn, bassoon, string quintet.
Mozart, Wolfgang Amadeus. Serenade K. 384a, in C minor for pairs of oboes, clarinets, clarinets horns and bassoons.
———. *Gran Partita* K. 370a for 12 winds and string bass.
———. Partita K. 375 in Eb, for wind octet.
———. Quintet K. 452 for piano and winds.
———. *Symphonie concertante* for oboe, clarinet, horn and bassoon.
Novacek, Rudolf. *Sinfonietta*, for flute, oboe, 2 clarinets, 2 horns and 2 bassoons.
Oldberg, Arne. Quintet op. 18, for oboe, clarinet, horn, bassoon and piano.
Périlhou, Albert. *Divertissement*, for pairs of flutes, oboes, clarinets, bassoons and 4 horns.
Pierné, Gabriel. *Pastoral Variee dans le style ancien*, op. 30, for flute, oboe, clarinet, trumpet, horn and 2 bassoons.
Quef, Charles Paul Florimond. Suite op. 4, for flute, oboe, clarinet, horn, bassoons and piano.
Raff, Joachim. *Sinfonietta* op. 188, for 2 flutes, 2 oboes, 2 clarinets, 2 horns and 2 bassoons.
Reinecke, Carl. Trio op. 167, for oboe, horn and piano..
Rietz, Julius. *Concertstuck* op. 41, for flute, oboe, clarinet, horn, bassoon, and piano.
Rimsky-Korsakov, Nikolai. Quintet for flute, clarinet, horn, bassoon and piano.
Röntgen, Julius. Serenade op. 14, for flute, oboe, clarinet, 2 horns and 2 bassoons.
Saint-Saëns, Camille. *Caprice sur des Airs Danois et Russes*, for piano, flute, oboe and clarinet.
———., arr. Taffanel, Paul. *Feuillet d'Album*, for flute, 2 oboes, 2 clarinets 2 horns and 2 bassoons.
Schmitt, Florent. *Lied and Scherzo*, op. 54, for solo horn, piccolo, flute, oboe, English horn, 2 clarinets, horn and 2 bassoons.
Schreck, Gustav. *Nonetto* op. 40, for oboe, and pairs of flutes, clarinets, horns and bassoons.
Schumann, Robert. *Fairy Tales* for clarinet, viola and piano.
Strauss, Richard. Suite op. 4, for 2 flutes, 2 oboes, 2 clarinets, 4 horns, 2 bassoons and contrebasse.
Strube, Gustav. Quintet, for flute, oboe, clarinet, horn and bassoon.
Thuille, Ludwig. *Sextuor* op. 6, for piano, flute, oboe, clarinet, horn and bassoon.
Volbach, Fritz. Quintet op. 24, for oboe, clarinet, horn, bassoon and piano.
Wagner, Ernest F. Suite, for 2 flutes, oboe, clarinet, bassoon and piano.
de Wailly, Paul. Octet, for flute, oboe, 2 clarinets, trumpet, horn and 2 bassoons.
Weingartner, Felix. Quintet in G minor, op. 50, for clarinet, strings and piano.
Woollett, Henry. *Octuor*, for saxophone, oboe, clarinet and string quintet.
———., Quintet *on French popular themes*.
———., *Cinq Pieces* for 2 flutes, clarinet, horn and piano.
Wooters, A. Adagio and Scherzando, op. 77, for 4 flutes.
Wouters, François Adolphe. Quartet for 2 flutes, oboe and English horn.

On the Search for the Longy Club Performance Materials

Taking advantage of a tip from Jimmy Brown, an oboist with the English Chamber Orchestra, on a trip to Boston I found the original scrapbooks which contained articles, reviews and programs by the Longy Club, a professional wind ensemble consisting of members of the Boston Symphony Orchestra.

The publication of a little book I wrote about the Longy Club prompted much interest, especially in the search for the actual music used by this wind ensemble. The book tended also to shine some light on the present Longy School of Music in Boston, which has ties to Longy and his Club.

Following are letters which I deem historically important for their detail of this search and for the much additional information about the players of this ensemble.

Stevens Hewitt to David Whitwell
Philadelphia, Pennsylvania, 15 October 1988

I would like to order a copy of your book on the Longy Club, as I was a student of Clemen Lenom [second oboist in the ensemble]—Michael Finkelman told me of your book and expressed interest in Mr. Lenom. It is about time—He was quite a man. I have a color photo of his Thomas Hart Benton portrait and a picture of his portrait bust—He took three first prizes at Brussels—oboe, composition and solfege – studied with Massenet and Tabuteau's teacher, Georges Gillet—heard Cesar Franck play, knew Debussy and Degas—conducted the Boston Pops—knew Arthur Fiedler as a little boy.

I have some English horn reeds from him from 1904—no tubes, made bassoon reed style. They still work.

His wife, Mary Lenom, still lives in Brookline. His niece has his considerable library of oboe music in Buffalo, but his library (mostly French) is still in the third floor at Brookline.

It is amazing how ephemeral the reputations of the peasants in the orchestra are in comparison with the Great Artist conductors. It is amazing how they get so many notes to come out of the end of that stick.

Maybe you could do an article on Mr. Lenom and rectify his obscurity.

Stevens Hewitt, whom I believe played with the Philadelphia Orchestra at this time, wrote again the following month with much interesting information on the Longy Club members and their repertoire. He mentions here that the second wife of Lenom, the second oboist with the Longy Club, was still alive, with great stories to tell. I made repeated efforts to get someone in Boston to go to her and make an oral history recording, but I was not able to find anyone to do this.

Stevens Hewitt to David Whitwell
Philadelphia, PA, 4 November 1988

Thanks for the Longy Club book. As to their ensemble music, Rosario Mazzeo, Boston Symphony Orchestra bass clarinet player, had some of it. I understand that he still lives in Carmel, CA. He could tell a lot about the Longy Club.

I have a couple of the pieces, but they are very few elucidating pencil marks and they are in fragile shape. The Longy music in my Library:

Lacroix *Pastorale*
Gouvy *Octette, Petite Suite Galoise*
Dubois *Premier Suite*
Cossart *Suite*
[illegible] *Paysanes Normands*
Bird *Serenade*
Lazzari *Octette*
Schreck *Nonetti*

Lenom's niece got all of Lenom's smaller things (Cheryl Boschkoff).

A copy of the Strunke *Quintet* is in the Peabody Library in Baltimore, Curtis Library and the Fleisher. New England Conservatory I think has some of the music.

The Library of Congress has most of it, and the xerox machine is immediately available there, to flout the copyright laws with …

The Chelsea Chamber Ensemble played the Beethoven *Sonata Pathetique* in NY this Summer, for wind octet and contra, which I edited from the original parts. Serkin told me that he has seen sketches in Beethoven's notebook of the last movement in wind format. At present the score and parts are on their way out to John Mack in Cleveland. I think it is well worth doing. In case you are interested, I rent it for $50.00, but since you sent me the book, I will donate it to the cause.

Lenom's second marriage was to a young student. She is still very much with us, although bothered by arthritis, and has many stories to tell. M. Lenom himself was a very modest man and did not say much about himself, but told me stories of Cesantranch, Saint-Saens, Debussy, Muck, Nikish, Longy, Lorie, etc.

Did you know that Longy conducted the first 'Afternoon of a Fawn' in the United States?

Although forgotten today, the Longy players were very famous. Lenom was a French Legion of Honor; had his portrait painted by Thomas Hart Benton; conducted the Boston Pops, wrote a wonderful Solfege book that I use to teach stuffed sheep-head students how to read music out of.

I would hope that you could interview Mr. Mazzeo if he is still around, Madam Longy-Miguelle's daughter, and Mary Lenom.

The music of the New England School with Chadwick, et.al., is in my opinion unjustly slighted nowadays. You could work up a doozy of an article.

I have your cover picture [of the Longy Club] upon my wall—except that mine is in excellent shape. Your book just got back from Tony Gigliotti—He enjoyed the Brahms reviews.

I wrote to Mary Lenom, widow of the second oboist in the Longy Club, sending her a copy of my book and eventually received the following reply.

Mary B. Lenom to David Whitwell
Brookline, Massachusetts, 21 January 1989

I'm afraid I am going to ask you to forgive the unforgivable. For the last few months health problems have prevented me from doing many of the things I would like to do and should have done. Among them is getting caught up with my correspondence, something Steve Hewitt will tell you that I'm not very good at anyway.

I do thank you for your excellent and detailed history of the Longy Club. I did not know M. Longy. He had left Boston before I came to the N. E. Conservatory as a student. I did enjoy many visits with his widow at their little country home near Abbeville [France] and his daughter Renee was a very dear friend.

A few years ago I gave most of my husband's library to my grand-niece, Cheryl Priebe Bishoff, also an oboist. Steve Hewitt has some and there is still a small part of it on my 3rd floor. Due to two stubborn fractures of my right leg, at the moment I can't get to it. There is much on my 3rd floor that needs attention and I hope to take care of it one day soon.

Cheryl lives in Buffalo, NY with a small son. I'm not sure whether or not she has had time to do any cataloging. Her address is … if you would like to write her.

Whenever you are in this area I would be very happy to receive your visit. The musicians mentioned in your book brought back many fond memories of the years my husband and I spent in Boston.

Following is a letter by Rosario Mazzeo, former bass clarinetists with the Boston Symphony Orchestra. He retired to Carmel, California, and built a marvelous home in the hills, where I once had the great pleasure of visiting him. At the time he was maintaining a class of fine clarinet students.

Rosario Mazzeo to David Whitwell
Carmel, California, 10 September 1989

Indeed I have not forgotten you! By no means! I still recall with pleasure your extraordinarily fine conducting. But I have been away the whole summer, part of the time in Amsterdam and London, in connection with the festivities of the publication of Pamela Weston's new book, *Clarinet Virtuosi of Today*, and then some weeks of photographing in the high Sierra, thus my desktop is now somewhat invisible. It will be easier on you if I sit at my computer to write this note.

We have changed homes, having outgrown the potential of the house you knew, after our children were grown and gone. Our new place (as of '80) is more attractive, on a mountain ridge overlooking the ocean, Monterey Bay, with no houses, lights or sounds of people and their activities. We call the new house *Casa Tre Viste* (the third view being Point Lobos). I hope you will come to visit us some time, perhaps at my annual Clarinet Day, when my present pupils, and some invited ones from the past (all the way back to 1926), come together for a day and evening of Clarinet Chitchat, playing of unusual tapes I have collected through the years, some summing-up remarks by me, ever more chitchat and music, a climb to the summit of our mountain—1,050 ft. summit, we being at 975 ft., thus making the 75 ft climb a possibility for all clarinetists—and finally one of my wife's and daughter's ever wonderful dinners ...

Now to your question. Of course I recall Longy, though he had left the BSO before I was invited to become a member in 1933. Curiously enough, I never applied for a position. Longy was a Major Musical Fixture in the Boston area in the first part of the century—not only because of his beautiful tone and phrasing, and leadership of the Longy Club, but for his much admired European and Very French Presence. He was an exceptional artist, and even in the first 20 years of my own membership colleagues still spoke often and admiringly of him.

Curiously enough, at some point I bought his entire library of the Longy Club. This must have been sometime in the middle '30s, and was from some member of his family, whom I have since forgotten. I kept the material (devoted mostly to large wind groups) for a good many years, during which my own library grew to rather overwhelming proportions (it now numbers some 3,000 sets of parts and scores) so that I had to narrow my outlook. I sold off all music for more than six players (except for such items as the Schubert *Octet*, Beethoven *Septet*, etc.), and cannot recall whether I sold it to one, or a number of people.

Before joining the BSO in 1933 I organized the Boston Chamber Music Society, which continued to function until the middle 40's. By that time I had become so much occupied, not only with my orchestral duties, but also had been appointed Personnel Manager and elected Treasurer of the BSO Pension Institution ...

Though the Longy Club existed when I first came to Boston it chanced that I never heard it, being much occupied in washing dishes, and other similar activities which made my clarinet lessons possible. But the group was a Boston Favorite, mostly used large wind groups, etc.

I am sad not to be able to give more specific information. And I am not sure to whom you might turn for more. Certainly no one in the BSO today could be helpful. The only historian-minded person (librarian Leslie Rogers) died some time ago ...

There is one story that I must tell you, because it was so characteristic of Longy that it has become a Boston Classic.

A young oboe player came to Longy, asking for the privilege of having oboe lessons with him. Longy said (in an accent which all who told the story used, and with great gusto and characterization), 'Oh no! I nevaire give lessons, nevaire!' The pupil, in despair, 'But I came all the way to Boston to have lessons with you!' Longy, 'Maybe, but that is too bad, I NEVaure give lessons.' Pupil, 'But I do not really want LESSONS, I really want only to know the secret of your vibrato.' Longy, 'Oh-ho, The Secret!' 'Ah!'

Longy, 'Take your oboe.' Pupil opens case, takes oboe, reed, etc. 'Now play for me one long tone.' Pupil plays a few warm-up tones and then plays a long tone. Longy, 'Now play it espressivo.' Pupil plays, presumably espressivo. Longy shakes his head, then says, 'now play it again' and as the pupil plays he reaches forward and gently moves the bell of the oboe from side to side. Longy, 'You hear Zhat?' Pupil (eagerly) 'Yes!' Longy, 'Good, now again.' The process is repeated. Longy, 'Vairy good, that will be Seventy five dollare, please.' ...

Without question, all reports of his playing indicate that he was a very special artist, and I am sad never to have heard him. Also I cannot recall clearly having heard him on any recordings, but I have a lingering suspicion that I did at some time.

The only two people living who might have some direct information would be Mrs. Fernand Gillet, widow of the long-time successor of Longy. But I feel certain that she would not be helpful, and at her age she might resent the question about her husband's predecessor—they were not mutual admirers. But more likely one would be Mrs. Camille Speyer, widow of Louis Speyer, the long-time English horn player of the orchestra, and an old friend of Longy ...

In an attempt to locate a recording of the Longy wind ensemble I turned to Frederick P. Williams of Philadelphia, a collector with a vast collection of recorded music. He not only produced two recordings of the Longy Club, but also recordings of two other famous wind ensembles from the early twentieth century. I have heard that Fred has recently decided to retire from collecting and is seeking to sell his collection.

Frederick P. Williams to David Whitwell
Philadelphia, Pennsylvania, October 6, 1989

As you can see from the record list apparently not much was produced ... I have all the Georges Barrere Columbia acousticals (10") from c. 1914. Let me know if you want the list. The Taffanel Woodwind Ensemble recorded during the depths of the depression and in the US was released on the RCA Victor label: Album M-137 (7578, 7579 & 7580) Mozart *Quintet* in Eb for Winds and Piano and Thuille: *Gavotte*. I have it ... somewhere!

Again, it will take a little time to get my colleagues to locate the precious few Longy's for taping. I simply don't know where mine are but will find them ...

Thanks for the copy of the book. Your major rediscovery of Longy helps us to understand so much more than we did.

PS: After this letter was written ... I received a call from Sue Stinson, Belfer Audio Labs at Syracuse University ... Sue came up with a single Longy-Maquarre-Grisez recording: Rex D-5034, which I have on the Rishell label.

Two months later Fred wrote again to report he had found a Longy recording. He also supplies much interesting information about early band recordings.

Fred Williams to David Whitwell
Philadellphia, Pennsylvania, December 2, 1989

Enclosed is a copy of 'Einsamer Wanderer and Elfintanz' (Grieg)—Longy Club, Phono Cut #5120-B, probably 1911 or 1912, all too brief. We owe this thanks to Martin Bryan, Editor of New Amberola Graphia, 37 Caledonia Street, St. Johnsbury, Vermont 05819 ...

Your programs are exceptional and I have long been aware of your research, especially overseas, into band history. I find the program reviews extremely interesting.

I will continue to look for my Longy recording and you will hear from me …

PS: While I went 'full blast on cylinders' [early recordings] late in the game (last 12 years) I have been able to locate the majority of Columbia's after 1901 and the bulk of Edison's output from 1900 to 1920. They get tough to find from 1921 to 1928.

Of course this leads to the US Marine Band compact disc released a year ago. Did I mention this to you? If you don't have a copy let me know. An 1890 version of 'The Washington Post' is on it (no one knows if Sousa was conducting) as well as another cylinder and four discs … I supplied them with 60 years of their recorded history.

The Banda di chieti (Mussolini's pride sent to the US in 1934 for goodwill purposes and to mollify us) is an incredible story that I must get to you one of these days. I had the good fortune to find almost all of the Associated Radio Transcription Recording Services 12" and 16" issues. I tape them for the two sons of the cornet soloists of the band, also a year ago. I'll probably wind up with the story in the ABA Journal. Don't know if Sonneck cares that much for band detail though my good friend and mentor, Alan Britton, encourages me to submit material.

Finally, there was a long letter regarding Longy by Michael Finkelman, a remarkable music-detective who always seems to know something about any topic dealing with wind music. When I first corresponded with him he had just finished the definitive study of the history of the tenor oboe.

Michael Finkelman to David Whitwell
Carbondale, Illinois, 29 November 1989

Greetings. Sorry for the slight delay in getting back to you since my trip to Boston last month … The trip to Boston was extremely fruitful as far as Longy documentation was concerned. I met with both of the heirs of his daughter, the redoubtable Renee Longy-Miquelle, a most remarkable teacher of advanced musicianship at Curtis, Julliard, etc. (d. 1979). I also visited the Longy School and picked up further data there & also a few tidbits elsewhere. In short, I now have enough info for a pretty decent article on this utterly extraordinary artist, who I have excellent reason to believe was the finest oboist of this century—really! Of course, the clincher on this would be an audition of those discs of his playing which you mentioned on the phone. I would be eternally grateful if you would please get after those collectors who have the Longy discs, and beg them for tape copies, and also (most important) label and number info. I am absolutely 'mad' to get those things, and will be happy to do ANYTHING you want within reason in return!! With these in hand, I will have a pretty rich array of Longy goodies, and will at least have a sufficient amount to begin to give a portrait of this magnificent but somewhat enigmatic artist. (It never ceases to amaze me how quickly even the greatest wind players are forgotten: your research on Longy is in fact the ONLY such work that has ever been done on him.)

With regard to Longy's rather extensive library, I had the luck (if you can call it that) to discover among the previously buried documents at the Longy School that his collection was apparently sold, piecemeal, ostensibly for the benefit of the school. It is clear that when he retired in 1925, he retired completely and did not even take his music back to France with him. (His grandson, Claude, with whom I met in Boston, was the only person with him when he died in 1930: they were out for a walk together. Claude was 5 years of age at the time, and soon went back to the US, where he had been born. He did not return to the spot until 40 years thereafter!) I have all sorts of interesting bits of local lore on Longy's life in France, including pictures! In any case, the outcome of matters, music-wise, is that while virtually all of the works performed by the Longy Club (in addition to plenty of others) were actually owned by Longy, they were simply sold to the first comers who had cash to pay. I even have the prices that were paid for most of these things: they are a joke, even by the standards of 60 years ago.

It is fairly clear that the single person who acquired the greatest quantity of Longy's music was his 'right-hand man' in the BSO, Clement Lenom, who also retired from the orchestra in 1925, but remained active in Boston & New York musical life for *decades* thereafter. (I am trying to cook up an article on him also, but this is tougher going, even though his wife, now 80, is still very much live. I had a most pleasant afternoon with her last month. She still lives in the same elegant Brookline townhouse she has lived in since shortly after her marriage to Lenom in 1932! Mrs. Lenom, a distinguished teacher of solfege and musicianship, as was Lenom himself, is very much together in the mental department, but unfortunately is physically rather handicapped, and has not been able to get upstairs in her 3-story house in quite a long time. Eventually, she hopes to be able to get upstairs and sort through all the documents, etc. Who knows what is there? … Various well-meaning fools, some of whom are old enough to know better, often badger me about why I haven't published any of these things—and there they are, with armies of grad assistants, full-time professional secretarial help, in-house and external grants, etc. etc.)

Mixed in with all of the rest of this year's brohaha, I managed to get to Buffalo twice to visit Mrs. Lenom's oboist niece, who actually owns what remains of her uncle's collection. I am told by her that I have now seen everything, and even though the list is not as 'clean' as I would like it to be, I thought you would like to see the wind ensemble pieces, so here is the list. I have now requested a copy of the Hure, *Pastorale*, which is clearly the most important thing there, in this respect. This is a very substantial work: the score alone is 64 pages long, many containing two systems! It took me a long while to find the time to collate and type up all of my notes on this collection, so I was only able to send out the request a very short while ago.

I was informed by Mrs. Lenom that the collection was once substantially larger than it currently is. Around about 1945, Boaz Piller apparently was given a substantial bit of it. (Piller was the contrabassoonist of the BSO early in the century, and quite a character, as I hear. He has been dead quite some time.)

…

The two Longy heirs have both seen the copy of your book on the Longy Club which you gave to Victor Rosenbaum at the school. Of course, they both want copies …

You are by now probably wondering how much overlap there is going to be between my eventual article and your book. The answer is that I intend to keep this at an absolute minimum. I do have some stray business bearing on the Club, but it is not a great deal: I only took down or collected items which were not in your book. Probably the niftiest item is a caricature of the entire Club, which exists at the school, and of which I have a copy on order. I will try to run off a photocopy of this for you later. In any case, the school is going to retain the negative, as I understand it.

I did manage to gather a few Longy anecdotes, but not a great many. I do have the address of an elderly lady who knew him well, and I will be writing her later today. As I am informed, she is really the last person alive in this country with any possibility of serious recollections of him. Mrs. Lenom, by the way, did not know Longy: she did not move into the Boston area until the year 1930 or so, and would have been way too young to have been in his circle even if she had been there. To confuse you even further, I managed also to see Louis Speyer's son … I finally finished picking up the needed documents on his father (on whom I am also writing an article, which began with a pair of interviews with the now-deceased elderly gentleman in 1978!) … Andy Speyer told me that he had to put his mother, who has to be about 90 now, in a home earlier this year, so I was certainly not about to press for a visit, nor to bother him about begging Longy anecdotes from her … At any rate, Speyer himself gave me a little Longy information when I spoke with him some 11 years ago, and that will just have to do. (It must also be kept in mind that Speyer was a fairly young man during the years he knew Longy, 1918–1930, and I doubt if he were that intimate with him, though he did visit Longy at the latter's house in France on several occasions). If only I had had any clear idea of the towering importance of Longy in 1978, I would have pumped Speyer relentlessly for information. Alas, I was but 24 at the time, and the Speyer meetings were the first oral history interviews I ever conducted.

About the Author

Dr. David Whitwell is a graduate ('with distinction') of the University of Michigan and the Catholic University of America, Washington DC (PhD, Musicology, Distinguished Alumni Award, 2000) and has studied conducting with Eugene Ormandy and at the Akademie fur Musik, Vienna. Prior to coming to Northridge, Dr. Whitwell participated in concerts throughout the United States and Asia as Associate First Horn in the USAF Band and Orchestra in Washington DC, and in recitals throughout South America in cooperation with the United States State Department.

At the California State University, Northridge, which is in Los Angeles, Dr. Whitwell developed the CSUN Wind Ensemble into an ensemble of international reputation, with international tours to Europe in 1981 and 1989 and to Japan in 1984. The CSUN Wind Ensemble has made professional studio recordings for BBC (London), the Koln Westdeutscher Rundfunk (Germany), NOS National Radio (The Netherlands), Zurich Radio (Switzerland), the Television Broadcasting System (Japan) as well as for the United States State Department for broadcast on its 'Voice of America' program. The CSUN Wind Ensemble's recording with the Mirecourt Trio in 1982 was named the 'Record of the Year' by The Village Voice. Composers who have guest conducted Whitwell's ensembles include Aaron Copland, Ernest Krenek, Alan Hovhaness, Morton Gould, Karel Husa, Frank Erickson and Vaclav Nelhybel.

Dr. Whitwell has been a guest professor in 100 different universities and conservatories throughout the United States and in 23 foreign countries (most recently in China, in an elite school housed in the Forbidden City). Guest conducting experiences have included the Philadelphia Orchestra, Seattle Symphony Orchestra, the Czech Radio Orchestras of Brno and Bratislava, The National Youth Orchestra of Israel, as well as resident wind ensembles in Russia, Israel, Austria, Switzerland, Germany, England, Wales, The Netherlands, Portugal, Peru, Korea, Japan, Taiwan, Canada and the United States.

He is a past president of the College Band Directors National Association, a member of the Prasidium of the International Society for the Promotion of Band Music, and was a member of the founding board of directors of the World Association for Symphonic Bands and Ensembles (WASBE). In 1964 he was made an honorary life member of Kappa Kappa Psi, a national professional music fraternity. In September, 2001, he was a delegate to the UNESCO Conference on Global Music in Tokyo. He has been knighted by sovereign organizations in France, Portugal and Scotland and has been awarded the gold medal of Kerkrade, The Netherlands, and the silver medal of Wangen, Germany, the highest honor given wind conductors in the United States, the medal of the Academy of Wind and Percussion Arts (National Band Association) and the highest honor given wind conductors in Austria, the gold medal of the Austrian Band Association. He is a member of the Hall of Fame of the California Music Educators Association.

Dr. Whitwell's publications include more than 127 articles on wind literature including publications in Music and Letters (London), the London Musical Times, the Mozart-Jahrbuch (Salzburg), and 39 books, among which is his 13-volume *History and Literature of the Wind Band and Wind Ensemble* and an 8-volume series on *Aesthetics in Music*. In addition to numerous modern editions of early wind band music his original compositions include 5 symphonies.

David Whitwell was named as one of six men who have determined the course of American bands during the second half of the 20th century, in the definitive history, *The Twentieth Century American Wind Band* (Meredith Music).

A doctoral dissertation by German Gonzales (2007, Arizona State University) is dedicated to the life and conducting career of David Whitwell through the year 1977. David Whitwell is one of nine men described by Paula A. Crider in *The Conductor's Legacy* (Chicago: GIA, 2010) as 'the legendary conductors' of the 20th century.

> 'I can't imagine the 2nd half of the 20th century—without David Whitwell and what he has given to all of the rest of us.' Frederick Fennell (1993)

www.ingramcontent.com/pod-product-compliance
Lightning Source LLC
Chambersburg PA
CBHW081350230426
43667CB00017B/2778